On Religious Freedom

On Religious Freedom

Jay Newman

University of Ottawa Press
Ottawa • Paris

BV
741
,N53
1991

© University of Ottawa Press, 1991
Printed and bound in Canada
ISBN 0-7766-0308-6

Canadian Cataloguing in Publication Data

Newman, Jay, 1948-
 On religious freedom

Includes bibliographical references and index.
ISBN 0-7766-0308-6

1. Freedom of religion.   I. Title.

BV741.N49 1991   291.1'772   C90-090520-4

UNIVERSITÉ D'OTTAWA
UNIVERSITY OF OTTAWA

This book has been published with the help of a grant from the Canadian Federation for the Humanities, using funds provided by the Social Sciences and Humanities Research Council of Canada.

Design: Marie Tappin

To my parents, Kate and Louis Newman

Contents

Acknowledgements   ix

Chapter 1   **The Idea of Religious Freedom**   1
1. A Valuable but Ambiguous Expression 3
2. Religion 4
3. Freedom: Lexical Analysis 7
4. Freedom: Theoretical Analysis 10
5. Types of Freedom 12
6. Determinism 16
7. Liberty; Religious Liberty; Autonomy 18
8. Types of Religious Freedom 19
9. Religious Freedom in Relation to Authority 24
10. "Internal" Constraints; Absence of Opportunity 30
11. The Ideal Beyond the Rhetoric 33

Chapter 2   **Religion as a Hindrance to Freedom**   35
1. The Theological Basis of Religious Repression: Hebrew Scripture 36
2. The Theological Basis of Religious Repression: The New Testament 46
3. The Psycho-social Basis of Religious Repression 52
4. The Philosophical Basis of Religious Repression 58

Chapter 3   **Religion as a Source of Freedom**   65
1. Theology of Freedom: Hebrew Scripture 66
2. Theology of Freedom: The New Testament 70
3. Faith as an Incentive to Moral Action 74
4. A Prime Example: The Virtue of Humility 78
5. The Social Consequences of Spiritual Freedom 85
6. Religion in Relation to Other Sources of Freedom 88

Chapter 4   **Religious Liberty   93**

    1. The Idea of Religious Liberty..94
    2. A Brief Historical Excursus..101
    3. The Separation Principle 113
    4. The Moral Justification of Religious Liberty: Theologico-
       ethical Arguments and Appeals to Conscience 123
    5. The Moral Justification of Religious Liberty:
       Utilitarian Arguments 130
    6. The Moral Justification of Religious Liberty:
       Matters of Consistency and Authenticity.................................135

Chapter 5   **Religious Liberalism   143**

    1. Liberalism 144
    2. The Idea of Religious Liberalism 151
    3. Philosophy and Liberal Religion 160
    4. Criticisms of Religious Liberalism 169
    5. Liberal Religion and Spiritual Freedom 176

Chapter 6   **Freedom and Authority   181**

    1. Resolving the Paradoxes 182
    2. The Marks of Legitimate Authority..186
    3. Charismatic Authority 197
    4. Authority and Love..204

Notes   **213**

Index   **229**

Acknowledgements

An earlier version of part of Chapter 1 was presented at the 1989 International Symposium on Truth and Tolerance at McGill University, and an earlier version of part of Chapter 3 was presented in a public lecture at the University of Calgary. I have benefitted from the critical suggestions made by people in attendance at those sessions. Chapter 3 incorporates a revised version of part of my article "Humility and Self-realization," which appeared in *The Journal of Value Inquiry* 16 (1982), and I thank the editor of the journal for allowing me to make use of the material here.

I am grateful to two institutions for facilitating my research and writing during the academic year 1988–89: the University of Guelph, which granted me sabbatical leave for the year and provided me with a travel allowance from the Discretionary Fund of the Dean of Research; and The Calgary Institute for the Humanities at the University of Calgary, which conferred on me the status of Visiting Research Fellow for the period of my visit. It is with great pleasure that I acknowledge the generosity and hospitality of my colleagues at the Institute, and especially of Harold Coward, the able and energetic Director of the Institute. Gerry Dyer and Cindy Atkinson of the Institute staff not only provided courteous secretarial assistance but did much to raise the spirits of all members of the Institute. The University of Calgary has on its faculty five of the most distinguished philosophers of religion in the English-speaking world — Harold Coward, Hugo Meynell, Kai Nielsen, Terence Penelhum, and Alan Sell — and I am grateful for having had the opportunity to discuss this project with them. I have also benefitted from conversations about subjects discussed in this book with Jakob Amstutz, Wayne Borody, Helen Diemert, Donald Evans, John Hick, James Horne, John Nota, Edward Synan, Elmer Thiessen, many members of the Canadian Theological Society, and my teacher and friend, Elmer Sprague. I am grateful to Janet Shorten and Jennifer Wilson of the University of Ottawa Press for their generous attention to the manuscript and their kindness to the author. Finally, it is my hope that some of what I have written in Chapter 6 will convey to those concerned some idea of my immense debt to my parents.

1 The Idea of Religious Freedom

As they meditate upon what they interpret as the moral decay in their culture, many people are given to pondering the general decline of religious zeal and the forms of institutional permissiveness — political, ecclesiastical, and academic — that have contributed to it. Such people usually regard religious faith as an irreplaceable stimulus to morality, and whether or not they themselves are capable of religious commitment, they regret its decline in society and worry about a future in which the primary source of moral incentive will be something as unreliable as subjective sentiment, philosophical speculation, or political rhetoric. Yet there are other people who look upon the persistence of hatred, injustice, exploitation, and callousness as representing the major part of the legacy of traditional religion, which they see as glorified, institutionalized superstition that must constantly be checked through the efforts of reasonable, liberal-minded people like themselves. The disagreement between these two camps is perhaps most strikingly reflected in their divergent conceptions of the relation of religion to freedom, which seems to have always been, on at least one level of consciousness, one of the highest human ideals. Defenders and promoters of religion have insisted time and again that it is only through religious faith — and perhaps only through their particular religious faith — that true freedom can be attained, and that other things called "freedom" are not nearly as important as this true freedom, while secularists, open or disguised, have protested that religion, as traditionally conceived, has been the greatest obstacle to the most important forms of freedom, those that correspond to self-realization (on the personal plane) and civilization (on the social plane). The philosophical core of this disagreement has rarely been considered in an unbiased manner, and despite their intense interest in religion and in freedom individually, philosophers have generally shown little interest in a systematic investigation of their relation.

Yet hardly a month goes by in which we do not hear someone mention "religious freedom," "religious liberty," "freedom of religion," "religious liberalism," "liberal religion," or something else that suggests that there is a middle ground between the two camps. For on the one hand, such expressions suggest that what is ordinarily regarded as religion may indeed be compatible with what is ordinarily regarded as freedom; and on the other, they remind us that there are important forms of religion that are not compatible with important forms of freedom. The idea of such middle ground is consoling and encouraging to anyone who wishes to believe that neither he nor his fellows must ultimately choose between reactionary religious authoritarianism and secularist materialism; and such a person is not easily fooled by the attempts of extremists to manipulate the definitions of terms like *religion* and *freedom* in such a way as to promote their own agenda. Unfortunately, when we begin to explore the middle ground, we may find ourselves mired in swamps of murky rhetoric, obscure theory, and noisome insincerity. Thus, in exploring such territory, it is helpful to have philosophy as a guide, and despite its countless other obligations, philosophy must be willing to accept the assignment.

In this philosophical investigation of some of the more important relations between religion and freedom, we shall proceed in five stages: (1) We shall begin by considering the idea of religious freedom, which appears to be a composite of the ideas of religion and freedom; and we shall also consider at this preliminary stage several other ideas often associated with these; (2) We shall consider some of the more important ways in which religion is a hindrance to freedom and some of the more important ways in which it is a source of freedom, and we shall try to determine whether on balance it is more a source of freedom than an obstacle to it. At this stage we shall also give some attention to the value of religion and of freedom; (3) We shall consider the nature and value of religious liberty and shall examine various aspects of the general relationship between religious and political institutions; (4) We shall scrutinize the major types of theological theory designated as kinds of religious liberalism and shall consider them in their relation to the development of liberal religion; and finally, (5) We shall survey the various paradoxes concerning religious freedom that have emerged in the course of our investigation, consider them in their relation to one another, and endeavour to resolve them in an intellectually satisfactory and practically efficacious way.

1 A Valuable but Ambiguous Expression

In considering the relations of religion and freedom, we may reasonably focus our attention, at least initially, on the expression "religious freedom," which occupies a fairly secure niche in ordinary, nontechnical discourse. We could instead begin by focusing our attention on "freedom of religion" or "liberal religion," but these expressions have a narrower application and can be recognized, on reflection, as referring to types or aspects of religious freedom. "Religious freedom" is an expression that may appropriately be applied to various phenomena. Indeed, although some scholars believe that there is widespread agreement on what "religious freedom" means,[1] others are struck by the ambiguity of the expression. For example, Maurice Cranston is impressed by the fact that "we find the expression 'religious freedom' used sometimes to mean 'freedom (from state interference) for religious institutions,' and at other times to mean 'freedom (for individuals) *from* religious institutions.' (People who want freedom *from* religious institutions often look to State interference to secure it.)"[2] Some scholars have attempted to define the expression, as does Jacques Ellul, for example, when he states that "Religious freedom is usually construed as freedom of belief . . . and then as political freedom to practice the religion of one's choice in a given society without fear of molestation."[3] But it takes little imagination to realize that the expression could also appropriately be used to designate the special "spiritual freedom" that religious apologists contend can be attained only through religion (or a particular religion); and while often it refers to a specifically *political* right, institution, condition, or objective, it is sometimes used to designate a more general *cultural* situation, one that fosters the growth of liberal religion or even secularism. Cecil Northcott has suggested that a distinction might be drawn between "freedom of religion" ("as concerned with rights which can be established in law") and "religious freedom" ("where the religious man moves in the world of duties and obligations").[4] However useful such a distinction could be, it is not one that is ordinarily made by speakers of English; and while there are kinds of religious freedom that we would never characterize as "freedom of religion," we normally would not hesitate to treat religious rights which can be established in law as constituting a kind of religious freedom.

I appreciate the expression "religious freedom" because, in the breadth of its applicability, it reminds us that religion and freedom are related in various ways and intersect on several different planes, such as the political, ecclesiastical, theological, psychological, and existential. M. Searle Bates has observed that part of the vagueness in usage of the expression "religious liberty" (which either is interchangeable in common use with "religious freedom" or designates a certain type or aspect of religious freedom) "derives from the complex relationships in issues of religious liberty, involving the individual, the religious body, the community, and the state."[5] This point, as I have suggested, applies at least as much to the expression "religious freedom" as it does to the expression "religious liberty," which seems to me to be narrower in applicability. Bates ultimately does offer a definition of "religious liberty" — as "actualized opportunity for individuals and groups to pursue high spiritual aims"[6] — but even so abstract and general a definition may be too narrow, for it does not appear to be able to accommodate the view of those who would regard religious liberty (or freedom) as something of intrinsic as well as instrumental value.

2 Religion

The idea of religious freedom would appear to be a composite of the ideas of religion and freedom; and since, in any case, we are ultimately concerned in our investigation with the relations of religion and freedom, it is appropriate at this point to turn our attention directly to the terms *religion* and *freedom*. Of course, in comparison with the vagueness or ambiguity of these two terms, the vagueness of expressions like "religious freedom" and "religious liberty" may seem almost negligible.

Prudence dictates that any scholar attempting to lay down even an informal, working definition of *religion* exercise great caution, for with advances in recent years in such academic disciplines as sociology of religion, comparative religion, and ecumenical studies, there has been a heightened sensitivity to the ethnocentric and theological biases underlying most traditional definitions of *religion*. Ordinary speakers of English, and even many scholars, tend to think of their own religious commitment as paradigmatic and to classify things as religions to the extent that they resemble or approximate the paradigm. An early eighteenth-century dictionary defines *religion* as "the worship of a Deity, Piety, Godliness";[7] and a late eighteenth-century dictionary defines it as "Virtue, as founded upon reverence of God, and expectation of future rewards and punishments; a system of divine faith and worship as opposite to others."[8] Whatever value these definitions once had, they would be regarded by most modern scholars in the field of religious studies as unhelpfully (and perhaps even offensively) narrow and as reflecting the lexicographers' limited experience with world religions. A careful modern scholar, when discussing religion as such, constantly reminds herself of differences between religions and, particularly, of differences between her own religion and other things that her fellow scholars — and broad-minded, thoughtful people in general — would see as qualifying as religions. So, if she is, say, an Anglican or Lutheran, she makes a conscious effort to work with a definition of *religion* that is not biased in the direction of Protestantism, or Christianity, or monotheism, or Western thought. In an effort to be broad-minded and to attain a deeper understanding of the phenomena she is investigating, she works with a longer list of paradigms than did the lexicographers, theologians, and churchmen of earlier periods. That list will include not only such major Eastern religions as Hinduism and Taoism but also less well-known forms of commitment, as well as, perhaps, "new" religions and even certain highly personal faiths manifested by a handful of exceptional individuals. Of course, a person of limited vision might insist that his religion is the only one that deserves to be called by that name, and that others are counterfeit approximations, or "pseudo-religions." Such a person would be dismissed by most scholars as an ignorant bigot, but perhaps more to the point, he will have failed to keep up with the way in which ordinary speakers of the language now use the term. Of course, there is a grey area here, and scholars often find themselves disagreeing with ordinary speakers of the language about whether certain things properly qualify as religions. For example, in our society, there have been bitter disputes about whether certain "cults" deserve to be granted the privileges extended by the state to "genuine" religious groups. Moreover, since *religion* is an English term derived from the same Latin root as corresponding terms in other Western European languages, and since Christianity has been in many ways (as in historical influence and in number of adherents) the dominant religion of the English-speaking world and of Western Europe, Christianity does remain in a sense the principal paradigm of a religion for most speakers of English and of several other European languages.

The term is derived from the Latin *religio*, which may or may not be related to the term *religare*, meaning "to bind up" (as to one's god, faith, or ethic).[9] We regularly use it to refer to a general form of culture or experience (in contrast with, say, philosophy, science, or art) and to particular systems of it (Christianity, Buddhism, and so forth). Modern dictionaries associate the form of culture or experience with belief in, service, obedience, and devotion to, reverence for, and worship of, a transcendent, supernatural power, which is often a personal God or group of personal gods.[10] Modern dictionaries also generally acknowledge the systematic character of the particular expressions of the form of culture or experience, and the things typically seen as being systematized are beliefs, attitudes, feelings, practices, values, and rites.

Lexical definitions give us a rather limited conception of the nature of a thing, and particularly of the nature of something as complex as religion, and it is not surprising that philosophers and social scientists have supplemented lexical definitions of *religion* with any number of theoretical accounts of the essence of religion. Many of these, particularly in the nineteenth century and the early part of this century, have involved speculations about the origin of religion and religions, though such accounts have become less and less fashionable. More sophisticated accounts tend to be descriptive, and are always accompanied by a list of qualifications, caveats, and apologies. A good, typical working definition of *religion* by a contemporary scholar is Peter Slater's characterization of a religion as "a personal way of life informed by traditional elements of creed, code, and cult and directed toward the realization of some transcendent end."[11] But we must always be mindful of the complexity of religion and of the significant differences in emphasis from one religion to the next. As Jean Holm has observed,

> To concentrate on one activity, such as worship, is to ignore the fact that a religious person sees the whole of life in a religious perspective, and the rites and customs he observes, the festivals he celebrates, the code of ethics he follows, are no less aspects of his religion than worship is. We are likely to gain a more accurate understanding of the phenomenon of religion, therefore, if we recognize its complexity and take account of all its aspects.[12]

Nevertheless, it must be recognized that working definitions do help us to get on with our work, and I feel obliged to indicate that I find it especially useful to conceive of religion as the acceptance of a spiritual world-view and the behaviour that is based on such a commitment; thus, a particular religion can be usefully regarded as the acceptance of a particular spiritual world-view and the behaviour that is based on that commitment.[13] You, the reader, may not find this conception helpful, and you may not even be clear as to precisely what such a conception involves; the terms *spiritual*, *world-view*, and *commitment* are indeed ambiguous and complex in their own right. But in any case, you and I almost surely agree that Judaism and Christianity are paradigmatic systems of religion, and these are the two religions that will, in fact, occupy the major part of our attention in this study. Of course, I shall not be ignoring the fact that these two religions are in certain important ways very different from most others.

3 Freedom: Lexical Analysis

The terms *free* and *freedom* are also notoriously ambiguous, and even if we consider only those usages of the terms that could be significantly relevant to religion, we find ourselves left with concepts that are difficult to pin down. As is perhaps also the case with respect to our own personal religious faith, we may well feel that we have an intimate, intuitive, direct awareness and understanding of our own personal freedom, but problems arise when we move to the plane of definition. As Ketcham and Day have noted, "We have known the immediacy of the phenomenon of freedom as lived experience, and we have also encountered the difficulties of disciplined effort to express such experience faithfully and clearly."[14]

John Walker's 1791 dictionary defines *freedom* as "Liberty, independence; privilege, franchises, immunities; unrestraint; ease or facility in doing or showing any thing." It defines being *free* as "At liberty; uncompelled, unrestrained; permitted; conversing without reserve; liberal; frank; guiltless; exempt; invested with franchises, possessing any thing without vassalage; without expence [sic]."[15] Most of the terms and phrases in these definitions still appear in modern dictionary definitions of *free* and *freedom*. Other terms and phrases that appear in modern dictionary definitions of *freedom* are "non-slavery," "power of self-determination," "exemption," "being unconstrained by fate or necessity" (or "by duty" or "by coercion" or "by the power of another"), and, with respect to a particular freedom, "a right" and "a privilege." In definitions of *free*, we find references to one's "having rights," and to one's being "independent," "unhampered," "unimpeded," "not dependent on others," "not determined by external forces," "relieved from a burden," and so forth.[16]

According to etymologists, the words *free* and *freedom* are ultimately derived from Anglo-Saxon terms referring to fondness; and the key to this strange connection is that the Anglo-Saxon terms for "beloved" and "friend" were applied to free members of the clan to contradistinguish them from slaves.[17] P. C. Hodgson has pointed out that the development of the English terms corresponds to the development of the terms used to designate freedom in all Indo-European languages. Thus, ancient Greek and Latin terms for freedom also developed as the result of the perceived need to contrast someone's condition with that of slaves.[18] Hodgson concludes that, "Linguistically, the word freedom is a product of those who are masters and who define their mastery vis-à-vis slavery."[19]

Several writers have attempted to clarify the ordinary person's fundamental conception of freedom without plunging into deep theoretical waters. One of these is H. J. Muller, who begins his analysis with the blunt assertion that, "To the ordinary man, freedom means the feeling of being able to do as he likes, act at his own sweet pleasure."[20] Appealing to common usage and common experience, Muller then associates freedom with being unconfined, unfettered, and unconstrained, and with "the condition of being able to choose and to carry out purposes."[21] This capacity requires three conditions: absence of external constraints; practicable purposes; and a power of conscious choice between significant, known alternatives. Thus, it involves freedom *from*, freedom *to*, and freedom *of*.[22] Acknowledging that human beings are always constrained to some extent by physical and social necessities, Muller then qualifies his earlier claim by observing that "Freedom is restricted only when the constraints appear to be arbitrary — unaccustomed, unnecessary, unreasonable, or unjust."[23] Thus, "freedom is broadened in so far as arbitrary power is limited, rule is constrained by the recognition of rights, and rights are extended to all members of a society, guaranteed by law."[24]

A more sophisticated attempt to clarify the fundamental significance of *freedom* has been undertaken by Maurice Cranston, who draws on various methods and insights of linguistic philosophy. Central to Cranston's analysis is the thesis that freedom is always freedom *from something*. According to Cranston, " . . . there is no *one* freedom but many freedoms; and they are as various as are constraints, impediments and burdens";[25] and, "If we are to know which of those innumerable possibilities is intended, we must know what it is that a man who says he is free, is free from. He must name a constraint, impediment or burden."[26] Such analysis is clear, straightforward, and useful; and on the surface it seems plausible enough. But we have seen how someone like Muller would object to Cranston's reduction of "free *to*" to "free *from*";[27] and some scholars feel that Cranston undervalues the basic unity underlying all particular freedoms.[28] Perhaps most importantly, Cranston himself recognizes that, by treating freedom as essentially involving something "negative," absence of constraint, he is going against a long and distinguished philosophical tradition that has preferred a more positive formulation.[29]

Cranston believes that freedom must ultimately be understood in relation to desire, for, "If we had no desire to do things, we should hardly know the meaning of constraint," and, "Constraints stand opposed to our desires; freedom stands opposed to constraints. A reason for liking freedom is that we do not like constraints."[30] It is not surprising, then, that *freedom* is a "*hurrah*-word"[31] or that philosophers and others have used it by giving "persuasive definitions" of it in order to promote their own special agenda.[32] The word has a "strong laudatory emotive meaning for English-speaking peoples,"[33] and, "We do not speak of ourselves as being free from something we should welcome."[34]

Cranston has attempted to clarify and to some extent to simplify the central lexical definition of *freedom* that we find in dictionaries, and in some ways he has accomplished his task. But we can see that even someone who tries as hard as Cranston does to avoid unnecessarily complex theorizing has a tough job on his hands when he gets down to the business of explaining what freedom is. There are scholars whose analysis of the basic nature of freedom comes close to Cranston's, as when the psychologist J. F. Rychlak asserts that "To be *free* is to be without constraint, open to alternatives, and not bound to a fixed course."[35] Yet there are others who approach the idea of freedom from a different angle, as when Daniel Callahan locates at the focal point of freedom "the possibility of making choices,"[36] or when Christopher Dawson proclaims that "the freedom of man is in the knowledge of God."[37]

One feature of Cranston's analysis that perhaps is particularly noteworthy is his reference to *freedom* as a "*hurrah*-word." Austin Farrer has put the point in a slightly different way by observing that the word *freedom* has a "hybrid" character: "It is always descriptive of a fact, at least in part; it is often in part evaluative."[38] Some words are essentially descriptive (such as *blue* and *pencil*), and others are essentially evaluative (such as *good* and *goodness*); but still others are normally partly descriptive and partly evaluative (such as *civilized* and *wisdom*). *Freedom* belongs to the last family of terms, and terms in this group pose special difficulties for both speaker and listener, for sometimes they are used primarily (or even purely) in a descriptive way and sometimes they are used primarily in an evaluative way, and often it is not clear as to precisely how they are being used in a particular context.

4   Freedom: Theoretical Analysis

Accounts of the nature of freedom are not always restricted to explanations of the meaning of *freedom* in ordinary language. Some are deliberately theoretical, and others are more theoretical than they were intended to be. Theories of freedom can be useful in drawing our attention to interesting aspects of at least certain kinds of freedom, although by their very nature they tend to be more speculative and more dogmatic than attempts at the lexical definition of *freedom*.

For example, when the Thomist writer Yves Simon writes that "Freedom is the power to make a choice between the means offered to our activity,"[39] it would appear that he is offering us something pretty close to a lexical definition. When he goes on to say that "The conquest of freedom in daily life implies above all else a daily fight against falsehood, a daily fight for truth," his analysis has become more theoretical; and students of the history of ideas will recognize the influence of traditional Roman Catholic thought on his perspective.[40] When, following another Thomist writer, Maritain, he distinguishes terminal freedom (freedom of authority) from "mere" initial freedom (free will, freedom of choice), we may find his analysis useful or we may find it arbitrary and manipulative.[41] By the time he gets around to stating that "One who is ruled for his own good or for the common good is a free man," we can see that Simon's analysis is marinated mediaeval apologetic.[42]

Consider again how the Jesuit Piet Fransen's conception of freedom differs from the "ordinary" conception of freedom that interests writers like Muller and Cranston. "Freedom never consists in the pure capacity of indulging in whatever fancy crosses one's mind, limited only by the fancies of others. This false conception of freedom was defended during the nineteenth century; it still has its extreme partisans among a few existentialists and anarchists today. Real freedom, however, is the spontaneous creativity of a human person to realize his own truth."[43] However superior Fransen's conception might be to the conceptions of "existentialists and anarchists," it is clear from his characterization of "real" freedom that he has developed his own theory, for most people who use the words *free* and *freedom* do not think about themselves in terms of their "spontaneous creativity" or realization of their "own truth." Perhaps they ought to; but then Fransen should perhaps be speaking of the "highest" freedom rather than "real" freedom.

Sometimes intellectuals theorize about freedom because deep thinking is their vocation, and freedom is as suitable a subject for investigation as any. But most people who present and promote theories of freedom in books, lectures, sermons, and discussions have very precise practical objectives. They want to change people — individuals and societies — by enabling them to be free in the particular way that they see *themselves* as being free. Efforts to help one's fellow creatures to be wiser, happier, and better should never be despised; only the irredeemable cynic is convinced that there is little of value for him to learn from others. Still, we must also remember that, like all proselytizers, most people who theorize aloud about the nature of freedom consider themselves to be superior to us in some very important way and feel that they are obliged to work at making us more like them in that way. Some of these people are indeed superior and have much to teach us; others are dangerously deluded. But it can never hurt us to ask ourselves why these people think that we will be wiser, happier, or better if we are more like them.[44]

Consider in this regard certain ideas about freedom advanced by Spinoza in the first half of his famous *Ethics*. Theologians, creative writers, and behavioural and social scientists all frequently theorize about freedom, but no group theorizes more regularly on the subject than philosophers; and Spinoza is justly one of the most celebrated of philosophers and also one of the most famous of all writers on the subject of freedom. Early in the *Ethics*, Spinoza announces that "That thing is called free which exists from the necessity of its own nature alone and is determined to action by itself alone."[45] This remarkable definition leads Spinoza to conclude that only God is free and that human beings are seriously mistaken in believing that they too are free:

> [M]en are deceived because they think themselves free, and the sole reason for thinking so is that they are conscious of their own actions, and ignorant of the causes by which those actions are determined. Their idea of liberty therefore is this — that they know no cause for their own actions; for as to saying that their actions depend upon their will, these are words to which no idea is attached.[46]

This is one of the classic statements of the doctrine that the fact of causal determinism counts against the possibility of human freedom, and the doctrine has been much criticized by writers who have insisted that causal determinism is compatible with, or even a necessary condition of, human freedom and responsibility. Indeed, in one of the strangest reversals in the history of philosophy, Spinoza himself goes on in the latter parts of the *Ethics* to explain how we human beings can be free. But why did Spinoza begin with the particular definition of *freedom* which he did? Why did he want us to think of freedom in that way? Perhaps the answer lies in Spinoza's agenda for social reform.[47] Towards the end of Part II of the *Ethics*, Spinoza explains to us why he thinks knowledge of his doctrine is of service to us. He suggests that it teaches us "how we ought to behave with regard to the things of fortune, or those which are not in our power," and, "with equal mind to wait for and bear each form of fortune because we know that all things follow from the eternal decree of God." Moreover, the doctrine contributes to social welfare and to the advantage of common society, since it teaches us "to hate no one, to despise no one, to mock no one, to be angry with no one, and to envy no one. It teaches every one, moreover, to be content with his own, and to be helpful to his neighbor, not from any womanish pity, from partiality, or superstition, but by the guidance of reason alone."[48] Interestingly, Spinoza maintains his agenda even after he introduces a new theory of freedom in the second half of the *Ethics* and argues, in effect, that the free man is the rational man. Those who approve of Spinoza's agenda may find one of his theories of freedom to be attractive. But it is hardly surprising that there are many who agree with Muller that Spinoza's talk about the "free man" is hollow, since "Spinoza was strictly defining a *wise* man — or more strictly a monster."[49]

Sometimes theorists are relatively open about the extent to which their conception of freedom reflects their agenda for political and cultural reform. For example, the theologians van Iersel and Schillebeeckx state bluntly that the classical definitions of *freedom* are "no longer entirely applicable to the modern situation"; in their view, "The main problem today is that of the dialectical relationship between the inner liberation of man himself (his conversion or change of heart) and his liberation from structural violence."[50]

5 Types of Freedom

An important way in which scholars theorize is by setting up classifications that, though ostensibly descriptive, are structured in such a way as to focus attention on some types at the expense of others. Sometimes, on careful inspection, the classifications turn out to be hierarchical; more often, however, the inclusion of an item on a list with more recognizable, more familiar types is all that is necessary to draw attention to it. If I talk about "such important painters as Raphael, Rembrandt, and Newman," people are likely to wonder who Newman is or was and why they do not know more about him than they do; they may even seek to find out more about Newman's work or even to examine some of his paintings. Thus, a good way for me to promote interest in Newman's work is to associate his name with more recognizable names. Or I may draw attention to his work in this way without even deliberately intending to do so. Now, interestingly enough, scholarly classifications are often constructed with the same objective, or at least the same effect. For example, if I refer to "the principal types of contemporary philosophy, that is, phenomenological, analytical, neo-Scholastic, Marxist, and Newmanist," I am not only indicating the importance that I attach to Newmanism but I am, deliberately or not, leading some people to take Newmanism more seriously than they now do. People who theorize aloud about freedom do this sort of thing all the time: they slip their pet freedom onto their list of the "main" or "important" types of freedom.

Of course, theorizing is involved more fundamentally in the choice of the principles by which one does one's classifying. We may, on various occasions, find it useful to classify common household objects according to colour, size, cost, or purpose, and the classifying we do will be based on what matter we consider to be important. A miser, for example, will think that cost is almost always the most important matter, and will classify the items accordingly, while many people will feel that different things matter at different times, and will classify the items accordingly. Similarly, when writers draw our attention to differences between Christian and non-Christian freedom, internal and external freedom, positive and negative freedom, and so on, they are not simply objectively describing different types of freedom but are indicating to us what they consider to be *important* types of freedom, and a certain amount of theorizing has gone into their judgement about what the most valuable principles of classification are.

Even if we restrict ourselves to the narrow view that freedom is essentially absence of constraint, there are still in a sense innumerable types of freedom, for, as Cranston says, freedoms are "as various as are constraints, impediments and burdens." And as we have seen, there are thinkers who believe that absence of constraint is itself at most only one type of freedom. Thus, the material here for classification is vast. However, as one peruses the literature on the nature of freedom, one notices that certain common themes underlie the classifications that are usually presented. One, again, is the distinction between negative and positive freedom. The negative conception of freedom may be, as N. O. Lossky has suggested, the most prevalent conception.[51] But even those theorists who believe that freedom is essentially a matter of being independent of some condition recognize that other theorists have preferred a more positive formulation. The positive formulations that have been given are often very different; for example, some are made with reference to God, while others are secularist. Yet it is widely believed by theorists that, despite the differences, such positive formulations have enough in common to warrant being contrasted with negative formulations.

A second theme that emerges in classifications of types of freedom is that, despite the countless number of things that could conceivably be regarded as constraints, some can be seen from history to be especially important. Thus, when classifying freedoms, many theorists refer to political and religious freedom, some refer to academic and economic freedom, and a few at most refer to athletic and culinary freedom. Theorists are influenced here by, among other things, their perception of what the freedoms are for which people have historically been prepared to struggle, sacrifice, and even die.

Another theme that sometimes emerges is the difference between basic freedom of the will, or personal autonomy, and a freedom rooted in communal responsibilities. We have already taken note of one formulation of this distinction, that of Maritain and Simon. The Jesuit Jean-Yves Calvez makes the point in somewhat different language when he asserts that,

> As long as one understands freedom merely as free will and autonomy, there will be a never-ending conflict between freedom and society, social determinisms, social powers.... Freedom does not principally consist in escaping social determinisms, which, after all, are the fruit of past actions of men laboring toward self-determination, toward realization of themselves. Freedom rather consists in the assumption of such given determinisms for the sake of new processes of self-determination.[52]

For the Protestant theologian H. Richard Niebuhr, it is crucial to contrast other forms of freedom with a Christian freedom that involves "the self's ability in its present to change its past and future and to achieve or receive a new understanding of its ultimate historical context."[53] And of course, the distinction between the "free will" of traditional metaphysics and the existential freedom of the creative, responsible individual is one of the major themes of recent European philosophy.[54]

A final theme that warrants explicit identification here is the distinction between internal and external freedom. The contrast made here is between spiritual, psychological, and existential freedoms on the one hand and freedom from constraints over which the agent ultimately has relatively little, if any, control, such as physical forces and rigid social structures. The internal constraints are, as Muller puts it, more "intangible, elusive, and ambiguous" than external constraints, and sometimes it is difficult to determine in which of the two categories a particular freedom or constraint belongs.[55] More often than not, writers who draw this distinction consider internal freedom to be more important than its external counterpart. Reinhold Niebuhr (brother of the aforementioned Richard) suggests that,

> When considering the problem of freeing the mind, we are too prone to think first of the various political and social restraints upon the free play of man's rational faculty. It would be more helpful to consider first the inner restraints which the self places upon its mind; for the mind is not a simple sovereign of the self, but the servant. It is one of the illusions of a rationalistic age that the mind would control the self, if only irrelevant political restraints were not intervening.[56]

Josef Neuner expresses this theme in a more radical way when he remarks that "Freedom is found in man himself; what takes place outside himself is not decisive."[57] But most theorists who make the distinction are prepared to allow that external constraints can prevent one from being free in significant ways, even if internal, interior, inner freedom ultimately matters more than freedom from external constraints.

There is virtually no limit to the imaginativeness that the theorist can bring to the classification of types of freedom. Consider Hodgson's list of the principal types of freedom as political-economic, rational-psychoanalytic, tragic-existential, ecstatic-vitalistic, and pragmatic-technocratic; just reading the labels is almost enough to convince one that one is destined for bondage.[58]

Perhaps the most frequently cited classification of types of freedom is that to be found in M. J. Adler's *The Idea of Freedom*. Focusing mainly on the ideas of celebrated philosophers, Adler and his associates conclude that it is useful to think in terms of five basic freedoms: circumstantial freedom of self-realization (being able, under favourable circumstances, to act as one wishes for one's own good as one sees it); acquired freedom of self-perfection (being able, through acquired virtue or wisdom, to will or live as one ought in conformity to the moral law or an ideal befitting human nature); natural freedom of self-determination (being able to change one's own character creatively by deciding for oneself what one shall do or become); political liberty (being able to participate in making the positive law under which one lives and to alter the political institutions of one's society); and collective freedom (being able to achieve the ideal mode of association that is the goal of mankind's development and to direct one's life in accordance with such necessities).[59] Recognizing the value of a general formulation, Adler states that a person is free when he "has in himself the ability or power to make what he does his own action and what he achieves his own property."[60] One of the strengths (though some might consider it a weakness) of Adler's analysis is that it takes account of the ideas of a wide range of philosophers, even (in the case of collective freedom) those of Bakunin, Comte, and Marx, for whose ideas Adler obviously has very limited affection. Yet Adler, a well-known Aristotelian, is the object of sardonic remarks by Muller, who sees Adler's analysis as overemphasizing acquired freedom of self-perfection at the expense of other freedoms.[61]

6 Determinism

We took note earlier of the widely held belief that human beings are aware of their freedom through some intuitive or otherwise direct experience, but the fact remains that there have been philosophers and others who have expressed grave doubts about the possibility of freedom. We have considered the case of Spinoza, who, while not consistent on the subject, does in places articulate the position that human beings are not free and that "will" is an empty term. In every generation, there have always been thinkers who have been attracted to the view that ultimately human beings are not free and responsible agents, and history has produced a wide range of fatalisms and determinisms. Lossky characterizes fatalism as the position that "the chief events of human life, death, serious illness, marriage, etc., are predetermined by a higher power, God, Fate (*Fatum*) and so on, and are conditioned by the action of that power, against which man is helpless."[62] He contrasts such fatalism with the more modern, more sophisticated type of theory known as "determinism," according to which "a man's fate does partly depend upon his own conduct, but that conduct in every one of its manifestations is not free; it is necessarily conditioned by the nature of the man's body, or by his character, by the influence of environment, heredity, etc."[63] Not all philosophers will approve of these definitions, but they are as good as any we are likely to come upon, and in any case, it is not hard to see what kinds of positions Lossky has in mind. Among the types of determinism that Lossky singles out for special mention are materialism, psychological determinism, and super-naturalistic (or theological) determinism.[64]

Of course, we all recognize that a large part of our behaviour (and our thought) is shaped by various determining factors, but we ordinarily see such determining factors as constraints that limit but do not totally prevent personal freedom. Even metaphysicians who profess to be "hard determinists" almost always behave in a way that indicates that they do hold themselves and others morally responsible for much of their behaviour. And while some philosophers still believe that the fact of causal determinism in general or a particular kind of determinism (such as physical, psychological, or theological) is incompatible with "free will" or "freedom of the will," many more philosophers, theologians, and behavioural and social scientists now seem to believe that determinism is a condition of personal autonomy. For example, the Roman Catholic theologian Calvez asserts that freedom is self-determination within necessity;[65] and the psychologist Rychlak observes that "A free-will psychology is not inconsistent with the view of behavior as also determined. Moving determinately toward a predetermined end is what *will* or *will-power* means!"[66] In a similar vein, the psychologist J. A. Easterbrook suggests that "The alleged incompatibility of free will and determinism . . . involves a misconception of will. It is based on a biased question — one that implies that will must work in a causal vacuum."[67] Indeed, "compatibilism" or "reconciliationism" is now the most popular philosophical position on this subject, though some critics of "hard determinism" hold the more radical position that some human behaviour can be wholly independent of determining factors.

Lossky may well be correct when he states that the problem of "free will" has been the subject of more discussion than any other philosophical problem.[68] But while consideration of the problem has sometimes resulted in changes in a society's moral and legal conceptions, the fact remains that almost all people ordinarily act in accordance with the belief that their reflective, rational, and emotional capacities provide them with sufficient conditions of freedom and responsibility. Even the ancients were cognizant of the *practical* limitations of fatalist theory, as is perhaps best illustrated by Diogenes Laertius' famous anecdote about Zeno, who found himself in the position of chastising a slave who was familiar with Zeno's Stoical outlook. When the slave pleaded that he was fated to steal, Zeno replied, "Yes, and to be beaten too."[69]

7 Liberty; Religious Liberty; Autonomy

Many theorists see the words *freedom* and *liberty* as synonymous.[70] Even Hans Hofmann, who wishes to distinguish the two, grants that in popular usage the terms are generally considered synonymous.[71] Dictionary definitions of the two terms do appear to sanction treating them as synonyms. The first part of the definition of *liberty* in John Kersey's 1708 dictionary indicates that liberty is to be understood as "Freedom, Leave or Free-leave"; and modern dictionaries invariably follow suit by identifying "freedom" or "being free" as a primary meaning of *liberty*.[72] Moreover, as we saw earlier, dictionaries generally take "liberty" to be a primary meaning of *freedom* and "at liberty" to be a primary meaning of *free*.[73] However, one dictionary notes that, while *freedom* has a broad range, *liberty* "may also imply more strongly than *freedom* a release from restraint or compulsion."[74]

When Massimo Salvadori defines *liberty* as the "right, to be exercised within limits dictated by the requirements of the social order, of each and all to act according to their own decisions," his definition of *liberty* may well strike one as being extremely similar to general definitions of *freedom*.[75] However, Salvadori's use of the word *right* is suggestive, for it reminds us that *liberty* does, in ordinary language, have a narrower range than *freedom*, and is usually used with reference to absence of political constraints; for while political rights are not necessarily the only rights we can enjoy, they are certainly the paradigmatic rights that come to mind when we hear the word.

Given our interest in the relations of religion and freedom, we must wonder whether the common expression "religious liberty" is generally used to refer to all of the phenomena that are or might be designated as "religious freedom." While such a distinguished authority on religious liberty as Bates sees the terms *liberty* and *freedom* as largely interchangeable in common use (with both referring to "absence of compulsion or restraint"),[76] I am inclined to believe that "religious liberty" is an expression customarily used to refer only to certain types or aspects of religious freedom, or to certain religious freedoms. Specifically, I am inclined to share Hofmann's intuition that the expression "religious liberty" is not ordinarily applied to many of the things that are or might be characterized as "spiritual freedom" or "inner freedom."[77] Carrying this point further, I suggest that the expression would not normally be used to designate even "theological freedom" or all forms of "ecclesiastical freedom." Moreover, I am inclined to believe that, when seen as a positive freedom, religious liberty is usually associated with enjoyment of political rights and privileges; similarly, when seen as a negative freedom, it is normally associated with absence of constraints that are primarily political.

Intuitions, especially about something as plastic as ordinary linguistic usage, are not always reliable. But I shall follow my intuitions here throughout this investigation and shall associate religious liberty only with those types or aspects of religious freedom that have an important political dimension. And even if my intuitions are wrong in this case, you at least now know more about how I shall be using certain key expressions.

Another term widely regarded as synonymous with *freedom* is autonomy, and I have already treated the expression "personal autonomy" as interchangeable with the expression "freedom of the will." The word *autonomy* is quite similar to the Greek term from which it is derived, and can easily be seen to refer to self-government or self-determination, or to the right or power of self-government, and it is not hard to see why it is often properly interchangeable with *freedom*. However, *autonomy* is not used nearly as often as *freedom* (or even *liberty*) in everyday discourse, and some people might be tempted to regard it as a semi-technical term appropriately reserved for scholarly discourse. Moreover, general usage of it indicates that it has a narrower range than *freedom*. In fact, reduction of freedom to autonomy has been strongly criticized not only by theologians but by political theorists, particularly contemporary liberals.[78]

8 Types of Religious Freedom

We are now in a better position than earlier to understand the idea of religious freedom and some of the more important relations between religion and freedom. We can see now that the expression "religious freedom" is not ambiguous simply because of the casual way in which ordinary speakers of English and careless scholars bandy about words and phrases. The expression may be said to be "systematically" ambiguous for several reasons: there are serious disagreements about the precise meaning of the terms *religion* and *freedom*; there are different theories about the nature of religion and of freedom; both ordinary speakers of our language and scholars tend to be prepared to acknowledge that there are different types of religion and different types or aspects of freedom as well as different religions and different freedoms; the relative importance of the descriptive and evaluative aspects or uses of the expression may vary from user to user or even use to use; the expression is often used rhetorically in order to manipulate attitudes or behaviour; and high-minded thinkers sometimes feel that they have a moral right (or even obligation) to employ the expression in a more "valuable" way than ordinary speakers do. Thus it is prudent for us not to rush into trying to lay down a general formulation. A safer course to follow is to keep an eye on historical discussions of the relations of religion and freedom and to consider some of the more obvious ways in which a person might be said to enjoy religious freedom.

Let us begin by considering certain matters concerning agency. To have religious freedom can be a matter of being able to do certain things. Specifically, it can be a matter of being able to do various things directly associated with religion. Viewed positively, such a freedom involves simply having certain capacities, and viewed negatively, it is a matter of not being constrained in such a way that one cannot do religious things. A person who is religiously free in this sense ordinarily can do some of the following things: hold religious beliefs, attitudes, and values; observe religious rites and customs; belong to a community of religious believers; celebrate religious festivals; act in public as well as in private on the basis of his religious commitment; and promote his faith through teaching and proselytizing. This list is not exhaustive, but it takes into account the main religious activities that have been at the heart of historical struggles carried on in the name of religious freedom. It is clear that, even solely with respect to matters of agency, there are countless degrees or gradations of religious freedom. The more things directly associated with religion that one can do, the more religious freedom one enjoys. A person who can observe religious rites but cannot belong to a community of religious believers has a certain amount of religious freedom, but he obviously has, *ceteris paribus*, less religious freedom than the individual who can both observe religious rites *and* belong to a community of religious believers.

Moreover, a person who can act on the basis of the religious world-view she accepts is obviously very much freer than a person who can act only on the basis of *some* religious commitment. To be able to do things associated with religion as such, and not to be determined to be a secularist, constitutes something that can reasonably be regarded as a primary form of religious freedom. But one clearly enjoys *more* religious freedom to the extent that one has not been determined to act on the basis of a *particular* religious world-view, especially insofar as one finds that particular world-view to be unacceptable. A committed Protestant who is forced to behave at certain times as a Roman Catholic behaves still enjoys religious freedom in that he is not forced to be, say, a secularist materialist (or even a non-Christian); but he does not have the degree of religious freedom that he would have if he were able to behave consistently as a Protestant, on the basis of a world-view that he genuinely, whole-heartedly *accepted*, and on the basis of the concomitant beliefs, attitudes, values, responsibilities, and special personal relationships. It is actually useful to distinguish *qualitatively* between freedom to do religious things and freedom to act on the basis of a specific religious world-view that one sincerely accepts.

With respect to agency, however, religious freedom can be a matter of being able to do various things only *indirectly* associated with religion. If we look at a wide range of historical struggles carried on in the name of religious freedom, we see that a person is often regarded as religiously free to the extent that, *ceteris paribus*, she enjoys the same civil rights and privileges and the same social courtesies that are enjoyed by people in her community who do not share her particular religious commitment. If someone is not permitted to own land or to attend a university because she is a Methodist or a Jew, then she is in one important sense not religiously free even though she is not being directly prevented from doing the things that being a Methodist or Jew involves. She would be freer if she were able to do those things without suffering disabilities in the civil and other secular domains of culture. Also, religious freedom has often been associated with one's ability to *avoid* religious activities; thus we can understand what, say, a secularist materialist means when he says that by being forced to practise certain religious rites — or being prevented from avoiding the practice of those rites — he is being denied religious freedom. Religious freedom is often construed to include the capacity or right to avoid religious activities of any kind.

When one does things "associated" with religion — in the various ways indicated above — one's religious freedom involves either doing what one wants, or doing what it is prudent for one to do, or doing what it is morally right for one to do, or some combination of these. Of course, ideally one always wants to do what it is prudent and morally right for one to do; but this ideal, like all ideals, is one that mere mortals can only hope to approach. In the sphere of religion, as in other spheres, we can conceive of conflicts between what we want to do, what it is prudent for us to do, and what we ought to do. One kind of religious freedom is the power to do whatever things "associated" with religion one wants to do, regardless of prudential or moral considerations. This may well strike one as being as close to the "ordinary" conception of religious freedom as we are likely to get. But think carefully. If we prevent a person from practising a bizarre religious rite that involves the death of thousands of innocent people, we are in a sense restricting his religious freedom; yet we do not *normally* think of religious freedom as involving one's capacity or right to do such a thing. And that is not simply because our religious views differ from those of such a fanatic, but because we believe that religious freedom must always be understood within a wider moral context, one that involves the agent's other interests, the interests of his fellow human beings and other creatures, the interests of civilization, ideals other than freedom (such as justice), and forms of culture or experience other than religion (for important and embracing as religion is, human beings are never *simply* religious). Of course, we can say that preventing the fanatic from carrying out his bizarre rite is a restriction of his religious freedom in one sense of the expression. When one does what one wants, then, regardless of whether one's action is prudent or morally right, it is a manifestation of a certain form of personal autonomy. Nevertheless, the case of the fanatic illustrates something that also applies in less extreme cases: that there is nothing especially "ordinary," "basic," or "fundamental" about the conception of religious freedom as doing whatever things "associated" with religion one *wants* to do.

Yet we can also see from history that the idea that religious freedom is properly understood only within a wider moral context is a potentially dangerous idea that can be mischievously exploited by those of a reactionary, authoritarian disposition. Such a position, after all, has often been cited by people unjustifiably professing to be moral experts when they have argued that the restrictions they have placed on someone's religious activities cannot be regarded as restrictions on his religious freedom in the "true" sense of the expression. It is hardly coincidental, then, that some of the major disputes about religious freedom over the centuries have turned on the questions of what constitutes the difference between the virtue of tolerance and the vice of permissiveness and what constitutes genuine moral and spiritual authority. Nor is it surprising that people of a liberal inclination are invariably suspicious when they hear theologians, politicians, and ideologists insist that "true" religious freedom is essentially a matter of doing what is prudent and right. We may think back here to Yves Simon's assertion that "One who is ruled for his own good or for the common good is a free man."[79] When we hear such a statement, we should immediately consider whether there are good reasons for sharing the speaker's view on who is fit to do all this ruling.

The issue of religious freedom does not arise solely with reference to agency; we can contrast freedom to do with freedom to be. To have religious freedom can be a matter of being able to be a certain kind of person. Of course, some types of freedom to be can be explained by reference to freedom to do. There are circumstances in which it is appropriate, for example, to understand being a Muslim or being a religious person as being someone who does certain things. Hence, if a person is unable to do various things "associated" with religion, he is not free to be a certain kind of religious person. However, such reduction is not always appropriate.

I particularly have in mind here the various types of "spiritual" and "psychological" freedom to which I alluded earlier. Viewed positively, these freedoms are optimum states of the "soul" or "mind." Viewed negatively, they involve one's personality's (the "internal," "interior," or "inner" self's) not being constrained in such a way that it is unable to attain a well-being variously conceived (or characterized) as health, peace, happiness, blessedness, and salvation. In the case of spiritual freedom, this well-being is seen as involving the individual's relationship with a transcendent or ideal order, while in the case of psychological freedom it is normally analyzed in a purely functional manner or in terms of pleasure.

Most religions teach that it is only through a religious faith and life (either a particular religious faith and life or one from among several adequate religious faiths and lives) that one can attain spiritual freedom or psychological freedom or both. In fact, I cannot think of any prominent religion, living or dead, that has not taught some version of this proposition. The proposition is usually, if not always, seen as having the corollary that only through a religious faith can one live well, for spiritual or psychological well-being is a necessary condition of behaving consistently in a virtuous and socially constructive, as well as satisfying, way. To the extent that one does what one does because one is what one is, we may say that freedom to be is a condition of freedom to do.

There is another kind of freedom to be that has been much discussed in recent years, and it is quite different from the freedom to be *well*. The most poignant comments on this form of freedom have been made by philosophers and other writers associated with the intellectual movement known as "existentialism," and in their honour I shall characterize this freedom as "existential" freedom. Existentialist writers, along with such celebrated precursors as Pascal, Kierkegaard, and Nietzsche, have stressed the extent to which at least some human beings have the capacity not only to determine much of what they do, but, more radically, to determine much of what they are. Interestingly, most of these writers have been religious, although perhaps not in a traditional or conventional way, while a few of them, such as Nietzsche and Sartre, have been among the most passionate and most powerful critics of religion. In either case, the phenomenon of religion and the question of its precise relation to human self-determination have occupied a large part of their attention.

To some who are concerned with existential freedom, the expression "religious freedom" must seem hollow, if not self-contradictory. But to others, religion, perhaps more than any other form of experience or culture, makes possible the kind of insight into oneself and others that stimulates one to abandon deterministic notions and transcend other determining factors and get on with the human project of self-determination through choice and commitment. A central theme of Christian and Jewish existentialism is the importance of this kind of freedom to be, a freedom at least partly known through religious experience and one which qualifies for the title of "religious freedom" along with the other types or aspects of freedom we have been considering.

9 Religious Freedom in Relation to Authority

Although I have indicated how various things that can be usefully characterized as forms of religious freedom can be seen as involving absence of constraints, I have not directly addressed the matter of what the actual constraints are. Even if freedom as such is not simply the absence of constraint, constraints are important in relation to freedom because they prevent one from enjoying the various types or aspects of "positive" freedom.

In a sense there is no limit to the number of things that might prevent one from enjoying the various religious freedoms. If one is hit by a truck while one is crossing the street, one's religious activities and one's chances of attaining spiritual and psychological well-being may be dramatically curtailed. But it would be foolish to brand the driver of the truck as "an enemy of religious freedom." The constraints that concern us are those that we can see from history to be directly relevant to religious freedom.

The most obvious of all "external" constraints related to religion are those involving authority, illegitimate authority, and abuse of authority. We would not be far off the mark if we concluded from historical studies that the major struggles for religious freedom have been attempts to shake off constraints established and justified in the name of authority. The pattern is familiar: Individuals and groups have wanted to do certain things and be certain types of people, and then someone "in authority" or some supposedly "authoritative" group or institution has stood in their way. Sometimes the dictates of those rightly or wrongly in authority have been accepted with humility, sometimes they have been accepted only grudgingly, and occasionally they have been met with rebelliousness.

The idea of authority has received much attention from theologians and political philosophers and has been the subject of considerable theorizing. For example, in a study of the idea in Christian literature, J. H. Schütz, drawing on theological and sociological sources, concludes that authority is the "interpretation of power" and corresponds to what Weber calls "legitimate domination."[80] The term *authority* appeared in English as far back as the thirteenth century and is ultimately derived from the Latin *auctoritas* (meaning, among other things, "advice," "opinion," and "command"), which is related to the term *auctor* (meaning "master" or "leader"), a term also related to the English term *author*.[81] In Kersey's 1708 dictionary, two distinct but related definitions of the term are worth noting: on one hand, the word refers to "Power, Rule, Preheminence [sic]," but it also refers to "a Testimony, or passage of an Author, quoted to make good what one says."[82] Reflecting on these two usages, which are still employed today, we can see how systematic ambiguities arose with respect to the term. We still often use the word to indicate power to command, enforce obedience, influence opinion and behaviour, judge, and so forth; and often we use the word to indicate some person, group, or institution that possesses such power. At times, however, we also imply that the power possessed by the people in question is in fact legitimate; we then mean to suggest by use of the term that we accept or endorse their exercise of power. At still other times, we play a more active role in determining authority by appealing to what we consider to be the wisdom or other virtue of some person, group, or institution that we have determined to treat as an authority (whether or not she, he, or it wishes to be treated that way); and thus we may say, "My authority on such matters is so-and-so."[83]

Authority is derived from very different sources. Actual authority may be derived from the ability of leaders to inspire fear, sincere respect, or even just a sense of the futility of attempts to overthrow it. Legitimate authority is derived from the ability of leaders to convince those subject to it that the leaders merit obedience; those who exercise legitimate authority are perceived by the totality of subjects as representing the most competent and trustworthy leaders available. "Availability" is an amorphous criterion, and legitimate authority almost always falls far short of being ideal authority.

Many disputes over religious freedom arise as a result of the perception that there is an intolerable gap between actual authority and legitimate authority. Sometimes these arise because those hitherto subject to an authority have lost confidence in the competence of the present leadership or the integrity of an institution. Sometimes they arise because people believe that more competent leaders are now available. Sometimes they arise because people no longer consider it futile to attempt to overthrow the entrenched leadership, or because they are not as worried as they once were about the danger of anarchy or disorder setting in once the present leadership has been abandoned. Sometimes they arise because people have gradually become convinced that what is legitimately authoritative in one sphere is only actually authoritative in another. Sometimes they arise because people have developed radically individualistic, anti-authoritarian, anarchical ideas, at least with respect to religious matters. When the actual authority of leaders is put under attack, they may respond with repressive measures or reasoned defences, and occasionally they may even abdicate. Disputes over religious freedom often develop into violent conflicts; indeed, they have figured prominently in many of the most infamous wars that have been waged throughout history and in all parts of the world.

Actual authority, even when legitimate or ideal, represents a limitation on personal autonomy to the extent that there is regret or dissatisfaction on the part of those acquiescing to it. However, it is reasonable to expect less regret and dissatisfaction from those who quite willingly acquiesce to actual authority that they regard as legitimate than from those who grudgingly acquiesce to actual authority that they do not regard as legitimate. Where one recognizes authority as legitimate, one will be prepared to grant that, though one's personal autonomy has been to some extent limited by such authority, one has religious freedom in a more profound sense, one that takes into account such factors as one's actual interests, one's communal responsibilities, and the need for guidance and order in one's community. Of course, when one sees one's spiritual and psychological well-being and one's existential integrity as threatened, one may no longer be willing to regard any authority that poses such a threat as legitimate, at least where religious matters are involved. Authoritarian leaders and institutions sometimes defend their repressive handling of dissent among their subjects by insisting that in the long run those subjects will be compensated for restrictions on their religious activity by the spiritual freedom that is so much more important. But the fact remains that dissenters have lost confidence in the ability of those in authority to deliver on precisely that promise.

The form of authority that represents perhaps the most obvious possible interference with religious activities and the religious quest for well-being is political authority. Leaders of the *polis* can have all sorts of motives for restricting the religious activities of at least certain subjects. They may fear the danger of religious pluralism as a source of conflict within the community; they may be heavily under the influence of the leaders of a particular religious denomination, either because they require the political support of those leaders or are committed members of the denomination; they may find it politically useful to curry favour among religious (or secularist) bigots who wish to see religious minorities humiliated and kept down; they may sincerely find the rites of some denominations abominable; they may feel it prudent to remind religious leaders that they have the power to inconvenience them and their flock; and so on. Sometimes disputes over religious freedom arise because the civil government is too closely involved with a particular denominational hierarchy (and in theocracies, there is more than just "involvement"); sometimes they arise because the civil government is militantly secularist and anti-religious; sometimes they arise because the civil government has failed to keep the peace among conflicting denominations and has failed to establish and safeguard civil liberties with respect to religion; and sometimes they arise because political leaders are prepared to try almost anything that might conceivably secure or extend their power and influence.

Another major threat to religious freedoms is posed by denominational hierarchies themselves. Here, mediaeval popes and bishops may come to mind; but the fact is that almost all clergymen of all faiths — and lay religious leaders — are constantly working to see to it that those subordinate to them in the pecking order, and particularly the ordinary members, are doing what they think such people should be doing. It was, of course, religious institutions that endowed the world with such categories as heresy, heterodoxy, apostasy, nonconformity, and idolatry. It was high-ranking clerics who created the Inquisition and hundreds of less conspicuous institutions that foreshadowed it or copied it. But of equal importance is the clergyman who lives next door or down the street who uses his power as pastor and teacher to limit the activity and influence of co-religionists with "strange" notions; and so is the academic theologian, in his clerical garb or his tweed suit, who through clever mockery of unpopular opinions may induce those who look up to him to follow the straight and narrow course of consecrated tradition and established truth. These people are not only eager to limit the activity and influence of "wayward" members of their own denomination, but are often at least as zealous in their attempts to limit the capacities of upstarts and overreachers in rival denominations.[84] It is hardly surprising, then, that despite their fears of state interference in religious matters, many of the greatest advocates of religious freedom have looked to the state to promote and protect it by checking the influence of high-handed ecclesiastical bureaucrats.

Even if we consider only the two aforementioned types of authority, those involving political and denominational (in the case of Christianity, ecclesiastical) leadership, we can see that it may be an oversimplification to characterize the constraints they represent as purely "external." For often, if not typically, the agent who considers herself constrained by such forms of authority can choose to reject the dictates of leaders, risk the consequences, and carry on with the religious activities that the leaders have called into question. If, say, fear of loss of property or social position is a factor contributing to her acquiescence, then clearly there is an "internal" dimension to the constraint, no matter how arbitrarily and aggressively the leaders have been exercising their authority. Some notable passages in Aristotle's *Nicomachean Ethics* come to mind. At the beginning of Book III, Aristotle makes some famous distinctions that have greatly influenced subsequent philosophical reflection on freedom and responsibility. He asserts without qualification that actions are compulsory when the cause is in the external circumstances and the agent contributes nothing. But he recognizes that in many important cases compulsion is not as obvious as in the case of someone being carried somewhere by a wind. He allows, then, that some acts are "mixed," for while not involuntary in the strictest possible sense of the word, they are involuntary in another sense, for people would not choose to do such acts unless they were under some significant pressure. Aristotle recognizes that it is often difficult to determine the degree of an agent's responsibility under such circumstances.[85] Still, we can see that the "internal" dimension of constraint is more significant in the case of a person who acquiesces to authority because of fear of loss of social position than in the case of a person who acquiesces to authority because of torture. Even in the former case, however, we must not forget that the political or denominational leaders' repressive exercise of authority is an important "external" dimension of the constraint limiting the agent's activity. "External" constraint is present even when the political and denominational leaders limit their subjects' although when no pain is involved in these processes, one might be inclined to believe that the constraint is primarily "internal" or even to agree with Aristotle that there is no compulsion at all.[86]

Political and denominational authority are not the only forms of authority that constitute a threat to religious freedoms. Much less discussed but perhaps more important in the long run is parental authority. Parents normally do not offer their children a choice of what religious world-view to accept, nor do they typically encourage their children to visit various religious communities in order to decide which one they will join. Parents exercise tremendous power over their children, and it is no coincidence that most children grow up to worship according to the "faith of their fathers." The main reason why this form of constraint historically has not received as much attention as the others we have considered is that it has been widely and rather arbitrarily assumed over the centuries that children, being immature, have few, if any, rights because they are incapable of responsibly exercising freedoms. There is perhaps no more dramatic instance of the importance of parental authority in the religious sphere than the not uncommon situation in which parents decide for ostensibly religious reasons that their child should not receive life-saving medical treatment.

A related form of authority that receives too little attention is academic and professional authority. For example, if a pseudo-liberal professor gives a student low grades solely because he is offended by certain religious assumptions and attitudes that the student brings to her philosophical and social-scientific essays, or even if he simply encourages other students to ridicule their classmate's piety, he may well be abusing authority. So too may be the fundamentalist teacher who uses his position to intimidate or otherwise indoctrinate those who are disinclined to interpret historical and scientific matters as he does. The social influence of academic "experts" — and professional "experts" in general, particularly journalists, broadcasters, physicians, lawyers, and economists — is even greater in highly advanced societies than in others and, because it is usually more subtle and indiscernible than most traditional forms of the exercise of political and ecclesiastical power, it is often an even more dangerous threat to religious freedoms than they are. For example, in recent years the periodical press in North America has perhaps done more, on balance, to limit the religious activities of individuals and churches on this continent than any group of elected politicians has.[87] I grant, however, that the exercise of authority tends to be more subtle and indiscernible in precisely those situations in which the "internal" dimension of constraint is more significant.

The "internal" dimension figures even more significantly in cases in which an individual acquiesces to the authority of such things as tradition and convention (including "peer group pressure"). And the authority of such faculties as reason and conscience is usually deemed to be primarily an "internal" constraint despite the fact that such faculties are heavily influenced by input from "external" authorities.

10 "Internal" Constraints; Absence of Opportunity

We have already considered in passing certain things that may qualify as "internal" constraints and how they blend together with "external" constraints to limit religious activity in such a way that one may be said to have been prevented from doing what one wants to do. There are many reflective people who are troubled by the notion of an "internal" constraint. They see this notion as leading us down the garden path to radical determinism of a kind that leaves no room for personal responsibility. However, in everyday life people recognize the existence of not only the kinds of acts Aristotle characterized as "mixed" but also various kinds of mental or psychological compulsion. Outside of mental illness, the most obvious of these is addiction. Alcoholism, for example, not only prevents one from attaining spiritual and psychological well-being but prevents one from performing certain activities that one considers as religious obligations. Even if a person were largely responsible for allowing himself to turn into an alcoholic, we would still recognize that in his present state he does not enjoy certain religious freedoms. Certain habits that are seen as falling short of being outright addictions are also often regarded as qualifying as "internal" constraints. Since the time of the ancients it has been recognized that, while people usually are largely responsible for their vices, vices are sometimes instilled in a person through poor upbringing and other corrupting influences, and deep-rooted vices are extremely difficult to throw off. The same applies to certain rigid ways of thinking that have been derived mainly through corrupt systems of "education" that amount to little more than indoctrination and conditioning. Although many children, as well as most adults, have highly developed powers of critical reflection, open-mindedness is an important and often undervalued *virtue* that needs to be patiently and carefully nurtured, and people cannot always be fairly blamed for having failed to cultivate it on their own without any support from parents, teachers, and broad-minded peers.[88]

One could say, perhaps, that ignorance itself — combined with the atrophy of the rational and other cognitive faculties that remove this obstacle to religious and other freedoms — is the most important "internal" constraint. There are, as Aristotle observes in the *Nicomachean Ethics*, intellectual as well as moral virtues.[89] We should remember, however, that many people dismiss as "ignorance" any worldview that differs significantly from their own, even if commitment to it has been the result of lengthy and disciplined reflection. When, say, a shallow Christian asserts that it is the thoughtful Buddhist's "ignorance" that is preventing him from attaining spiritual freedom or well-being of one sort or another, she is not saying much more than that her views differ from the Buddhist's, although she is also giving us an indication of her own shallowness.

Those who distinguish between "external" and "internal" constraints tend to think of the latter as constraints that *as individuals* we are in a substantially stronger position to remove. However, as we have now seen, this view may involve wishful thinking. Moreover, the various constraints typically characterized as "external" and "internal" are often blended together in such complex ways that it is impossible to determine whether the dominant aspect of a particular constraint is "external" or "internal." With respect to this point, let us consider one more major obstacle to religious freedoms.

Although we may not think of it as such, absence of opportunity represents a very significant constraint in the sphere of religion. For example, if one lives in a part of Asia or Africa where one has little, if any, contact with Christians or Christian literature, then, as Christian missionaries are given to reminding us, one is lacking a certain kind of freedom: if one is not actually being deprived of the possibility of spiritual freedom, one is at least being deprived of the possibility of doing certain religious things that, were one offered a choice, one might elect to do. In a certain sense, one is not free to the extent that one is not able to choose from among more alternatives than one is now. The more alternatives open to one, then, *ceteris paribus*, the freer one is. We think in these terms particularly when we recognize that, in a specific situation, an agent has fewer alternatives to choose from than other people have, either because she lives in a certain place, comes from a disadvantaged socio-economic background, has the wrong social connections, has a physical handicap, or whatever. There are obviously countless reasons why a person, in the religious sphere or any other, might have fewer alternatives from which to choose than other people do, even the people who live next door, or her own brothers and sisters.

These countless ways in which one may be constrained by absence of opportunity would seem, for the most part, to be "external" constraints. No one chooses to be born in a particular place, to particular parents, in a particular socio-economic stratum, with such-and-such ailments, and so on. It is a fact of life that some people are born with advantages that you and I were not given at birth; similarly, some people inherit burdens that you and I will never have to bear. And as life goes on, each one of us picks up more advantages and more disadvantages in relation to one's various fellows.

But we need not be fatalistic about all of this. Social theorists and social reformers have always been sensitive to the extent to which absence of certain kinds of opportunity is a function of systematic exploitation and oppression of the disadvantaged by cultural and even trans-cultural elites. Opportunities in the realm of religion are among others that have been systematically denied to oppressed people. Often such oppression is directly related to abuse of political and denominational authority. Sometimes, however, it is a result of more complex factors, such as social structures themselves. (This is a major theme of recent liberation theology.) In any case, we are obliged to recognize that absence of opportunity, whether an obstacle to our own personal freedom or to the freedom of others, is often something that we are in a position to do something constructive about. To regard absence of opportunity as invariably something that we and others simply must learn to accept stoically is itself to be incapacitated by a constraint that has a significant "internal" dimension. No one can single-handedly solve all of the world's social problems or ameliorate the condition of all of the oppressed people of the world; but almost all of us are in a position to make some *contribution* towards eliminating hindrances to freedom that severely disadvantaged people have had to suffer. And most of us are also often in a position to do something to remedy our own lack of opportunity. There are many ways in which one can better oneself; and although it may be unfair that one should have to work at achieving a condition (intellectual, economic, or whatever) that is not nearly as desirable as that for which others have not had to expend the slightest effort, this does not justify a fatalistic attitude. To some extent people are free to make themselves freer through disciplined and imaginative efforts at personal growth. As Fransen has observed, "Freedom never comes to us as full-grown adult creativeness but is given to us as a risk-fraught and daring adventure, as a splendid human task in fulfilling which we must freely grow toward an even deeper, fuller and more ample freedom, an ever more transparent authenticity. We are called to freedom rather than being empowered with freedom or set up in a completely free human situation."[90] Yet however we may be inspired by evidence of what courageous people have managed to accomplish under very difficult circumstances, we must always be mindful of those things that are genuinely beyond our control, or the control of the agents whose situation we are considering.

11   The Ideal Beyond the Rhetoric

No general definition of the expression "religious freedom" will be offered here. Such a definition would inevitably be either vacuous ("religious freedom is freedom somehow related to religion"; or "religious freedom is the ability to do or be something involving the spiritual or transcendent"), or too narrow ("religious freedom is the absence of political constraints upon one's religious worship"; or "religious freedom is spiritual health"), or convoluted and ever expanding. We could perhaps say that there is at most a family resemblance between one and another usage of the expression. That does not mean, of course, that the expression is so ambiguous that it is consistently worthless and misleading and should be scrapped. But why, you may wonder, have I concentrated on the expression rather than just on the relations of religion and freedom? Part of the answer is that use of the expression gives us some guidance as to what people consider to be the most important relations of religion and freedom; and in any event, the ambiguity of the expression mirrors the ambiguity of its component terms. Part of the answer is that it may be contrasted with such expressions as "freedom of religion," "liberal religion," "religious liberty," and "religious autonomy," all of which have a narrower range of applicability that may lead us to neglect certain important relations of religion and freedom. But most importantly, when we focus on the expression itself, we are reminded of all that rhetoric by which people with one or another axe to grind try to influence the attitudes, policies, and practices of political and denominational communities. Thus, we hear references to religious freedom and related matters by defenders of religion, critics of religion, politicians, jurists, orthodox clerics, radical religious reformers, theologians, social scientists, resentful laymen, and many others; and they all want to see something changed. But somewhere in the distance there is an ideal — a moral and intellectual ideal, an ideal of civilization — and it should not be left to careless or sophistical rhetoric to determine our vision of that ideal.

I have indicated in the opening paragraphs of this study what the basic problem is that concerns me and how I intend to approach it.

This investigation is philosophical, or at least it tries to be. Philosophers sometimes indulge in rhetoric; they too have axes to grind, and when they theorize aloud and lay their classificatory schemes before us, they are letting us know that they think we would be wiser, happier, and better if we were more like them. But any philosopher worth the name is at least sometimes a "lover of wisdom"; and if we are to take the view of Socrates and Plato seriously, then the primary motives and skills of the philosopher and the rhetorician are wholly different.[91]

2 Religion as a Hindrance to Freedom

While prepared to grant that some forms of religious life are freer than others, critics of religion itself, or of the monotheistic, prophetic type of religion that has long been dominant in the Middle East and the West, have frequently pronounced that religion as such, or at least Western religion, is, as a form of culture and experience, inimical to the most important kinds of freedom. This is a radical thesis that we usually associate with such controversial thinkers as Nietzsche, Marx, and Freud. However, even religious apologists have felt obliged to acknowledge that there are important ways in which religion as such, or at least Western religion, is by its very nature a hindrance to freedom. Such people sometimes add that we must be careful not to overestimate the importance of freedom in relation to other ideals; and often, as we have noted, they see a higher freedom as compensating the believer for his loss of lower freedoms.

Many scholars have noted what they take to be the "paradoxical" character of Christianity's involvement with freedom; even when they do not actually use this term, one can see that they are struck by the tension in the most prominent Western religion's relations with the ideal. While recognizing that Christianity promises to its adherents a freedom of the highest order, they are not blind to the ways in which Christian thought and practice have systematically undermined some widely valued freedoms. What applies to Christianity in this regard may not apply to the same extent to other religions, but Christianity has, as a religion, much in common with other religions too; and special attention to Christianity is warranted here not only because of its historical importance in the West — and specifically in most of the places in which this volume will be read — but because of the imposing amount of philosophical, theological, and social-scientific theory that it has come to have associated with it.

Let us consider several attempts to formulate the paradoxes involved in the relations between Christianity and freedom. John

Macquarrie writes that "Faith in Jesus Christ has . . . been paradoxically described in terms of both grace and decision, and this is the familiar paradox of the divine and human action meeting together in the personal dimensions of the Christian life. This life is on the one hand obedience, which is an essential constituent of faith. It conforms the believer to Christ's own obedience. His own will is offered to God, so that the divine grace may work in and through him."[1] In Hans Küng's words, "The Christian's freedom, with its paradoxical harmonization of independence and duties, power and renunciation, autonomy and service, dominion and slavery, is a mystery to the world."[2] And focusing his attention on Holy Scripture, as is appropriate for the Protestant theologian that he is, Millar Burrows concludes not only that "No distinct conception of what we call the will as volitional effort is apparent in either the Old or the New Testament,"[3] but that "There is . . . no clear, consistent biblical teaching on the question of freedom versus predestination. Perhaps that is why it has aroused such hot controversy and even split Christian churches. The language of passages dealing at all with the subject is often ambiguous, and it is not always clear whether groups or individuals are in view."[4]

Adopting the perspective of the historian and social theorist rather than the theologian, Northcott observes that "It is one of the paradoxes of Christianity that it holds within itself revolutionary teaching about liberty for the individual and what often seems to be a reactionary intolerance in dealing with the results of liberty."[5] And Muller suggests that interpretation here depends much on perspective: "[M]any thinkers hold that Christianity is the fountainhead of Western ideals of freedom and democracy, and insist that only on a religious basis can we hope to maintain these ideals. Other thinkers see religion as a relic of primitive fear of the unknown, 'the sum of scruples that interfere with the free exercise of human faculties,' or even a calculated opiate for the masses, 'a device for keeping people quiet while skinning them.'"[6] Often a critic (or defender) of religion sees what she wants to see; but there is no dearth of open-minded scholars who are more impressed by the tensions themselves.

1   The Theological Basis of Religious Repression: Hebrew Scripture

Our starting-point for further reflection is a consideration of various passages in Hebrew Scripture, and particularly in the Torah or

Pentateuch. Hebrew Scripture not only is the first (and larger and older) part of Christianity's Bible, but is at the core of Judaism, one of the world's living religions and historically one of the most influential. According to Burrows, "The problem of freedom is not felt in the Old Testament. The facts of experience on both sides of the question are presented, and God's sovereignty and man's responsibility are both emphasized."[7] Whether or not the problem is actually "felt" in Hebrew Scripture, generations of philosophers and theologians have rightly seen it as arising there and have felt compelled to address it with their own theorizing.

The problem arises right from the start, for at Genesis 1:1 God is identified as having created heaven and earth and thus is indicated as the first and pre-eminent determining factor; and since at Genesis 1:2 God is identified as a spiritual being ("the Spirit of God moved upon the face of the waters"), we are led to conclude that God is responsible for things being the way they are.[8] The following verses indicate that God has (or at least once had) a plan and that He has employed something analogous (though superior) to human reason. The creation of man is described at Genesis 1:26–31 and 2:4–25: we are told that God created man in His own image, after His likeness, that He blessed the first male and female, and that He gave them dominion over all living things. God breathed the breath of life into man, who was formed of the dust of the ground, and man became a living soul. And God put man into the Garden of Eden and instructed him, "Of every tree of the garden thou mayest freely eat; But of the tree of the knowledge of good and evil, thou shalt not eat of it; for in the day that thou eatest thereof thou shalt surely die."[9]

Though countless pages have been written about these passages, most people are not as troubled as they might be by the philosophical problems that the passages pose for an understanding of personal autonomy. For, on the one hand, man is portrayed as a living soul, created in God's image, who has dominion over other creatures, may freely eat certain things, and has been given the option of choosing to disobey God's command (and die). On the other hand, man has not determined himself to existence but rather has been created by God, for unidentified purposes, to be as he is. Moreover, despite the dominion and freedom he has been given, man has been denied permission by the highest possible authority, the Creator, to eat from a particular tree. So, while he is free in one sense to eat from that tree, he is not free in another sense. Man was from the start, and continues to be, rather bewildered by the rules of this complex game; for if God could make man exactly as He wished him to be, why did He make him in such a way that he could (and perhaps inevitably would) defy God's command and interfere with God's plan? Why did He create a tree from which man could eat even though He did not want man to eat from it? We may perhaps assume that being a living soul created in God's image necessitated man's being free; but if man has been created after God's likeness, why would he be so stupid as to consider defying God? Why, if God has made him in His own image, has God refused man permission to behave with complete freedom? And why did God create the first man as free if he lacked, and was not permitted to attain, knowledge of good and evil? There have been some very profound and some equally silly answers to such questions over the centuries, but some reflective people are still troubled by those questions.

Genesis 3 describes the fall. A serpent allowed by God to hang around the Garden of Eden tempted the woman to eat the forbidden fruit; she ate it and induced her husband to eat it, and as a result God imposed all sorts of punishments on them. Interestingly, when interrogated by God, both the man and the woman denied that they were responsible for what they had done. The man pointed to the woman, and the woman pointed to the serpent. Had they been more sophisticated at metaphysics, they might have reminded God that prior to eating the forbidden fruit they had had no moral conceptions. But they were disobedient nevertheless, and God put enmity between them, and between them and their seed. He decided to make childbirth unpleasant for women, and to make man work hard for his bread, and He expelled man and woman — and with them all their descendants — from Eden. A naive or irreverent person might call into question God's severity. After all, God had made the man and woman what they were, and their decision to eat the forbidden fruit, if it indeed qualifies as a genuine decision, was uninformed by moral insight, which had been initially denied to them. Besides, though they were disobedient in some sense — in the way a very young child is, perhaps — they were acting according to their nature and, ironically, they had become the sort of creatures that henceforth God would constantly be demanding human beings to aspire to be, that is, morally responsible agents. Indeed, they had become freer and more like God Himself, as God readily acknowledged.[10] Genesis 4 relates the tale of Cain and Abel. Cain was angry because the Lord respected his brother's offering but not his own. In his anger, Cain killed his brother, and as a result he was severely punished by God. Again, a naive or irreverent person might ask why God, with all His power, allowed enmity to develop between the brothers, and even promoted it by respecting the offering of only one of them. And even if Cain was morally responsible in a way that his parents were not when they ate the forbidden fruit, it is not hard to understand why someone who had probably received little moral education lost his temper and became irrational when he came to perceive himself as the victim of a conspiracy between his brother and God.

Many theologians and high-ranking religious leaders have seen these events as having actually taken place and as having had tremendous implications for the human race — and for God. Intensely bitter theological disputes have been waged over the precise significance of these events, but it is enough for us to note here that the first chapters of Hebrew Scripture raise some awesome conceptual puzzles about what it means to be free in a world created and dominated by a transcendent Spirit.

For one thing, the opening chapters raise a classic version of the problem of causal determinism vis-à-vis freedom: how can a human being or community be free when everything has been determined to be as it is, was, and always will be by a first cause, a Creator-God? But even more striking is the way in which these chapters establish God as the eternal Authority of authorities. God is presented as supreme Father figure and King of kings, as the supreme paternal *and* political authority. God is to His subjects "our Father, our King," as a famous Hebrew liturgical expression reminds us. As Father, He was involved in bringing us into existence, has an intense and unflagging interest in our welfare, is principal teacher and guide, and is One to whom we must answer for our deeds. But this Father, unlike human fathers, has created the universe, is eternal, knows all the thoughts as well as all the deeds of all His creatures (and cannot be deceived or hidden from), and is absolutely perfect. As King of the universe, He has supreme dominion over everything, is He who must be obeyed by even the mightiest princes and pharaohs, and is the source of the Law which overrides (and is properly the inspiration for) any and every possible moral or legal code. And He is not only Father and King, paternal and political Authority of authorities, but He is the Lord God, the religious and spiritual authority *par excellence*, and we find in Scripture that He has many names, each of which gives to His subjects some insight — the limited insight of which a mortal is capable — into an aspect of His perfection. Moreover, not only does He judge one and all and dispense the ultimate rewards and punishments, but He is the Author of the Divine Plan, which only He knows and understands, and in which human beings are to play a role despite their inability to understand the ultimate significance of that role. Indeed, it is their primary function and purpose in life to fulfil their obligations on the basis of the little that they know about those obligations, which has been provided to them through Revelation, prophecy, and the guidance of those individuals and institutions chosen by God to be His special agents and instruments. The supreme, multiform Authority of God is perhaps nowhere else in Scripture more poignantly characterized than at Exodus 34:5–7, where we are told of how Moses brought the tables of the Law down from Sinai:

> And the Lord descended in the cloud, and stood with him there, and proclaimed the name of the Lord. And the Lord passed by before him, and proclaimed, The Lord, The Lord God, merciful and gracious, long-suffering, and abundant in goodness and truth, Keeping mercy for thousands, forgiving iniquity and transgression and sin, and that will by no means clear the guilty; visiting the iniquity of the fathers upon the children, and upon the children's children, unto the third and to the fourth generation.

These powerful lines underscore man's responsibility, but their description of God's sovereignty seems to leave little room open for the existential freedom to which so many noble, high-minded individuals have aspired.

Let us focus now on four themes in the Torah that are particularly troubling to those who attach great importance to the ideal of freedom: election, socio-economic slavery, the Law, and prophetic and priestly authority. The first is election. Throughout the Torah, God is portrayed as "playing favourites." Sometimes, as in the case of Noah, we are given some idea as to why God prefers some people to others;[11] but more often, God's special concern with some people — or peoples — at the expense of others may well appear to us to be somewhat arbitrary. The primary instance of this is the case of the children of Israel themselves. Hebrew Scripture is largely an account of various stages in the history of the Jewish people or, more exactly, of the descendants of the patriarchs Abraham, Isaac, and Jacob. Indeed, to these people, God is the God of their fathers — the God of Abraham, the God of Isaac, and the God of Jacob. Now, while only a fool would deny the historical and continuing importance of this people, the reader of Hebrew Scripture may well be troubled by the comparative unimportance of other peoples, such as the Egyptians, Babylonians, Hittites, Chinese, Ethiopians, and Greeks. God is so often seen punishing the children of Israel that other peoples might be thankful that they do not figure so prominently in the Divine Plan. But even if they are materially more prosperous than the children of Israel, other peoples may resent the fact that, if Hebrew Scripture is reliable as history and metaphysics, by an accident of birth they have been denied the opportunity to be of central importance in the unfolding of the Divine Plan. This resentment should not be taken lightly, for it is, among other things, one of the major pillars of anti-Semitism. What may be especially disturbing to these other peoples is that, throughout Hebrew Scripture, the children of Israel are not usually portrayed as a particularly noble people worthy of God's special attention but rather are commonly depicted as a stiff-necked, ungrateful, small-minded rabble constantly on the verge of slipping into materialism or idolatry.[12]

A corresponding arbitrariness may appear to mark God's election of prophets, leaders, and even victims. A notable example is that of Moses himself, greatest of the Hebrew prophets, who was ordained prior to his birth to deliver his people from bondage.[13] A very different example is that of the pharaoh with whom Moses had to deal, for as Burrows points out with reference to Exodus 3:19 and 4:21, "The idea of God's overruling control appears in its harshest form in the statement that God hardened Pharaoh's heart and yet punished him severely."[14] Again, "The use of Assyria and other nations as instruments of divine judgment, according to the conception of the prophets and historians, implies God's control of men's actions. Second Isaiah's argument for monotheism makes much of Yahweh's foreknowledge of history, and God knows what will happen because it is he who determines from the beginning what is to be, calling men and nations to work his will."[15]

A second noteworthy theme here is that of Hebrew Scripture's treatment of the subject of socio-economic slavery. It has often been observed that the exodus of the Hebrew slaves from Egypt is the central event of the entire Pentateuch. The Ten Commandments begin with the words, "I am the Lord thy God, which have brought thee out of the land of Egypt, out of the house of bondage."[16] Paul van Buren has rightly observed that the exodus from Egypt is the "greatest of all images of freedom in the Bible";[17] furthermore, "to the question of who they were and why they were what they were, Israel's classic answer was this: 'We were Pharaoh's slaves in Egypt and the Lord brought us out of Egypt with a mighty hand!' Slaves set free! That is the beginning of this people, and in the light of that happening (the Exodus, they called it), they interpreted their whole past and even the very creation of the world."[18] Countless generations of people of all faiths and cultures have looked to the story of the exodus as a classic affirmation of the primacy of freedom and an incomparably vivid celebration of the quest for freedom. And, on another occasion, Moses uttered the memorable words, "proclaim liberty throughout all the land unto all the inhabitants thereof."[19]

But does Hebrew Scripture ultimately affirm the primacy of freedom? Three rather different considerations may suggest otherwise. First, consider van Buren's further thoughts on the subject: "Slaves set free. And yet that is not really what happened. Israel's exodus was not the first nor the last time in human history in which slaves have been emancipated only to find their new freedom a condition worse than their old servitude. . . . They were set free, not to do as they chose or to go where they would, but to be the slaves of the One who had emancipated them. . . . They were set free to be the people of their Liberator."[20] Secondly, "Was it really *freedom* into which Israel was released? Free to worship a golden calf, free to demand a king against God's wishes, a king free to murder his trusted lieutenant in order to steal his victim's wife, Bathsheba? Is it a God of freedom who sets a people free to sell the needy for a pair of shoes, and then to be again made slaves in Babylon?"[21] Or, one might add, to be tortured to death in Nazi concentration camps and to be blown up by Arab terrorists?

Finally, the reader of Hebrew Scripture can hardly fail to be struck by the matter-of-fact way in which it sometimes appears to sanction slavery, even the enslavement of one's fellow Hebrews. So, for example, whereas at Exodus 20:2 we find God drawing attention to His having brought Israel out of the house of bondage, in the very next chapter, at 21:2, we read, "If thou buy an Hebrew servant, six years he shall serve; and in the seventh he shall go out free for nothing."

Hebrew Scripture's emphasis on the Law is familiar mainly through Christian caricatures of it. However, there is undoubtedly a genuine contrast between the Pauline and Mosaic views of the Law. In Galatians, for example, we read such things as, "Christ hath redeemed us from the curse of the law, being made a curse for us" (3:13), and, "Stand fast therefore in the liberty wherewith Christ hath made us free, and be not entangled again with the yoke of bondage. . . . Christ is become of no effect unto you, whosoever of you are justified by the law; ye are fallen from grace" (5:1, 4). In Deuteronomy, however, the theme is markedly different: "Therefore thou shalt love the Lord thy God, and keep his charge, and his statutes, and his judgments, and his commandments, alway" (11:1). Common to both faiths is the primacy of the commandment that "thou shalt love the Lord thy God with all thine heart, and with all thy soul, and with all thy might" (6:5); but in Hebrew Scripture, and most emphatically in the Pentateuch, love of God is primarily associated with observance of His commandments. It is not hard for someone unfamiliar with the Jewish tradition to understand why men and women should not feel free to kill, steal, and bear false witness against their neighbour;[22] but it is not unreasonable to expect him to be surprised at the importance attached to such things as not eating camel meat and not shaving around one's temples.[23]

A fourth notable theme concerns prophetic and priestly authority. In the Pentateuch, God is shown at times to be a very firm sovereign, as, for example, when He destroyed the corrupt cities of Sodom and Gomorrah.[24] Hebrew Scripture also draws our attention to the severity of God's agents. Consider Numbers 25 as a case in point, for we learn there that Moses instructed the judges of Israel, "Slay ye every one his men that were joined unto Baal-peor," and that Phinehas thrust a javelin through the abdomen of a Midianitish woman about to corrupt the congregation.[25] The text leaves no question about the integrity of such leaders; they were clearly agents of God's will. It is important to note, however, that while often God is portrayed in Hebrew Scripture as having acted directly, more often He is seen as having delegated authority to prophets, priests, and other agents.

When God intervened directly in human affairs, as when He performed miracles, the children of Israel were suitably awed. But when His agents issued directives, the mob was not always accommodating. In the time of Moses, as in our own time, many people resented and resisted claims to authority, even when such claims had been shown time and again to be reliable. They resented doing things that they did not want to do, they resented not being able to do things that they did want to do, and they resented having to believe, trust, and obey a fellow human being, and even their God. In light of the austerity of so many ostensibly prophetic injunctions, we may perhaps have some sympathy for them.

We may even be able to sympathize to some extent with Korah and his fellow rebels, whose stinging words against what they perceived as the authoritarianism of Moses have a remarkably modern ring to them, and are strikingly similar to the words of many of history's famous rebels, both high-minded and self-serving. "Ye take too much upon you, seeing all the congregation are holy, every one of them, and the Lord is among them; wherefore then lift ye up yourselves above the congregation of the Lord?"[26] Having had no trouble recognizing this play for power for what it was, Moses was nevertheless disconsolate; but

God interceded, and Korah and his gang were swallowed up by the earth.[27] Rarely, however, were Hebrew (or any other) prophets able to rely on such a decisive show of support from the Authority of authorities when dealing with a refractory rabble. Still, while the reader of Hebrew Scripture cannot help sympathizing or even identifying with the likes of an Elijah or Jeremiah, we may speculate that the children of Israel may have occasionally put their scepticism and recalcitrance to good use by refusing to follow certain self-professed prophets who were actually scheming or deluded imposters.

Much has been made by certain theorists, such as Spinoza, of the fact that Hebrew Scripture treats theocracy as the ideal constitution.[28] Although this interpretation is plausible, several qualifications should be kept in mind. First, as we have already noted, though God is sometimes portrayed in the books of the Torah and Prophets as having interceded directly in human affairs, more often than not He is seen as having worked through agents. Thus, even the Mosaic theocracy, while perceived by the faithful as ultimately being ruled by God, was ruled by Moses and his associates in God's name. Secondly, throughout most of Hebrew Scripture, there is a matter-of-fact acceptance of a certain degree of separation between political and spiritual authority. The case of the aforementioned Elijah comes to mind; for the point being stressed by Elijah was not that he himself was the rightful king but that the statesmen of Israel should be faithful to the high moral precepts of the Torah.[29] Thirdly, although Moses was certainly the supreme prophet, statesman, and military leader of his people, the priesthood itself was left to Aaron and his progeny.[30] Although the Torah associates priesthood primarily with the supervision of ritual sacrifice, the institution of the priesthood was destined to give a remarkable amount of power to a particular family, for not only was priestly authority to be passed on from one generation of Levites to the next, but the Levites were to receive a variety of economic and social privileges.[31] Whereas anyone could conceivably be chosen by God as a prophet, even an enemy of Israel such as Balaam,[32] the high spiritual authority of the priesthood was reserved for Levites alone.

We have considered several themes in a work — or, if you prefer, a corpus of writings — that has exercised unparalleled influence upon world civilization. Of course, Christian and Islamic conceptions of freedom, determining factors, and authority are not merely modest refinements of the corresponding conceptions in Hebrew Scripture; even in the Jewish tradition there has been considerable development in this sphere. And conceptions of freedom, determining factors, and authority had an independent development in the Orient. Yet the impact of the metaphysical, moral, and socio-political outlook of the books of the Torah and Prophets — an outlook that can itself be seen as having undergone significant development from the earlier to the later books — is immense and, on reflection, not a little awesome.

On the basis of what we have seen, it all but goes without saying that Hebrew Scripture has not always been looked upon as a classic of liberal or existential theory. J. B. Bury, the celebrated historian of freedom of thought, heaps scorn on Hebrew Scripture for being "full of savagery" and "corrupting the morals of men."[33] "It burnished an armoury for the theory of persecution. The truth is that Sacred Books are an obstacle to moral and intellectual progress, because they consecrate the ideas of a given epoch, and its customs, as divinely appointed."[34] While there is a useful insight here, Bury's point is overstated, mainly because it presupposes a crude form of cultural and historicist relativism. Bury's point is related to the anti-Semitic canard that it was the Jews who invented "exclusivism" and infected Christianity with it.[35] Even a sober scholar like Northcott is moved to suggest that "Historically it was the Hebrew and Christian conception of a single and universal God that introduced a religious exclusivism leading to compulsion and persecution in the realm of religion. Ancient religions were regarded as confined to each separate people believing in them, and the question of change from one religious belief to another did not arise."[36] Northcott and kindred writers fail to appreciate the extent to which monotheism promotes the ideal of brotherhood and breaks down the barriers between cultures in conflict.

A more profound criticism that might be leveled against the Hebraic world-view is that it left limited room for individualism. Here it must be remembered that in this regard the ancient Hebrews resembled other peoples. As A. J. Carlyle writes, "the characteristic of a primitive and in a large measure of a barbaric society, is the solidarity of the group, the fact that the individual counts for little or nothing compared with the group, and has little autonomy or independence in the group."[37] Carlyle is particularly critical of seventeenth- and eighteenth-century political theorists who naively assumed that in the beginning human beings were separate and isolated units; in his view, the development of the Western idea of individual personality belongs to the period between Aristotle and the rise of Christianity.[38] However, while it is true that Hebrew Scripture often uses broad strokes to characterize such peoples as the Egyptians, Edomites, Moabites, and Israelites themselves, it cannot be reasonably maintained that Hebrew Scripture, with its focus on charismatic figures, its keen psychological analyses of saints, sinners, and morally ambiguous types, and its fascination with the theme of the lonely hero versus the crowd, wholly ignores individual personality and is thoroughly anti-individualistic in tone.

2   The Theological Basis of Religious Repression: The New Testament

Since Christianity was heavily influenced by Hebrew thought, we can expect to find some of the themes we have considered appearing in some form in the New Testament. But Christianity not only was also influenced by Greek thought and by the highly personal visions of its founders, but was in important ways built upon a reaction against the basic Hebrew world-view. We have already seen the apostle Paul's attitude towards the Law to be a case in point; there and elsewhere, Christological ideas contributed to the modification or abandonment of Hebrew conceptions of freedom, determining factors, and authority. And these Christological ideas did not constitute the sole impetus to change.

Hodgson holds that "'Freedom' is a distinctively Greek concept, and it was above all Paul who took this concept and transfigured its meaning in light of what had happened in and through Jesus."[39] Although Hodgson has exaggerated both of his points, there can be no question either that the Greek influence on Christianity made the founders of the religion more aware of problems concerning freedom or that the apostle Paul was largely responsible for laying the foundations of all subsequent Christian reflection on the nature of freedom. Since Jesus is not depicted in the Gospels as having preached a systematic doctrine of liberty,[40] much of the theory surrounding freedom that we associate with Christianity must ultimately be traced back to Greek and Pauline influences. And much of this theory has been extremely troubling to those who seek to promote various freedoms.

"And ye shall know the truth, and the truth shall make you free": here we have one of the most famous lines not only in the New Testament but in world literature.[41] Although these words do not indicate that a particular type of freedom is being promised, we need only ask ourselves what freedom knowledge in itself can bring to realize that what is at stake here is essentially a spiritual freedom rather than one of several freedoms from actual external constraints. The emphasis on this specific freedom is one thing that distinguishes the New Testament from Hebrew Scripture, and the freedom is associated with something else that does not figure prominently in Hebrew Scripture: salvation in the form of personal immortality or eternal life.[42] Corresponding to the New Testament's emphasis on this freedom is a devaluation of others, undue concern with which is treated as a distraction from what is of genuine importance.

The Pentateuch theme of election recurs in the New Testament but is strikingly transmuted. Whereas Hebrew Scripture emphasizes God's election of a people and its prophets, the New Testament focuses instead on God's election of individuals. Often, the New Testament language used in connection with grace and predestination has a sharply deterministic ring to it and, although Christian theological disputes over the extent to which human beings have personal autonomy have played a tremendous role in the development of Western thought, there can be no doubt that in some sense predestination is for Paul a central article of faith[43] and that there are significant adumbrations of his doctrine in the Gospels. Thus at John 8:36, for example, we find Jesus telling some Jews, who are "Abraham's seed, and were never in bondage to any man," that, "If the Son therefore shall make you free, ye shall be free indeed." At Luke 10:19–20, Jesus says, "Behold, I give unto you power to tread on serpents and scorpions, and over all the power of the enemy; and nothing shall by any means hurt you. Notwithstanding, in this rejoice not, that the spirits are subject unto you; but rather rejoice, because your names are written in heaven." These notions, which are developed by Paul in Ephesians and elsewhere, have been criticized by detractors of Christianity as leading to a paralyzing fatalism. The rationalist or existentialist mind cannot easily accommodate Paul's teaching: "For by grace are ye saved through faith; and that not of yourselves; it is the gift of God: Not of works, lest any man should boast. For we are his workmanship, created in Christ Jesus unto good works, which God hath before ordained that we should walk in them."[44]

Two distinct problems concerning freedom are actually involved here. One concerns justification by faith alone: "He that believeth and is baptized shall be saved; but he that believeth not shall be damned."[45] The difficulty is that the idea of believing freely is rather more problematic than the idea of acting freely (in other ways); we usually know how to go about doing something, but how are we to go about inducing ourselves to believe? But then the second problem arises, for if this faith is God's gift to particular individuals, then there is not much incentive to work at acquiring or keeping the faith. But, of course, there is a paradox here, for not only does even Paul himself enjoin others to *do* certain things and *behave* in certain ways,[46] but Christians are enjoined to promote the faith through proselytizing: "Go ye therefore, and teach all nations, baptizing them in the name of the Father, and of the Son, and of the Holy Ghost; Teaching them to observe all things whatsoever I have commanded you; and, lo, I am with you alway, even unto the end of the world."[47]

This last point brings us to a certain aspect of Hebraic exclusivism that recurs in the New Testament; it too is strikingly transmuted. Like Judaism, Christianity is on at least one level a monotheistic faith, and Christians believe that their God is the God of all peoples and ages. However, the Israelites, partly because they perceived themselves as constituting a holy people, did not aggressively seek converts; and while they and their descendants have always accepted proselytes, they have primarily served as teachers of the peoples of the world in a different way, by participating in the maintenance of a model community. In Christianity, with its repudiation of tribalism, and its emphases on God's election of individuals and the duty of aggressive proselytizing, there is obviously a new theological impetus to the kind of assertiveness that, when not kept under control, might quickly degenerate into intimidation and ultimately persecution.[48] History teaches us that some of the worst atrocities have been perpetrated in the name of saving souls. As we have seen, Jesus is pictured in the New Testament as commanding his followers to teach and baptize, and fanatics of various stripes have interpreted this injunction in some truly remarkable ways. Even relatively reflective Christians have sometimes countenanced persecution as a way of saving souls and protecting the community from corrupting influences. It is strange indeed how some Christians have even managed to take the gentle shepherd of the Gospels to be a prototype of the modern fascist hatemonger.

The New Testament has been seen by certain progressive social theorists, some of them theologians (for example, those affiliated with the "Social Gospel" and "liberation theology" movements), as demanding commitment to the aggressive promotion of a wide range of social freedoms, particularly among the oppressed of the world. But when we return to the three themes we considered earlier — socio-economic slavery, the Law, and priestly authority — we find that the New Testament historically has not been much of an incentive to reform in these areas. In a sense, the New Testament has even less to offer here than Hebrew Scripture, because it not only focuses on spiritual freedom at the expense of other types but stresses the relative unimportance of matters pertaining to the temporal realm. Consider first the case of socio-economic slavery. While A. J. Carlyle believes that Christianity can be seen as promoting the general principle that men are all equal before God and capable of a life of communion with God, he is struck by the fact that the Christian church in its earliest years tended to strengthen rather than attack the institution of socio-economic slavery.[49] In fact, theological ruminations confirmed the suspicion of the Fathers that slavery is "one of those disciplinary institutions which are necessary under the actual condition of human nature — that is the actual sinfulness and viciousness of human nature. . . . The Church, then, not only recognised slavery, but lent some of its authority to enforce it; and it should further be noticed that the Church was itself even a slave-owner on a considerable scale, and that the Church rigorously prohibited the ordination of the slave."[50] A similar point can be made with respect to the Law, for while the apostle Paul railed against the Law of the Hebrews, and even ridiculed those who perform ascetic practices, the most prominent and influential churches have been legendary for the restrictions that they have placed on believers (and sometimes non-believers). One needs only to think here of the complex canon law of the Roman Catholic church, with all its restrictions on even the most intimate forms of behaviour, or one may think instead of John Calvin's Geneva, where the famed Reformer demonstrated to the world that a Protestant can be as repressive and dictatorial as any pope. And thus, finally, we come to the matter of priestly authority, and one does not have to be a great scholar in the field of mediaeval and modern European history to know that some ecclesiastical dignitaries exercised an actual authority that easily surpassed that exercised by even some of the most powerful figures that we meet in Hebrew Scripture. Christendom has produced most of the world's theocracies.

A popular Protestant writer, Leonard Griffith, has remarked that "no man can be free from the restrictions imposed on him by God."[51] But many observers have lamented that the New Testament has often been used to sanction arbitrary restrictions imposed by one's fellow mortals. Defenders of Christianity, while acknowledging that many prominent churchmen have abused their authority, have usually insisted that such people have been unfaithful to the true spirit of Christian teaching. Yet some writers, such as F. J. Foakes-Jackson, have been prepared to acknowledge that there is a paradox at the heart of Christian teaching about freedom, and that it is represented by Paul himself: "His glory was that he renounced his liberty that he might serve others. The paradox is that man has to give up liberty to be really free; but, if he hates the sacrifice, he is only exchanging one servitude for another."[52]

There have been attempts to get beyond this paradox, and Pelagianism is perhaps the most famous of these; but Augustine of Hippo succeeded in convincing his most highly placed fellows that they should have none of the Pelagian "heresy," and though earlier in his career he had himself been prepared to regard freedom as the right use of free will, this extremely influential Christian thinker ultimately "chose" the way of paradox. The Augustinian position on the "free will" question not only won out over the Pelagian position among theologians but paved the way for increased authoritarianism on the part of ecclesiastical leaders. (One might well wonder whether its practical implications made the position more attractive to high-ranking clerics.) For one can reasonably argue that people *should* be free only if one holds that they *can* be free; and if personal autonomy is a mythical phenomenon, then there is no point in trying to help people to exercise it.

It was, in fact, Augustine who more than any other early Christian thinker established systematic persecution as a central feature of ecclesiastical strategy. As Bury says, "He formulated the principle of persecution for the guidance of future generations, basing it on the firm foundation of Scripture — on words used by Jesus Christ in one of his parables, 'Compel them to come in.'"[53] It was he who more persuasively than any other early Christian thinker stressed the necessity of the intolerance of "error";[54] and his influence in this regard extends even to our own time.[55] If Augustine had not promoted these ideas, perhaps some equally talented ecclesiastic would have done so at a later time. Augustine, after all, was not alone among the church Fathers in favouring persecution.[56] Still, the direct personal influence of this brilliant psychopath should not be underestimated.

As for the mediaeval period, Northcott is only being slightly extravagant when he remarks that, "To look for the idea of religious liberty, or even the idea of toleration, in the Middle Ages is to look for something of which that great period of religious history had no knowledge."[57] This was the period that produced such monstrosities as the pontificate of Innocent III, the Inquisition, and the reign of Emperor Frederick II.[58] Neuner sees the church's commitment to theocratic principles as the principal corrupting factor in the Middle Ages. In his view, the early church did show itself to be a power of social liberation when it attacked the totalitarian pretensions of the Roman state;[59] but "once the Church became the state religion, it had to integrate itself into the existing order," and, "As partner of the existing system it often ceased to fulfil its prophetic role to stand up for the sovereignty of God and the freedom of men, and became a power of preservation of the existing order, even when this order was unjust."⁶⁰ Surely Neuner is too generous here to the mediaeval clergy and too severe with the secular order; there were plenty of popes, bishops, and priests who proved themselves quite capable of being corrupt even without the help of their secular counterparts.

The Protestant Reformation did much to change this picture. There is much to be said for Roland Bainton's thesis that "Catholicism is capable of tolerance on far fewer counts than Protestantism,"⁶¹ and we shall explore this position when we consider the growth of religious liberty in a later chapter. Yet we cannot forget that the Protestant Reformers were as committed to the abuse of authority and the arbitrary restriction of freedom as the Roman Catholic prelates whom they relentlessly attacked. "Just as the Catholics burned Hubmeier (1528)," Preston King reminds us, "so the Calvinists burned Servetus (1553), the Lutherans, Muntzer (1525) and the Zwinglians drowned Manz (1527)."⁶² This may be puzzling to those who associate Protestantism with such things as individualism, pluralism, and the priesthood of all believers. But two separate facts must be taken into consideration. First, as Northcott has noted, "It was not . . . to be expected that the leaders of the Reformation could, or would, suddenly be men of religious toleration in the modern manner. . . . Luther and Calvin were men linked by birth and education with the Catholic tradition of medieval days, and the violence of both of them was not only characteristic of the two men but of the age which moulded them."⁶³ Equally important is the fact that, as J. F. Hayward has observed, the substance of classical Protestantism is for the most part decidedly illiberal.⁶⁴ Many people associate Protestantism primarily with varieties of modern liberal Protestantism that they contrast with a repressive Catholicism. The fact is that the major Protestant Reformers were very Augustinian in many of their theological — and social — views. We may think back, for example, to the famous disputations between Luther and Erasmus, in which Erasmus, who remained loyal to Rome, clearly emerged as the champion of freedom. Or consider Calvin's views on election. "Protestant Christianity," Hayward notes, "affirms that God judges and redeems human life. Man is justified in the midst of his imperfections by God's grace. Freedom is not a natural endowment; it is a divine gift deriving from the loving initiative of the Almighty and overcoming the bondage of man's will to sinful compulsions. Man may wish to be free, but he is not actually free except by grace."⁶⁵ In our own age, fundamentalist Protestants, along with their counterparts in other faiths, are among the most militant critics of religious and other freedoms.

3   The Psycho-social Basis of Religious Repression

Defenders of religion as a form of experience and culture are usually inclined to dismiss most abuse of actual authority by religious leaders as somehow "incidental" to religion itself — or at least to their own religion. These people usually feel that too much is made of things like religious persecution by people who have an axe to grind and are mainly interested in promoting their own secularist ideology. Though they may grant that there have been many corrupt religious leaders, and that many laymen too have perpetrated evil deeds in the name of religion, they tend to see all this corruption as a minor theme in the history of religion. They may dismiss the corrupt figures as "not truly religious," or they may remind us of the fact that religions like their own have long acknowledged man's sinfulness and need for redemption. Nevertheless, many critics of religion, or at least of "institutionalized" religion, and even some troubled religionists, have been prepared to entertain the possibility that there is something about religion itself, or at least the kind of religion that is dominant in the West, that generates constraints to freedom. What is it about such religion, then, that might lead it to generate such constraints?

One possible answer is that religious people are basically stupid, and being so, they either do not understand what freedom involves or make very foolish judgements about how it is to be attained. G.E.W. Scobie, a serious psychologist of religion, reports that, "Despite some conflicting results and the possibility that social factors have been inadequately controlled, general research evidence seems to indicate that religious people in general are less intelligent and that religious conservatives seem to be less intelligent than religious liberals."[66] However, I do not find this answer to be satisfactory, partly because I suspect that my concept of intelligence is rather different from Scobie's, partly because I do not have as much confidence in academic psychological research as Scobie has, and partly because I have known so many very intelligent religious people.

A second possible answer is that religious people, or at least many of them (or many of the most influential among them), are mentally sick, and their psychopathy leads them to truncate their own freedom or that of others. This is a more profound answer than the previous one, and this thesis has been defended at great length by such notable thinkers as Nietzsche and Freud.[67] Undoubtedly religion is a rich field for the development of psychological disorders; even if one has never personally encountered somebody who thinks he is God, murders innocent people he takes to be "sinners," or practises bizarre rites, one should know from history books and newspapers that there are and have always been all sorts of religious crackpots, many of whom have managed to attain positions of authority in ecclesiastical, political, or other institutions. Many of these people practise strange forms of asceticism and self-denial; and although most of us believe that it is sometimes ennobling to give up certain pleasures, at least temporarily, few of us can fathom the behaviour of people who, say, mutilate themselves. Again, while most of us believe that it is sometimes appropriate to encourage others to be less preoccupied with pleasures, few of us can approve of the behaviour of religious leaders who convince their followers to engage in self-mutilation and other bizarre practices. But while I can accept that mental illness can be a factor contributing to religious constraints to freedom, I cannot agree with those who contend that it is the primary factor. For one thing, most religious people I know seem to be quite "normal." For another, numerous scholarly works have argued thoughtfully and eloquently that religion more often than not promotes healthy-mindedness, a sense of well-being, and sympathetic concern for others.[68] Furthermore, valuable though they may be in their own way, radical theories like those of Nietzsche and Freud are always highly speculative. Most importantly, I am persuaded that other factors contribute far more significantly to religious constraints to freedom.

A still more subtle answer is that religion is by its very nature a form of experience and culture that enables people to cope with their fear of freedom. This service may be only one of many that religion performs for us, or it may even be the primary service it performs, the one that is the key to its longevity. The answer comes in several forms, but at the heart of all of them is the idea that human beings are involved in something akin to self-deception: while in their rhetoric they indicate that they regard freedom as one of the highest ideals, and while they justify many of their actions by insisting that they are exercising or striving for personal freedom or the freedom of their fellows, in reality most people are rather terrified of freedom. Since they usually desire security, order, or pleasure rather than freedom, and since they are especially afraid of being ultimately responsible for what they do, they find it prudent on some level of consciousness to turn to religious conceptions and institutions, for religion solves their problem in three ways. First, religion, with its metaphysical and ethical conceptions, provides order and direction in their lives, and saves them from the onerous task of thinking deep thoughts for themselves. Secondly, with its idea of a transcendent Spirit, religion enables people to cope with their failings. It enables them to muse, for example, that God is ultimately responsible for all things and that in the end God will clean up all the messes that they and other people have made. The consolation offered by such determinism should not be underestimated, for according to this view, those who are more talented and more successful than we are simply beneficiaries of God's grace; whenever confronted with limitations and obstacles, we can explain them with reference to God's Divine Plan, whatever it may be. Thirdly, while helping them to cope with their fear of freedom, religion provides believers with the feeling that they have actually managed to attain the highest form of freedom, either through God's grace, the act of faith, sacrificial rites and sacrifices of a more personal nature, or some combination of these. If God is a dictator, He is nevertheless an infinitely wise, just, and compassionate one, and what freedom can be better than that allowed to us by this benevolent Father, grateful for our respect and affection?

In the period of the Enlightenment, Immanuel Kant, reflecting on the self-imposed immaturity of his fellows, their submissiveness to all sorts of authority, and their refusal to think clearly for themselves, sardonically observed that it is all too comfortable to be a minor and to have life's biggest decisions made for one by other people.[69] But the most dramatic expression of some of the ideas we have been considering is to be found in the "Legend of the Grand Inquisitor" in Dostoevsky's famous novel, *The Brothers Karamazov* (1880). There, Ivan Karamazov tells of how Jesus, having returned to earth at the height of the Spanish Inquisition, finds himself in prison, conversing with the Grand Inquisitor, who tells Jesus that freedom only makes people miserable. Hence, the church, the Inquisitor tells Jesus, has substituted security, order, and direction for the Christian freedom with which the masses are simply unable to cope. People do not need freedom; they need miracles, mystery, and authority. The original failure of Jesus, the Inquisitor tells him, was that he overestimated the capacities of those in his flock, and since he is still going to be a disruptive force in society, and will only give people ideas that will ultimately make them unhappy, it is necessary that once again he be removed from the human scene.

This is a good story, and though subject to many interpretations, particularly in light of its context in Dostoevsky's novel,[70] it expresses, among other things, the view that "institutionalized" religion can play the role of providing people with a security that may be more useful to them than freedom. But Ivan's story indicates that such religion is very different from that of Jesus himself, who is portrayed as having brought freedom to mankind. In any case, it is not enough simply to dismiss religion as repressive, for not only are there different types and aspects of religion but, even when religion appears to be at its most repressive, it makes allowances for the human being's need to believe that he is free in some important sense of the word.

A related view is the widely held view, not restricted to Marxists, that religion functions as an opiate to those who have been denied socio-economic opportunities. Critics of "organized" religion have long observed that religious institutions have helped some people to get rich and fat at the expense of others. This was a favourite theme of writers of the Enlightenment period, and particularly Voltaire. The basic thesis is that religious institutions constitute a convenient and reliable device for exploiting the disadvantaged by reducing their rebelliousness, enabling them to tolerate the socio-economic status quo, providing a sanction for their obedience to the actual political authority (which co-operates with the denominational authority insofar as it is to their mutual advantage), and generally diverting their attention away from matters related to their material, socio-economic interest. We can understand why the socio-economically privileged classes would want to use religious institutions for such purposes, but how is it that the victims allow themselves to be taken in by this scheme? To some extent the answer lies in their lack of educational opportunity, and to some degree it lies in the existence of a vicious circle whereby people come to suspect that rebellion is futile and turn to religion for a consoling world-view that reinforces their original sentiment that rebellion is futile. But the major part of the answer lies in the nature and value of religion itself, which offers believers things that are so significant to them that they are prepared to be diverted from the pursuit of purely temporal freedoms.

Referring to the founders and apostles of all religions, Muller suggests that, "In offering man higher hopes, they deprived him of other hopes, in effect declared that religion is his only hope. Often they taught that natural desire is evil, or at least more evil than suffering and pain. The great religious teachers have mostly offered man freedom *from* anxiety or spiritual want, seldom freedom *to* choose and carry out his earthly purposes."[71] The theologian Nicholas Lash wonders whether it is even possible for a denomination with deep historical roots ever to mend its ways, for he respectfully acknowledges the opinion of those who would say that

> [T]he Church is too deeply enmeshed in a web, woven by history, which has irredeemably entwined its structures and attitudes with just those economic, social and political forces which, at least on a world scale, stifle or inhibit man's search for freedom. Moreover, if men are to be freed, they

must be enabled critically to confront, and come to grips with, the roots of their alienation; whereas Christian preaching and worship are characteristically ideological, and thus effectively distract men from the task of liberation. In other words, the Church, in its structures and its consciousness, masks rather than expresses, frustrates rather than proclaims, the freedom of man, the freedom of the sons of God.[72]

Finally, it is useful here to consider certain ideas of atheistic existentialism. In his most straightforward and accessible explanation of his philosophy, Jean-Paul Sartre focuses on what is probably the favourite theme of existentialist writers, the primacy of freedom.[73] Sartre writes: "When I declare that freedom in every concrete circumstance can have no other aim than to want itself, if man has once become aware that in his forlornness he imposes values, he can no longer want but one thing, and that is freedom, as the basis of all values. . . . [T]he ultimate meaning of the acts of honest men is the quest for freedom as such."[74] Unlike most major existentialist writers, Sartre is an atheist, and he sees his atheistic existentialism as more coherent than the theistic kind because belief in God is not consistent with the existentialist idea that existence precedes essence, that is, that a human being is genuinely self-determining. "When we conceive God as the Creator, He is generally thought of as a superior sort of artisan. . . . Thus, the individual man is the realization of a certain concept in the divine intelligence"; but if God does not exist,

> [T]here is at least one being in whom existence precedes essence, a being who exists before he can be defined by any concept, and . . . this being is man, or as Heidegger says, human reality. What is meant here by saying that existence precedes essence? It means that, first of all, man exists, turns up, appears on the scene, and, only afterwards, defines himself. . . . Thus, there is no human nature, since there is no God to conceive it. Not only is man what he conceives himself to be, but he is also only what he wills himself to be after this thrust toward existence.[75]

For Sartre, then, religion is a form of experience and culture that is necessarily repressive insofar as it involves the agent's (and his society's) refusal to come to grips with the fact that "man is nothing else but what he makes of himself."[76] Thus, religion not only paves the way for the individual's flight from responsibility but imposes upon him a conception of his "human nature" that is the creation of other human beings.

Sartre, like all major existentialist writers, was much influenced by Nietzsche, a philosopher famous for announcing the death of God and for his vituperative but often perceptive criticisms of, among many other things, religion and morality, and particularly Judaism and Christianity. We have already taken note of Nietzsche's view that religion involves sickness on several planes, perhaps most noticeably in its association with ascetic ideals. But Nietzsche's critique of Western religion is actually rather more profound. Unlike his fellow atheist Sartre, he is not concerned with human freedom as such, for he has little regard for most people, with their "slave morality." As Paul Roubiczek has observed, Nietzsche sees both morality and Christianity as vicious because they prevent the superior man from being the master that he is entitled to be:

> If the natural order — which would then necessarily be the ideal order — were left intact, all those who are weak would be subjugated by those who are strong; to defend themselves, according to Nietzsche, the weak ones therefore invented what we usually accept as normal or Christian morality.... Thus all our morality is seen as a slave morality, a morality of the herd, destined to break down the healthy man so that he may be subjugated.... With Christianity, especially, begins "the slave-insurrection in morals" which has justified and won over all those who are "misfits, the badly favoured, all the scum and the outcasts of mankind."[77]

This admirably clear and concise summary of some very complex ideas shows us how Nietzsche would explain the repressive nature of Western religion. The Jews were slaves in Egypt, and their religion was the invention of slaves who never ceased to require a Master. The Jews, nevertheless, were brilliantly creative in their own way, and altered the course of civilization by turning natural morality upside down and associating goodness and nobility with weakness and the virtues of herding-animals. Christianity lifted this morality from the Jews, removed the best elements from it, and spread what was left all over Europe and to other parts of the world, thereby infecting mankind for centuries to come.[78] Religion, then, at least in the West, is a form of experience and culture that stultifies the creativity of the higher man; promoting as it does the "virtues" of the small man, the herding-animal, it represents a conspiracy of the weak against the strong, of the slave against the noble person.

Neither Sartre nor Nietzsche has succeeded in convincing most of his fellow philosophers that his explanation of these matters is entirely plausible; and, as might well be expected, they have both drawn an especially cool response from most religionists. Sartre's position has been seen by its critics as particularly vulnerable to the standard objections raised to most versions of existential philosophy: irrationalism, amoralism, excessive individualism, excessively narrow humanism, pessimism, and morbidity.[79] Nietzsche's position has been attacked on the additional grounds of historical inaccuracy and incoherence. A notable problem for Nietzsche is his inability to explain why it is necessary for him to free the supposedly higher men, the masters, from the remarkably effective domination that the supposedly weak have had over them. But what is perhaps most striking about both positions, especially in light of our concerns in this study, is their excessive voluntarism. Both underestimate the importance of determining factors, and thus their homage to freedom and the will makes for better rhetoric than philosophy.

Nevertheless, we may say of these explanations of religious repression what may also be said of the others that we have considered: they contain a certain amount of truth, are applicable in certain situations, and give people sufficient insight into the phenomenon they address to warrant their having been taken seriously for many years by disciplined, responsible scholars. Most of the great philosophers have overstated their positions, which is one reason why we find them so interesting; painting their picture in broad strokes and bright colours, they enable us to see something that might escape our attention if it were presented in the work of a more cautious craftsman. Still, some of the writers I have mentioned — Freud, Marx, Sartre, and Nietzsche — have had major intellectual cults formed around them; and unfortunately, when enthusiasts become convinced that a particular thinker has provided them with the key to understanding the ultimate but normally hidden source of all human behaviour, they usually become insufferably dogmatic and lose touch with reality.

4 The Philosophical Basis of Religious Repression

In examining the psycho-social basis of religious repression, we have considered the phenomenon as possibly involving stupidity, sickness, something akin to self-deception, exploitation and manipulation, immaturity, naiveté, fear of freedom, irresponsibility, conspiracy, and other phenomena that do not show human beings at their best. But is it not possible that practical reason has also contributed to the emergence of the constraints we have been considering? Specifically, is it not both reasonable and ethical for the religious person to be ever mindful of his weakness in relation to the power of a transcendent Spirit and its agents in this world? And is it not also both reasonable and ethical for the religious person who finds herself in a position to exercise actual authority to promote what she considers to be the only true faith and the only sound way of life, even at the cost of having to limit severely the freedom of those she considers to be in error?

As I suggested earlier (when I cited the famous anecdote about Zeno and the slave), radical determinism, theological or otherwise, does not prevent one from going about the business of living, that is, from reflecting, making decisions and choices, and acting on the basis of one's judgements. However, deterministic inclinations often lead a person to be more forgiving of the trespasses of his fellows; and on the basis of deterministic notions, the criminal justice systems of many nations have to a great extent done away with the categories of guilt and responsibility. Whether determinism has led in such cases to a sensible compassion or to an irresponsible permissiveness is a question that must be left open here. But we should also take note of the fact that radical determinists are often believers in "social control." Once one has become convinced that people are not free in the sense of having the capacity for personal autonomy, one is apt to worry much less than others about such procedures as indoctrination and conditioning when they are promoted by imposing authority figures as being for the good of the individual and his society. Unfortunately, unscrupulous or deluded people often find themselves in positions of actual authority, and with the help of experts in the field of public relations, they can even manage to be quite imposing; and these people, even when they know what is in the interest of their subjects and their community, care little about the interests of others and are mainly guided by self-interest. So a person who, for theological or other reasons, is extremely conscious of his own limits and incapacities, may put himself (and his fellows) at the mercy of the operators and schemers of the world who have much more confidence in their abilities. Interestingly, however, some of the most aggressive promoters of deterministic ideas, from Augustine to B. F. Skinner,[80] have seen themselves as representing the sort of people who are in the best position to plan other people's lives for them.

Still, the question remains as to whether it can be both reasonable and ethical for a religious person to be constantly mindful of his weakness in relation to the power of a transcendent Spirit and its earthly agents. There is no simple answer to this question, and many factors need to be weighed. For example, has a particular person's theological determinism prevented him from fulfilling obligations that are entailed by his own religious commitment? Has it prevented him from striving conscientiously to realize what reflective and high-minded people of all cultures have consistently recognized to be trans-cultural ideals?[81] Has his adoption of the doctrine been self-serving? Is he confused about what the doctrine entails? If these and similar questions can be answered in the negative, then perhaps this person provides us with evidence that it can be both reasonable and ethical for a religious person to be constantly mindful of his weakness in relation to the power of a transcendent Spirit and its agents. But, of course, some people will still insist that theological determinism is a metaphysically unsound position, and that there are compelling arguments against it. Even setting aside all of the utilitarian, deontological, and perfectionist arguments that might be given to establish the immorality of failing to exercise and cultivate one's freedom and responsibility, and setting aside any theological grounds for rejecting determinism, some people might reasonably insist that theological determinism rests on a false assumption or presupposition about the existence of God, the nature of causation, the relation of God to human beings, the marks of true prophecy, and so forth.

Reasonable or not, the agent's beliefs, arrived at on the basis of at least some reflection, explain in part a constraint to his freedom. The same circumstances apply in the case in which one acts to restrict the freedom of another. Obviously, if one asks someone in a position of actual authority why she has prevented people from doing certain things in religion or some other sphere, she will probably not admit to being stupid, sick, or exploitative. Rather, she will give an answer that makes her seem as fair and reasonable as possible, whether or not that answer actually reveals why she is exercising authority in the way she is. (She may be lying, or she may be lacking in self-knowledge.) Often, restrictions to the religious and secular freedoms of others are justified by reference to one's own theological views or those of the leaders of one's denomination: "The Bible commands me to do this," "The leaders of my church command me to do this," "I am obliged to save souls," and so on. The views of the victim and his co-religionists are not deemed relevant here. Sometimes, however, defences of a more general ethical or political type are offered, such as, "Religious pluralism threatens the unity of the community," or "Practice of the forbidden rites interferes with the fundamental freedoms of other citizens."

We are not concerned at this point with purely ethical or political defences; our interest here is in how religion as a form of experience and culture generates constraints to freedom. And outside of the plainly theological doctrine that salvation is to be found exclusively in a particular faith, no doctrine has historically been more often cited by religious persecutors, or persecutors of the religious, than the general epistemologico-ethical position that error has no rights. Now, intolerance and persecution do not normally arise solely as a result of an individual's belief that his faith is the one true faith. If that were the case, every sincere religious believer, every genuinely committed religionist, would be intolerant and persecute others, at least when he had the power to do so without fearing retaliation. Hence, we may give an affirmative answer to a troubled Northcott's question, "Is it possible . . . for the religiously convinced to be tolerant?"[82] But Northcott poses a more difficult question when he asks, "Can a religious body which believes it has the truth necessary to save men afford to tolerate error?"[83] It is here that the problem arises. As Preston King has helpfully remarked,

> Virtually all religions are dogmatic. Most of them appear to suppose not only that there is an absolute truth but also that their doctrine encapsulates this. Such a belief, however, while it may create a sufficient, does not create a necessary, ground for intolerance. The intolerance tends to follow not merely from believing that there is a truth, nor even from thinking that one has it, but from these two conditions joined with the assumption that this truth is the most important thing in the world — both on the individual and the societal level.[84]

One does not have to believe that one's truth is the truth that saves souls, although historically this has been a very common assumption. It is enough to believe that one's truth is, for one reason or another, among the most important things that one's fellows must know and among the most basic principles by which communal life must be organized and directed.

In so-called "liberal democratic" societies, the doctrine that error has no rights is, in a way, as thoroughly applied as in others. Under no form of constitution do people believe that the state should accommodate itself to every individual's or every group's opinion on every matter. A community that is not guided by truth and does not promote respect for truth cannot develop into a just society. Therefore, there is a sense in which it may reasonably be said that error has no rights. On the other hand, people who make errors do have rights. A child who makes a mistake on his arithmetic quiz does not forfeit his right to live, or to grow up to enjoy the same opportunities as his classmates will, or to be treated throughout life with dignity and courtesy both as a human being and in proportion to his positive contributions to communal life. Of course, religion is much more important than an elementary school arithmetic test. But one reason why religion is so important is that it involves personal commitment rather than the methods of objective verification that apply in mathematical and empirical studies. The bigots who shout that error has no rights are almost always among the ranks of the least sophisticated epistemologists. One's belief that someone is in error, no matter how sincere that belief is, does not in itself establish that the person is in error; and one of the great lessons of history, philosophy, and theology is that no religious proposition is incontrovertible.

Some may want to say, in defence of bigots, that their behaviour is consistent with their frame of mind, and that it is unrealistic to expect people who are as firmly convinced of the soundness of their world-view as they are to be anything but fanatics. This position is certainly false; fanaticism is a vice, and we have as much right to expect people to cultivate a healthy, socially constructive commitment as we have to expect them to cultivate such dispositions as justice, wisdom, temperance, and compassion.[85] Moreover, there is no good reason why we should assume that most bigots are fanatics rather than hypocrites, although I grant that it is not always easy to distinguish the two types. Lecky reminds us that, for Voltaire and others of his school, hypocrisy was seen as the usual concomitant of persecution, and while Lecky himself disagrees and sees most of history's worst persecutors as having spent their lives in absolute devotion to what they believed to be true, matters are undoubtedly rather more complex than either Voltaire or Lecky would allow.[86] Fanaticism and hypocrisy are the complementary vices of overcommitment and undercommitment, and for the improperly committed person, they often blend together or are converted into one another in perplexing sequences.[87]

Yet let us grant, for the sake of argument, that someone like Augustine of Hippo, who established a long tradition of persecution, was absolutely committed to the primacy of salvation and truth as he understood them. How, then, could he have ended up as being anything other than repressive towards those "in error"? And is it not unreasonable to have expected an ancient thinker such as Augustine to have thought about religious persecution in the way that contemporary liberals do? Whatever considerations influence one's judgement here, one should not lose sight of the fact that, when they and their fellow believers were persecuted in the period prior to the ascendancy of their church, early Christian leaders defended toleration on the ground that religious faith is a commitment that cannot be compelled.[88] After Christianity became dominant in European affairs, this early Christian ideal of tolerance — along with other early Christian ideals — receded into the background, to be superseded by rhetoric about the primacy of salvation and truth. We are being indiscriminately tolerant of ancient and mediaeval persecutors when we assume that their attacks on freedom were sincerely and exclusively based on a pure philosophical conception of the primacy of salvation and truth. Most of them knew better, and well they might have, for they had received a clear warning from their Bible in the form of a Divine commandment to Israel: "Also thou shalt not oppress a stranger; for ye know the heart of a stranger, seeing ye were strangers in the land of Egypt."[89]

3 Religion as a Source of Freedom

Religion has been so often condemned by its critics as a hindrance to freedom that some religious apologists have deemed it appropriate to concede that the two are incompatible and to defend religion by questioning the value of freedom. When Ivan Karamazov's Grand Inquisitor argued that the masses need security and order rather than a freedom that in the end will only make them unhappy, he was defending a type of religion that he regarded as quite the opposite of the religion of freedom that he saw Jesus attempting to establish. Yet some ecclesiastics who have been detractors of freedom have seen their position as orthodox. The Jesuit Fransen admits that, even in recent years, the word *freedom* has been regarded by many leading figures in his church as designating a dangerous idea and "a way of life thoroughly alien to a true son of the Church."[1] The Protestant Leonard Griffith, troubled by how "The desire for freedom, even to a point of permissiveness, has become a prevailing characteristic of our culture,"[2] suggests at one point that, though we are not free from God's rules, those rules do not "insult" our freedom.[3] But Griffith goes on to make the stronger claim that "Freedom is an illusion. Always you will be in some kind of bondage. The question is, What bondage?"[4]

The overwhelming majority of religious apologists sing a different tune. They argue that religion is the form of experience and culture that more than any other represents, manifests, promotes, and protects freedom in its most important forms. According to some of these people, religion is actually the principal source of freedom, the phenomenon that gave birth to freedom and continues to nurture it; according to others, religion, though not the principal source of freedom, is complementary to freedom. Focusing again on major Western faiths, we shall now consider some ways in which religion seems to be anything but the obstacle to basic freedoms that its detractors make it out to be.

1 Theology of Freedom: Hebrew Scripture

Returning to Hebrew Scripture, we shall consider some passages in it from a different perspective. We are told in Genesis 1 that God created man in His own image and that He told the male and female to have dominion over fish, fowl, and every other living thing. These words certainly exalt humanity, regardless of whatever paradoxes emerge at the beginning of Genesis. We are told that the human being not only has been given dominion over all other creatures but has actually been created in the *image* of God, whatever that may be. Moreover, God, the Creator of the universe, is portrayed not only as having regarded the creation of man as the culmination of a process but as having talked to the first man and woman and having expected them to understand Him, to reflect on His instructions, and in some sense to comply with His wishes.[5]

At Genesis 3:1–6, we are told how the woman and her husband did the one thing that God commanded them not to do. Whatever the limits of their understanding, they were clearly considered in some sense to be defying the authority of God. As a result of having eaten from the tree of the knowledge of good and evil, they were exiled from Eden but, their eyes also having been opened, they left Eden with moral conceptions. "And the Lord God said, Behold, the man is become as one of us, to know good and evil."[6] Although man's disobedience had resulted in calamitous consequences of exile and suffering, his act had at the same time ennobled him and made him even more in the image of God than God had apparently originally intended him to be.

At Genesis 4, Cain is shown to have been held responsible for the first murder, that of his brother. For his act, that of having deprived his brother of all the freedoms of life, he was severely punished. The issue of freedom is less equivocal here than in the case of the first man. The text leaves no doubt as to the basic culpability of Cain; we are led to conclude that he should have known better than to do what he did. Thus, the ideal of freedom has been to some extent fixed. Throughout the remainder of Hebrew Scripture, and throughout the New Testament as well, it is made clear that the writers consistently assume that human beings are for the most part free to do what they do and responsible for their actions and the consequences of their actions. Whatever the paradoxes involved, the believer is clearly obliged to see substantial freedom of choice and action as underlying not only the vast majority of the events that are recorded in the principal sacred works of Western culture, but also most of the human behaviour that she encounters in her own life and learns about through reliable testimony. The theologian Burrows suggests that, "Perhaps the conception which best does justice to the biblical representation as a whole is that the possibility of salvation, including all the historical and social media by which it comes to the individual, is God-given; but the individual is left free to accept or reject and to act accordingly, and is held responsible for his choice."[7]

One of the most striking features of Hebrew Scripture is its emphasis throughout the narrative on the importance of human judgement, which is often considered in relation to the reflection that preceded it and the actions that followed upon it. The main figures of the books of the Pentateuch and Prophets think, observe, reason, evaluate, weigh alternatives, and deliberate; they make plans, choices, decisions, and commitments; they do things and refrain from doing other things; and their actions (and, in certain cases, their lack of action) often influence various aspects of their own lives, the lives of others, institutions, communities, the course of history and civilization, and God Himself.

Equally striking is the extent to which these figures are, and perceive themselves to be, intimately involved with (and somewhat responsible to) fellow members of several communities: their immediate family, the extended family, their people (including their ancestors and descendants), the righteous of the world, humanity, and the order of living things. Central to their lives is the dialogue into which they enter with one another and, occasionally, even with God. Interestingly, God Himself is pictured at certain key moments in the narrative as talking *with* rather than *to* His creatures, as when He allows Abraham to negotiate with Him concerning the fate of Sodom,[8] and when Moses persuades Him to spare His people after the episode of the golden calf.[9] Sometimes the text stresses the importance of the human being's acting as an individual, as for example at Exodus 23:2, when each and every Israelite is admonished, "Thou shalt not follow a multitude to do evil; neither shalt thou speak in a cause to decline after many to wrest judgment." Elsewhere in the text, individuals are reminded of the fact that their destiny is associated with the destiny of the several communities to which they belong, as in the many passages in which families, tribes, or peoples are blessed or cursed.[10]

As we noted earlier, God's deliverance of the children of Israel from bondage in Egypt is not only the greatest image of freedom in Hebrew Scripture (and perhaps world literature) but the central event in the long and continuing history of Israel. Even here, though it is God who has liberated them, the Israelites have not been mere pawns in some incomprehensible cosmic game; they have participated in the Divine Plan. As van Buren notes, "It is the mystery of God's freedom that he will not exercise it apart from us. The freedom of God waits upon us."[11] Whatever else Hebrew Scripture says about freedom and slavery is ultimately overshadowed by the importance attached to the liberation of Israel from captivity in Egypt. To this very day, Jews interpret all other events in their history by reference to this central event.

Let us return now to some themes in Hebrew Scripture that we considered in Chapter 2. First, there are the matters of election and authority. Israel, we are told, is a holy people: "And the Lord hath avouched thee this day to be his peculiar people, as he hath promised thee, and that thou shouldest keep all his commandments; And to make thee high above all nations which he hath made, in praise, and in name, and in honour; and that thou mayest be an holy people unto the Lord thy God, as he hath spoken."[12] It is enough simply to consult the Scriptural narrative itself, without even bothering to look at other historical accounts, to know that Israel has suffered at least as much as any other people. Thus, the Israelites were not simply elected to privilege; they were primarily elected to service, although for playing their special role they would be accorded a particularly important place throughout history.[13] It was made clear to the Israelites from the start that they would continue to be judged on the basis of their actions, as would members of all the peoples of the world: "Behold, I set before you this day a blessing and a curse; A blessing, if ye obey the commandments of the Lord your God, which I command you this day; And a curse, if ye will not obey the commandments of the Lord your God."[14]

A similar point can be made with regard to the authority of priests, princes, and prophets. Authority in Israel was to involve more than just privilege and glory: leaders would be judged not only directly by God but by their fellow Israelites. It was made clear from the start that priests who abused their position would be severely punished,[15] and corrupt leaders of all kinds were to be relentlessly attacked by the righteous.[16] Indeed, we must not underestimate the importance of the fact that the idea of a God whose Authority and Law transcend and overrule all merely human authority and law, even in a so-called "theocracy" in which the leaders have failed to follow Divine injunctions, is a powerful incentive to rebelliousness against corrupt leaders and an unfailing encouragement to the oppressed. Finally, Hebrew Scripture underscores the failings and limitations of even the greatest prophets, such as Abraham and Moses, who are themselves shown to have been chastised by their Creator.[17]

With respect to the Law itself, we must bear in mind that, despite the apostle Paul's caricature of it, it was a blessing to Israel, and in a sense God's greatest gift to His people and to the world. For not only were the Israelites and others to be rewarded for their obedience, but the ways of the Torah are ultimately pleasant and, most importantly, the Torah was to be a vehicle for the advancement and progress of the people, and through them, of civilization. And it would protect the Israelites and others from the arbitrary legislation of self-serving, incompetent, or otherwise corrupt leaders.[18]

Perhaps most importantly of all, we must never in our minds dissociate Divine authority and human freedom from the love — which includes compassion — that is ideally to govern not only the relationship between God and His creatures but the relationship between creatures themselves.[19] This theme of Hebrew Scripture was carried over in some form to the New Testament and to many of the ethical systems of the great philosophers, jurists, and humanitarians. "And thou shalt love the Lord thy God with all thine heart, and with all thy soul, and with all thy might";[20] "The Lord, The Lord God, merciful and gracious, longsuffering, and abundant in goodness and truth, Keeping mercy for thousands, forgiving iniquity and transgression and sin";[21] "Thou shalt not hate thy brother in thine heart; thou shalt in any wise rebuke thy neighbour, and not suffer sin upon him. Thou shalt not avenge, nor bear any grudge against the children of thy people, but thou shalt love thy neighbour as thyself."[22] These themes were emphasized over and over again by the Hebrew prophets, who, in attempting to instil a sense of the unique importance of the ideas in the minds of their fellows, used what is perhaps the greatest poetic imagery ever created by human minds.

Consider the book of Jonah, which, though less grandiose than other books of the Prophets, has a simple, straightforward charm. There, we find the prophet Jonah rather less than delighted about the authority given to him by God. He flees, but no one can hide from God. In time, he comes to realize that God is not a killjoy or a tyrant or a fool,[23] and he goes off to Nineveh to inform the unrighteous inhabitants that God will punish them for their evil ways. But the people of Nineveh repent and are spared. Displeased by the turn of events, a petulant Jonah longs for death, but God enlightens him by creating for him a gourd to shield him from the hot sun, for when Jonah is dejected again after God's removal of the gourd, God sends him His key message: "Thou hast had pity on the gourd, for the which thou hast not laboured, neither madest it grow; which came up in a night, and perished in a night. And should not I spare Nineveh, that great city, wherein are more than sixscore thousand persons that cannot discern between their right hand and their left hand; and also much cattle?"[24]

Paul van Buren has spoken well in reminding us of the continuing importance of the Jewish people, who, despite being the objects of unparalleled slander and persecution, have not only survived through the centuries but have so often and in so many ways provided the vanguard for liberal and progressive movements in politics, the arts and sciences, philosophy, and, of course, religion itself: "They are what God made them, a people with a special role in history, living lights to humanity, if humanity cares to notice, given over to the worship of the Creator of this world and the One who wills its liberation."[25] The historic and continuing presence of Israel is a true mystery to any deeply reflective person; God loves the wise but leaves them mysteries to remind them that He is not intimidated by human reason.

2   Theology of Freedom: The New Testament

We noted in Chapter 2 that the promise of freedom runs right through the books of the New Testament. Throughout the New Testament, freedom is assumed to be desirable and attainable, and regardless of the paradoxes that are generated by certain New Testament teachings, and regardless of the views of exegetes who saw fit to play down the importance of freedom, the promise of freedom is as pronounced in the New Testament as the promise of salvation, with which it is regularly associated and in places identified. We have seen that the focus is on something, or some things, that can be characterized as "spiritual" freedom. However, as many theologians have observed, the approach to freedom in the New Testament is multi-faceted, and issues concerning freedom from oppression are not entirely ignored.

How, then, are Christians to regard themselves as free people? Christians must see themselves as having been redeemed, as having been set free. But free from what? For one thing, their faith is to be seen as having somehow liberated them from the Law. And in being free from sin, they are also ultimately free from death, for "the wages of sin is death; but the gift of God is eternal life through Jesus Christ our Lord."[26]

Clearly, the approach to freedom here is quite different from anything that one encounters in Hebrew Scripture; to some extent we see the influence here of Greek thought, but even Greek ideas have been radically transmuted.²⁷ As numerous theologians have pointed out, it would be a great mistake to identify the principal forms of Christian freedom with basic personal autonomy. It has been suggested that one reason why the New Testament's references to grace confuse many readers is that these readers have failed to appreciate that Christian freedoms are of a different order from the kind of freedoms they have in mind. Consider first Macquarrie's characterization of Christian freedoms:

> [Faith] conforms the believer to Christ's own obedience. His own will is offered to God, so that the divine grace may work in and through him. Yet on the other hand this very obedience is freedom. It is freedom from the tyranny of things, if these have been idolized, and it is freedom likewise from the frustration and meaninglessness of a life impotent in the face of guilt. The strange paradox is that the man who asserts his freedom and autonomy loses it through his self-idolatry; while the man who lives in obedience and dependence toward God is set free from the very things that are most oppressive and distorting, and becomes most responsibly his true self. God's service is found to be perfect freedom.²⁸

In Macquarrie's view, many people who fail to understand the New Testament's message here do so because they associate freedom with autonomy and independence,²⁹ while others who fail do not recognize the need to steer a middle way between extreme Augustinianism and Pelagianism.³⁰

A similar point is made by Hodgson, although his language is somewhat different from Macquarrie's. In Hodgson's view, autonomy is only one of three structures of freedom; community and openness are equally important.³¹ Thus, he writes:

> Jesus was the radically free person who proclaimed a gospel of liberation: liberation from law and religious piety, from social and political powers, from sin and death.... Freedom for Christians entailed not merely a liberation *from* bondage but also *to* or *for* something. However, this positive sense was understood neither as autonomy nor as membership in a privileged group, but as openness to liberating power ("faith"), which was not at the disposal of men and women but was the gift of the transcendent yet near God.³²

Hodgson does not deny that Christianity offers only one of many ways in which freedom might be conceived;³³ still, he praises it for providing an alternative to older definitions of freedom that are "oriented to the concepts of mastery, autonomy, private property, privileged community, and divinely sanctioned state."³⁴ With Hodgson's analysis, then, unlike Macquarrie's, we get a clear insight into the social implications of New Testament teaching on freedom; these are implications that are stressed by theologians associated with the Social Gospel and liberation theology movements.

Gustavo Gutiérrez, a leader of the liberation theology movement, underscores the socio-economic implications:

> At present, we are more sensitive to the social and political implications of freedom and salvation. Large sectors of humanity live in situations of misery and exploitation. The struggles for the *freedom from* become more urgent every day. A broad and deep aspiration for liberation inflames the history of humanity in our day. That is the case of Latin America. This aspiration is lived with distinctive characteristics by exploited classes, oppressed cultures and discriminated races in Latin America. This peculiarity does not limit the question only to the political field. On the contrary, it permits us to see from a concrete viewpoint all the human dimensions which are involved in the relation between freedom and salvation, that is to say, in the process of liberation. In a word: all the exigencies of *freedom to love*.³⁵

At this point, we may recall that deeply committed Christians of many denominations have been conspicuous in countless struggles against tyrants, persecutors, and exploiters, often even when their personal interests have been in no way directly threatened.

A. J. Carlyle has pointed out that one important dimension of New Testament teaching is its emphasis on the individual: "[I]t is clearly assumed by the New Testament that the relation of the human soul to God is an individual relation, and that the moral responsibility of the individual man or woman to God and his conscience is one which cannot be subordinated to the authority of any group or society."³⁶ But Carlyle adds some important qualifications: "This does not, of course, mean that the social relation is unimportant even in the most intimate matters of moral life or of religion. It does not mean that the relation of man to God may not be said, in a certain sense, to be mediated by the society or Church of which the Christian man is a living part."³⁷ Many bitter quarrels, even wars, have been fought over the issues of how and to what extent that relation is to be "mediated"; and some of the most vicious and arbitrary restrictions of freedom have been justified in the name of such mediation. But, in any case, we must acknowledge that Christianity recognizes the need for political as well as ecclesiastical authority, as is perhaps best indicated by the much-quoted if ambiguous injunction at Matthew 22:21: "Render therefore unto Caesar the things which are Caesar's; and unto God the things that are God's." However critical the New Testament is of corrupt authorities, it is not in the least opposed to authority as such, which it clearly treats as a condition of communal life.[38] As for ecclesiastical authority itself, one needs only to think of the famous passage of the New Testament in which Jesus is shown saying to Simon Peter, "That thou art Peter, and upon this rock I will build my church; and the gates of hell shall not prevail against it. And I will give unto thee the keys of the kingdom of heaven; and whatsoever thou shalt bind on earth shall be bound in heaven; and whatsoever thou shalt loose on earth shall be loosed in heaven."[39]

Yet despite the qualifications, which historically have left considerable room for various sorts of institutional authoritarianism, Carlyle's fundamental point is well made. Unlike Hebrew Scripture, the New Testament does not concentrate on the history and destiny of a particular people; for this reason, among others (notably among these its emphasis on witnessing and proselytizing),[40] the New Testament has a type of universal appeal that Hebrew Scripture does not. It places more emphasis on the situation of the individual than on the situation of any community, even the church itself. It makes its main appeal directly to the individual: "He that believeth and is baptized shall be saved; but he that believeth not shall be damned."[41] And in memorable lines from the Beatitudes, it singles out for a special blessing those who defy corrupt authority for sound reasons: "Blessed are they which are persecuted for righteousness' sake; for theirs is the kingdom of heaven. Blessed are ye, when men shall revile you, and persecute you, and shall say all manner of evil against you falsely, for my sake."[42] Some defenders of religious liberty and liberal religion have suggested that, by making its appeal directly to the individual, the New Testament indicates the absurdity of attempting to force people to comply with the demands of institutionalized religion. Northcott writes that Jesus "knew that His Kingdom could only be established upon the voluntary allegiance of men, and that no compulsion could be justified."[43] Jacques Ellul insists that "Christianity carries with it the proclamation of religious freedom,"[44] for "when the church and Christians reject religious freedom they deny themselves. They do not speak the word they are charged to speak. They ruin their message and Christ's own work. When the church denies this freedom, it destroys its own freedom."[45]

3 Faith as an Incentive to Moral Action

Muller, who is highly critical of institutionalized religion for interfering with personal freedom on many levels, admits that, "in their beginnings the higher religions were subversive, revolutionary movements, undermining worldly or priestly authority. They periodically inspired other such movements because their essential spirit was a quest of the Good. . . . They preached a disinterested love, which makes for freedom of spirit. With the higher religions the service of God ceased to be mere servility."[46] In a related vein, Foakes-Jackson has made the interesting point that the very thinkers who stressed the election of those who were to be saved (such as Paul, Augustine, Calvin, and Pascal) were often among the most energetic of personalities despite the fact that — or perhaps even because — they perceived themselves as instruments in the hands of God.[47] We have seen that such existentialist critics of religion as Nietzsche and Sartre saw Western religions as severely limiting the freedom, creativity, individuality, and assertiveness of their adherents. But it is surely no accident that most of the principal figures associated with existentialism (Kierkegaard, Buber, Marcel, Unamuno, and Shestov, to name a few) have had a positive attitude towards at least certain kinds of religion, and in explaining why they have, they have pointed to the relations of religion and freedom. Nor is it coincidental that, as Macquarrie has remarked, "In recent decades existentialism has in fact been the type of philosophy most influential with theologians. The early Barth, Bultmann, Tillich, Buri, Ott, Ebeling, Rahner — these are only some of the theologians of recent and contemporary times who have been significantly and, in some cases, deeply influenced by existentialist philosophy."[48]

Those who associate existentialism primarily with Sartre's version of it may well be puzzled by the very notion of religious existentialism, for obviously a religious thinker cannot endorse Sartre's claim that existence precedes essence (at least in the sense in which Sartre understands it). But long before Sartre took upon himself the task of explaining existentialism to a generation, Kierkegaard, the most important of the movement's fathers, had proclaimed himself to be a religious writer and had spoken about, of all things, a "leap of faith."[49] When we consider the major themes of all existentialist literature, even the atheistic, we eventually realize that it is not at all strange that so many existentialist writers have looked to religion to save humankind from the inauthenticity promoted by such fashionable modern outlooks as rationalism, positivism, Marxism, psychoanalysis, and sociobiology.

Existentialism, after all, is largely an attack on determinism; and religion, with its emphasis on the spiritual, may offer an escape route from the various determinisms preached by scientists and ideologists. Consider these typical comments from a typical book by one of the most important of religious existentialists, the Russian Orthodox philosopher, Berdyaev:

> Reflection upon the forms which godlessness takes in our time leaves us with the conviction that the most difficult problem is still the problem of the relation between faith in God and the acknowledgment of freedom for human creative power. Luther raised this question in an acute form in his day. There is only one possible way out of this difficulty and that is to recognize the great truth that God and the divine find visible expression not in domination but in freedom itself, not in authority, but in humanity, in God-manhood. Then it is that God is understood not as a diminution of human freedom and activity but as the condition upon which they are possible. If there is no God there is no truth and right which rise above the wrong of nature and society, man is wholly subject to nature and society, and he is the slave of natural and social necessity. Belief in God is the charter of man's liberty.[50]

Religion and freedom are also linked by such humanistic pragmatists as William James and F.C.S. Schiller. One of the major inspirations for their pragmatic approach to religion and freedom was Immanuel Kant's *Critique of Practical Reason*, the second of the celebrated philosopher's three famous critiques. Kant argues there that morality requires the postulates of freedom, the existence of God, and the immortality of the soul. He grants that freedom, God, and immortality cannot be known; but he believes that we are somehow obliged to postulate them if we are to behave as moral agents. Of special interest to us here is the way in which Kant associates religion with autonomy in analyzing the foundation of morality: "[T]hrough the concept of the highest good as the object and final end of pure practical reason, the moral law leads to religion. Religion is the recognition of all duties as divine commands, not as sanctions, i.e., arbitrary and contingent ordinances of a foreign will, but as essential laws of any free will as such."[51] Although Kant is famous as an advocate of a deontological moral philosophy, his position foreshadows humanistic pragmatism in recognizing the psychotherapeutic value of the postulates of pure practical reason, although this psychotherapeutic value is secondary to the moral value: "[M]orals is not really the doctrine of how to make ourselves happy but of how we are to be *worthy* of happiness. Only if religion is added to it can the hope arise of someday participating in happiness in proportion as we endeavored not to be unworthy of it."[52]

These Kantian themes were developed by numerous voluntarist philosophers of the nineteenth and twentieth centuries, but the most famous elaboration of them is undoubtedly that to be found in the works of William James. In an 1897 essay, James writes,

> [I]n a merely human world without a God, the appeal to our moral energy falls short of its maximal stimulating power. Life, to be sure, is even in such a world a genuinely ethical symphony; but it is played in the compass of a couple of poor octaves, and the infinite scale of values fails to open up.... When, however, we believe that a God is there, and that he is one of the claimants, the infinite perspective opens out. The scale of the symphony is incalculably prolonged. The more imperative ideals now begin to speak with an altogether new objectivity and significance, and to utter the penetrating, shattering, tragically challenging note of appeal.[53]

In his famous 1902 study in the psychology of religion, *The Varieties of Religious Experience*, James offered to the world a carefully documented defence of a position that too many of his readers already took for granted: that certain kinds of religion make people better and happier human beings. And in his most famous volume of lectures, *Pragmatism*, a work in which he defends a pluralistic, moralistic, melioristic theism, he goes far beyond anything that Kant would have countenanced: "If theological ideas prove to have a value for concrete life, they will be true, for pragmatism, in the sense of being good for so much."[54]

Ironically then, whereas writers like Nietzsche and Sartre are critical of Western religious conceptions because they see them as ultimately leading to the atrophy of the will, some of the most important modern philosophers and theologians defend religion on the ground that it alone can ultimately save us from the determinisms underlying increasingly popular kinds of scientific naturalism and socio-political ideology. The disagreement here parallels that revolving around the relation of religion to evil, for while some thinkers argue that the existence of evil in the world is all the evidence we need that an omnipotent, benevolent Spirit does not exist, other thinkers argue that it is precisely the limitations of worldly justice that lead us to regard a higher realm as necessary. How are we to explain the fact that deeply reflective people have interpreted the same data so differently? We might simply say that different thinkers have taken different "perspectives," and leave the matter at that. But why do they have such different perspectives? One answer, of course, is that they have been conditioned to see things in the way they do by such factors as parental influence, enculturation, and so forth. Another answer is that they interpret things according to a worldview that they have adopted on the basis of a highly personal commitment or faith that involves to some extent a "will to believe." Undoubtedly, defenders of religion can produce all sorts of evidence to show that critics of religion overgeneralize when they say that religion invariably stultifies creativity, deprives people of a sense of personal responsibility, or is little more than an opiate administered to the naive and manipulable. But defenders of religion also have a way of turning a blind eye to the evidence that the critics themselves produce.

Nevertheless, the defender of religion is justified in associating religion with a kind of personal spirituality that is rooted in a spiritual vision of the world. To what kind of freedom — and for that matter, what kind of joy — can the materialist lead us back? What is left of the concept of freedom by the time that a Spinoza, Comte, Marx, or Freud has whittled it down with the analytical knife that reveals long-obscured determining factors? Whatever challenges theological determinism poses for our conceptions of freedom and responsibility, religion is at least a coin that can be flipped to give us a sense of the worth and meaningfulness of human life, a feeling that the universe is not entirely alien to us, and an incentive to contribute to culture. Moreover, religion being the pre-rational, pre-philosophical, pre-scientific, and indeed pre-historic form of experience and culture that it is, we cannot even be sure that the concepts of freedom, responsibility, will, and action are not themselves the inventions, the creations, of Religious Man.

We may say here, in defence of the atheistic existentialist, that he is as critical as the religious apologist is of the scientific and ideological determinisms of the day. But what does he leave us? When Nietzsche goes on to tell us what kind of human being is noble, he ends up sounding just as dogmatic and overbearing as any other missionary; and while Sartre does not sound quite as dogmatic, his phenomenological analyses suggest that he is a person whose feelings and aspirations are very different from our own. And in any case, no one is entirely self-determining; and in particular, no one creates all of his own values. Though the concept has been abused by proselytizers of one stripe or another, we all have and all need a concept of human nature (and a related concept of humanity), and we can never be more or less than human beings.

4   A Prime Example: The Virtue of Humility

Now that we have taken a general view of the position that religious faith can be an incentive to free action, and particularly to moral action, let us move to the plane of the concrete and concentrate our attention on a particular virtue associated with Western religions (and to some extent Oriental religions): the virtue of humility. This analysis will help to crystallize the abstractions involved in the philosophical debate about religion and freedom.

It is a sign of the times that the subject of humility is not discussed by philosophers as much as it once was; yet even in our relatively cynical age, most of us are still impressed when we hear someone praised for her "true humility." Philosophical theories of morality come and go, but new generations continue to be Judaized and Christianized — as Nietzsche says[55] — and so humility survives in one form or another as an ideal of our civilization. No one who ignores humility can understand the ethical dimension of Western religion: "He hath shewed thee, O man, what is good; and what doth the Lord require of thee, but to do justly, and to love mercy, and to walk humbly with thy God?";[56] "Though the Lord be high, yet hath he respect unto the lowly; but the proud he knoweth afar off";[57] "The fear of the Lord is the instruction of wisdom; and before honour is humility";[58] "But the meek shall inherit the earth; and shall delight themselves in the abundance of peace";[59] "Blessed are the meek; for they shall inherit the earth";[60] "Take my yoke upon you, and learn of me; for I am meek and lowly in heart; and ye shall find rest unto your souls."[61]

Long before Nietzsche initiated the modern diatribe against Jewish–Christian slave morality, the more dignified Spinoza had already concluded by geometrical method that humility is not really a virtue at all;[62] and the clever Scottish empiricist David Hume had already observed that "no one, who has any practice of the world, and can penetrate into the inward sentiments of men, will assert, that the humility, which good-breeding and decency require of us, goes beyond the outside, or that a thorough sincerity in this particular is esteem'd a real part of our duty."[63]

What could have led the gentle Spinoza to conclude that humility is not a virtue? In Spinoza's view, humility is an emotion, the sorrow or pain arising from one's contemplation of one's weakness.[64] Though he has a secondary motive for defining *humility* as he does (that is, finding some niche for it in his conceptually frugal metaphysic), his primary motive is that of a moralist and critic of the dark side of religion. A central theme of his most important work, the *Tractatus Theologico-Politicus*, is that the major churches (and non-Christian denominations) have traditionally fostered superstition more than true religion. By emphasizing such dispositions as humility, religious leaders have led people to undervalue the truly important elements of religious life. When people concentrate on their lowliness, on their weaknesses and limitations, they are diverted from the intellectual love of God, self-perfection, self-assertion, and self-realization. As human virtue is, according to Spinoza, nothing but human power, why should human beings accept their servitude when they can be striving to achieve fuller freedom? What point is there in their dwelling on what they are not and what they cannot do when instead they can be enhancing what they are? If Spinoza overstates his point by saying that the essence of a human being is his striving, he at least declares himself at the same time to be a true successor to Plato and Aristotle, the great classical defenders of a self-realization ethic.

It is only a small step from Spinoza's view of humility to Nietzsche's. "Christian faith is a sacrifice from the start: sacrifice of all freedom, of all pride, of all spiritual self-confidence; at the same time, servitude and self-mockery, self-mutilation";[65] "One despises the cowardly, the anxious, the petty, those who think only in terms of narrow utility; also the distrustful with their unfree glances, those who humble themselves, the doglike people";[66] "The noble soul has reverence for itself."[67] Nietzsche too is a proponent of a self-realization ethic, though he does not share Spinoza's conception of what self-realization involves;[68] but he seems to be more sensitive than Spinoza to his debt to the un-Judaized, un-Christianized classical Greek philosophers. No matter how thoroughly one scrutinizes the texts of Plato and Aristotle, one will not find any equivalent of the Scriptural Hebrew concept of *anavah*, humility or meekness; what one will find instead is an aristocratic contempt for servitude in any form and for the qualities of the small-souled man. At *Nicomachean Ethics* 1107b, Aristotle tells us that the virtue or trained habit that represents the mean between the excess of foolish vanity and the deficiency of smallness of soul is *megalopsychia*, greatness of soul, which he characterizes at 1124a as a sort of "crown" of the virtues. Notice that the emphasis here is not on anything like humility, but on greatness of soul.

There is a certain fascination in how some of the most perceptive psychologists disagree on the extent to which human beings have a propensity to humility. The great seventeenth-century maximist La Rochefoucauld is struck mainly by how common *false* humility is; he tells us that "Humility is often just a sham submissiveness by which one tries to subordinate others. It is a contrivance of pride, which lowers itself in order to raise itself up."[69] Hume, as we have seen, sees humility as common enough, but only as a matter of custom and good manners, not of genuine commitment. In characteristic fashion he observes:

> [T]he *Christian* religion . . . places humility in the rank of virtues, and corrects the judgment of the world, and even of philosophers, who so generally admire all the efforts of pride and ambition. Whether this virtue of humility has been rightly understood, I shall not pretend to determine. I am content with the concession, that the world naturally esteems a well-regulated pride, which secretly animates our conduct, without breaking out into such indecent expressions of vanity, as may offend the vanity of others.[70]

In Nietzsche's view, however, humility is one of the defining characteristics of the modern Western herd-man with his Jewish–Christian slave morality.[71] Self-diminution is almost everywhere; only the rare "higher man" avoids it.[72]

These three great psychologists do agree on this much: there is something unnatural about Christian humility. In La Rochefoucauld's view, even those who characterize it as an ideal have no desire to cultivate it. To Hume it is a mysterious abstraction far removed from the prosaic social grace that we now call by the same name. And even Nietzsche, who sees it as being at the heart of a contemptible value-system by which the masses of herd-men really do lead their lives, sees it as having risen to prominence at a particular point in history: it was with the ancient Jews that the slave rebellion in morals began; they turned natural morality upside down.[73] Our three psychologists may seem to be overstating the point; after all, as I suggested earlier, even now many people are impressed when they hear someone praised for her "true humility." But what is the student of Christian ethics to make of humility when he reads the words of no less influential a figure than Bernard of Clairvaux, who defines humility as "that thorough self-examination which makes a man contemptible in his own sight"?[74]

So, if humility is so unnatural, what has commended it, at least in theory, to so many generations? How could anyone have ever taken seriously such a constraint to free and creative self-assertion? For one thing, there is a certain kind of social utility in it. In Nietzsche's jargon, a quality like humility makes a herd-man "tame, sociable, and useful to the herd." Spinoza, while regarding humility as a sorrow that does not arise from reason, follows the Biblical prophets in recognizing it as an effective means of controlling the irrational masses.⁷⁵ Where there is humility, there is rarely resentment, the primary condition of rebelliousness and defiance. Alas, the price paid for the resultant social stability may be a very high one, involving emasculation of the spirit, atrophy of the will, suppression of creativity, abolition of the righteous pursuit of social justice, and even a paralyzing fatalism. The leaders to whom the herd defers are usually lacking in the humility that they so vigorously commend to the herd; and such leaders are easily corrupted by their great power. On the other hand, when the leaders themselves are genuinely self-effacing, they may be incapable of strong, inspired leadership.

Humility can have personal as well as social utility. Ludwig Feuerbach is not speaking of *false* humility when he remarks that Christian humility is an inverted arrogance: the believer feels himself pre-eminent, though as a result of grace rather than his own striving.⁷⁶ In a more appreciative spirit, Kant argues that true humility, *humilitas moralis*, is accompanied by exaltation and self-esteem.⁷⁷ One must remember that Christian (or Jewish) humility is not cultivated *in vacuo*. It is one element in a complex world-view and form of life. To the lowly, there is no small consolation in the fact that they and their kind "shall inherit the earth." Such satisfaction is but one of the satisfactions that humility provides. Though the humble person is aware of her limitations, she accepts them, and she accepts herself. Acceptance is an important dimension of humility; the humble person does not allow self-knowledge to breed envy, bitterness, or frustration. The humble man can cope with his failures in a way that the "higher man," obsessed with achievement, cannot. What a relief it is to know that one does not have to reaffirm one's self-respect time and time again. So, when Spinoza associates humility with sorrow, he is not at his best.

We are scratching the surface but have gone some way towards understanding the "mystery" that undermines a large part of Nietzsche's analysis: the slaves *won*. If La Rochefoucauld and Hume are right, then the slaves did not win as much as Nietzsche thinks they did. But they defied the mighty Egyptians, subdued the noble Romans, and came to dominate Western civilization. In some sense, then, their humility was a source of strength for them.

When it has been established that there is utilitarian value in cultivating the virtue of humility, what light has been cast on the question of whether humility promotes or retards self-realization, self-assertion, and creativity? Nietzsche associates utilitarianism with slave morality; in his view, the "higher man," conscious of his creative powers, has no use for humility. And many ethics textbooks treat self-realization theories and utilitarian theories as rivals for the moralist's affection. But the most important self-realization theories pay utility its due. The utilitarian value of cultivating humility lies at least partly in the way in which it promotes conditions favourable to self-realization. Where there is no social stability, communal self-realization — civilization — is impossible, and individual self-realization is possible only for those who are comparatively privileged. To the extent that it promotes the stability of a progressive and civilized society, humility is indirectly an aid to individual and communal self-realization. If humility is also of psychotherapeutic value, then it is an aid to self-realization in that way too. And it can promote self-realization in a third and more fundamental way, as the Thomist Walter Farrell notes:

> Humility, as a matter of fact, places the very first condition of progress towards a full life, the condition of subjection. Showing a man his limitations, keeping his hopes within the bounds of his abilities, humility keeps a man in his proper place; and this is not in a particular respect, but universally. Consequently it cuts out at the roots the great obstacles to happiness, the obstacles that consist in putting ourselves above all others.... [78]

Promoters and detractors of humility agree that humility is a quality involving self-determination based on self-evaluation. The self-determination is a matter of choice and action, and it may be perceived as anything from self-knowledge to self-hatred. In evaluating oneself, one considers oneself in relation to something external. But what? The two most obvious answers are God and other people.

In explaining humility, Thomas Aquinas and other religious philosophers stress the importance of subjection to God.[79] In their view, all humility is rooted in this basic subjection. In the Jewish and Christian traditions, the primary condition of obedience is recognition of the Lord as God. In handing on the two tables of testimony to Moses, God began by saying, "I am the Lord thy God, which have brought thee out of the land of Egypt, out of the house of bondage."[80] Subjection to God is at the core of the religious believer's humility and follows directly from faith. One cannot truly believe in God without understanding one's lowliness in relation to Him. Of course, a *weak-willed* believer can fail to observe God's commandments, but when he does, it is not because of pride or because he has an exaggerated opinion of himself. The true man of faith understands his lowliness in relation to God and, to the extent of his ability, acts accordingly. Here, then, it is not humility that is a bone of contention; it is faith itself. A

Nietzsche can attack subjection to God because he is not a believer, but a true believer is necessarily humble in this way, though he may disagree with other believers as to what specific behaviour subjection to God involves.

Humility in relation to other human beings is more problematic. It clearly does not involve respecting all other people for all of their qualities. What it does involve is respecting other people for those of their qualities that merit respect. In his statement of the Thomistic position, Farrell writes:

> Every man is a mixture of the divine and the human in the sense that in every man there are the things that are God's, namely, perfections; and in every man there are things that are his very own, i.e., defects and deficiencies. . . . So that if we consider what has come from ourselves, each of us not only can but should be subject to what there is of God in every other man: in that sense, and in that sense alone, humility makes a man subject to every other man, even a saint to a sinner.[81]

It must be added, however, that this form of humility requires a special kind of sensitivity or perceptiveness. The humble woman sees herself as inferior to others in certain significant ways partly because she has made a serious effort to find "the things that are God's" in all the people with whom she comes into contact. This form of humility requires more than self-examination; it also requires a certain way of looking at one's fellow human beings. Here, two points should be noted. The first is that this humility involves more than a "realistic" appraisal of oneself and others; it requires a severe appraisal of oneself combined with a reasonably generous appraisal of others. The second is that this humility requires one to be capable of discerning "the things that are God's" in one's fellow creatures.

These various points suggest a third answer to the question of external arbiters for self-evaluation, an answer that does not conflict with the first two and yet is broad enough to be of interest even to a secularist. No matter how virtuous and talented we are, we necessarily fall short of being what we are capable of being. In evaluating himself, the humble man considers himself in relation to ideals that he is only in the process of realizing. If we think of humility in this way, we must regard it as a necessary condition of self-realization. The humble man strives to realize ideals in the knowledge that, no matter how successful he has been in realizing them in the past, he can never fully realize them but can only come closer to a complete realization. The self-impressed person, on the other hand, concentrates on how much more he has realized ideals than other people have, not on how much more fully he himself can realize his ideals. He looks backwards rather than forwards. So, we can see why so many great men and women have been capable of humility: the respect for ideals which has led them to their advanced state of civilization never ceases to inspire them to further striving. Whether they are more advanced than other people is of comparatively little interest to them.

Kant comes close to articulating this view of humility when he asserts that true humility follows from our comparison of ourselves with *the moral law*, and that exaltation and self-esteem arise from our recognition of what we are capable of achieving.[82] If humility involves our recognition of our distance from ideals, it is also a reminder of the higher dignity that awaits us. The humble man does not dwell so much on what he cannot do as on what he has yet to do. From this awareness he derives both sorrow and joy, but these are of secondary importance. He derives, above all else, a sense of his "mission" — so some would say — as a creature created "in the image of God." A paralyzing fatalism is not appropriate for one who has been enjoined by the prophet to *walk* humbly *with* God. In fact, Hebrew Scripture's most striking paradigm of the humble person is none other than Moses himself, who is described in Numbers as "very meek, above all the men which were upon the face of the earth."[83] Here is the principal role model commended to the reader: not a cringing slave but a person who manifested a nobility of the highest order in many domains — as prophet, philosopher, statesman, military leader, poet, jurist, and so forth.

The virtue of humility thus constitutes a prime example of a device through which religious faith can be an incentive to free, moral action and to creative self-determination, self-assertion, and self-realization. It is of special interest here because it is a virtue appropriately associated primarily with the major religious or spiritual world-views of Western civilization, and unlike such virtues as justice, temperance, courage, and wisdom it has no direct counterpart in the ethical systems of the classical philosophers. It is also of particular interest here because it has been targeted for explicit criticism by those philosophical critics of traditional Western forms of religion who have seen it as a typical but especially noteworthy device by which religion destructively restricts freedom, both by weakening personal autonomy and by encouraging unwarranted tolerance of constraints to freedom. However, other virtues promoted by religious ethics deserve a similar scrutiny. It is clear, for example, that Nietzsche, Sartre, and many other critics of traditional forms of religion have virtually no understanding whatsoever of what *love* represents to the religious believer, not only as a theological virtue but as an emotion, a need, an ideal, an inspiration, a consolation, and a principle of action. And in their efforts to ridicule *asceticism*, how many of those critics appreciate the extent to which ascetic practices represent the affirmation of the power of the will rather than its negation?

5 The Social Consequences of Spiritual Freedom

Having examined a particular virtue, humility, we have seen one way in which religion influences not only the individual believer himself but other people. A virtue, as the classical Greek philosophers observed, is a disposition or trained habit that helps one to live well, not only as an individual but in relation to one's fellows.[84] Humility is a virtue because the proper cultivation of it ordinarily contributes both to personal well-being (in the form of happiness, satisfaction, peace of mind, psychic health, salvation, and so forth) and to socially constructive behaviour (in the form of honest labour, good citizenship, participation in worthy projects, acts of kindness, and the like). The same, it would seem, is true of spiritual freedom itself: on the one hand, it is the well-being to which one aspires; yet it is also a condition that promotes the ability to contribute to the well-being of one's fellows. A mentally or spiritually troubled person may be able to help others, or even to make a substantial contribution to the advancement of civilization; and there are actually certain unusual cases in which being depressed, confused, or emotionally unstable enables one to make a social contribution that a healthy-minded person cannot. But it would appear that, as a general rule, the spiritual freedom of individuals contributes to the well-being of the communities to which they belong.

Hebrew Scripture does not address itself only to the needs of the individual believer; if anything, as we saw earlier, it tends to emphasize the interests of the community at the expense of those of the individual. The New Testament appeals more directly to the individual's desire for personal salvation; yet it associates salvation with social responsibility and generosity. Think back, for example, to the Beatitudes, where we are told that those are blessed who "hunger and thirst after righteousness," and are "the merciful," "the pure in heart," and "the peacemakers."[85] Such being the case, we may conclude that it is inappropriate to characterize either the pursuit of spiritual freedom or the manifestation of it as being necessarily selfish or self-centred. Nevertheless, we know that many people who claim to be spiritually free or to be promoting spiritual freedom for others do not always act in socially constructive ways.

Moreover, all sorts of terrible evils have been perpetrated in the name of religion and on the ground that they will ultimately contribute to the promotion of spiritual freedom.

Not much is to be gained by attempting to determine whether religion has, on the whole, made the world a better place than the world would have been without it. Defenders and critics of religion will be debating this issue until the end of time. Neither side is apt to be very impressed by the other side's historical, psychological, and social-scientific data. More often than not, one's assessment will probably be a concomitant of one's own world-view. But while critics of religion will almost always grant that religion has had some positive influences, particularly in inspiring people to do good deeds, the defenders of religion tend to be more reluctant to admit that religion has had bad influences. What they are more inclined to say is that religion is sometimes perverted or corrupted, and that whenever religion seems to be resulting in evil and misery, the blame lies with those who have corrupted it rather than with religion itself. Critics of religion are rarely impressed by this argument; they may well muse that the same argument could be made in defence of art or politics, in which case its absurdity would be more evident. For religion, as a form of experience and culture, is a human phenomenon, and it is ultimately what human beings make of it.

However, there is something distinctly sophistical about the argument, heard all too often, that "Religion is a bad thing because without it there would not be any religious persecution." It is obviously true that, if there were no religion, there would be no religious persecution; and there is a sense in which religion may be blamed for at least some of the evils committed in its name. But one would have to be taking a perversely narrow view of things to conclude from these facts alone that religion is a bad thing. First, victims of religious persecution are usually religious people themselves (although sometimes secularists are the victims too); and religious people are persecuted by religious bigots and schemers precisely because they refuse to abandon certain religious ways that they deem important enough to suffer for. Secondly, if religion is to be blamed for the religious persecution carried on in its name, perhaps it must also be praised for the religious tolerance that it provides religionists with the opportunity to manifest. Without religion, there would be no religious tolerance, no religious dialogue, and no religious harmony. Thirdly, we must not forget the many forms of secular persecution, those involved in racism, sexism, totalitarianism, militarism, colonialism, imperialism, chauvinism, speciesism, and so on.

If there were no such thing as religion, there would probably still be many areas left in which the vicious person could do his persecuting. Of course, the person who persecutes others in the name of religion is apt to be more *hypocritical* than other persecutors, and for this reason we may find him particularly loathsome. But if we find him to be hypocritical, it is because we expect better from him than we do from the secularist persecutor; we see the religious persecutor as committed on some level of consciousness to lofty ethical principles. Fourthly, the influences of religion are not restricted to the spheres of interdenominational relations, intradenominational relations, and relations between religious and political institutions. A person is not only manifesting his religious commitment when he persecutes or tolerates another person. His religious commitment manifests itself in countless ways; and so, measuring the ultimate influence of religion on an individual person or group — not to mention civilization — is no easy task.

The objection might be raised that, even if religion makes people more moral, it does not follow that it makes people freer. That is to say, religion may promote morality solely with respect to other ideals, such as justice, temperance, and the "virtues of the herd" that Nietzsche enumerates, such as tameness. It may even promote the other ideals at the expense of freedom, for ideals can sometimes come into conflict. (Nietzsche himself does not deny that religion promotes a morality, but he contrasts this morality with what he takes to be a higher morality; and he attacks Western religionists for identifying their own morality with morality as such.[86]) The basic objection is a fair one: religion does not necessarily make people freer in the process of making them more moral. For that matter, religion *may* actually make people freer in some of those cases in which it tends to make them *less* moral. However, it is appropriate to think back to a point raised in Chapter 1, that is, that we ordinarily believe that religious freedoms and most other freedoms must be understood within a wide moral context, one that involves the agent's other interests, the interests of his fellows, other ideals, and so on. Furthermore, we should not underestimate the extent to which religion is a *field* for creativity and the manifestation of freedom. Nietzsche naively (or perhaps manipulatively) characterizes Western religion, and particularly Jewish–Christian slave morality, as essentially the same in its many manifestations; although he sometimes contrasts Judaism and Christianity, and different types of Christianity, he tends to regard the common elements as more important than the differences. Perhaps the common elements are indeed more important than the differences, but the differences should not be undervalued. The history of Western religion is largely a tale of the formation of new denominations, churches, sects, and schools. The imagination of certain prophets, saints, reformers, theologians, religious philosophers, and propagandists has been as vivid in its own way as that of any poet or painter, and it is hardly coincidental that there has been as much interdenominational and intradenominational competition as there has been athletic or economic competition.[87]

6   Religion in Relation to Other Sources of Freedom

The defender of religion can take the offensive and pose the question to its critics as to what might qualify as a richer source of freedom than religion. Specifically, if we dismiss religion as a valuable form of experience and culture on the ground that it poses too many constraints to the most important freedoms, to what secular phenomena should we turn in an effort to enhance our own "internal" and "external" freedoms and those of others? Some may feel that such questions should be ruled out of order, for it could be argued that people are simply born free and do not need to turn anywhere at all in order to acquire or enhance their natural freedom. The famous words of Jean-Jacques Rousseau come to mind: "Man is born free, and everywhere he is in chains."[88] But most people nowadays regard this eighteenth-century position as naive and dated, or at least much overstated, and would probably be inclined to agree with R. G. Collingwood that "The facts of human infancy are dirtier and less picturesque, perhaps, than the fancies of Rousseau; but they are a safer foundation on which to build a science of the relations linking a man to his fellow men."[89] Collingwood could hardly be more straightforward in presenting those facts: "A man is born a red and wrinkled lump of flesh having no will of its own at all, absolutely at the mercy of the parents by whose conspiracy he has been brought into existence."[90] Even if one feels that Collingwood too has overstated his point, one will almost surely grant that the most important freedoms need to be cultivated and nurtured, and that an individual cannot do all the cultivating and nurturing for himself, at least in the crucial formative years of childhood and adolescence.

So, what secular phenomena might qualify? One obvious answer is the state, since almost everybody will allow that some political authority is necessary for the survival of the community, and as the years pass, people seem to look to the state to provide them with more and more services. But history teaches us that the leaders of the state can be even more repressive, exploitative, and arbitrary than religious leaders; and as we have noted, one form of religious freedom involves freedom from state interference. So, only a certain type of state will do, and many people would insist that it is what has come to be known as the "liberal democratic" state. Yet no amount of rhetoric has been able to convince everyone that the liberal democratic state is the solution to all our problems. Many critics of the liberal democratic state have argued that it cannot provide all the services that we may reasonably expect the state to provide. But some critics have also argued that the liberal democratic state cannot provide the protection for individual freedoms that its defenders so often vaunt as its most attractive feature. It was recognized even in ancient times that majorities can be as arbitrary as kings;[91] and many people over the centuries have received more justice at the hands of enlightened dictators than at the hands of a democratic electorate. Consider these observations of Lord Acton, a distinguished Roman Catholic liberal:

> There is a wide divergence, an irreconcilable disagreement, between the political notions of the modern world and that which is essentially the system of the Catholic Church. It manifests itself particularly in their contradictory views of liberty, and of the functions of the civil power. The Catholic notion, defining liberty not as the power of doing what we like, but the right of being able to do what we ought, denies that general interests can supersede individual rights. It condemns therefore, the theory of the ancient as well as of the modern State. It is founded on the divine origin and nature of authority. According to the prevailing doctrine, which derives power from the people, and deposits it ultimately in their hands, the State is omnipotent over the individual, whose only remnant of freedom is then the participation in the exercise of supreme power; while the general will is binding on him. . . . Christian liberty is lost where this system prevails: whether in the form of the utmost diffusion of power, as in America, or of the utmost concentration of power, as in France; whether that is to say, it is exercised by the majority, or by the delegates of the majority — it is always a delusive freedom, founded on a servitude more or less disguised.[92]

We may well be bothered by Acton's excessive generosity to (and confidence in) the leaders of his own church, but his worries about the abuse of authority in the liberal democratic state are not entirely unjustified.

Acton's point parallels one we considered earlier with respect to religion itself. We noted that religion, as a form of experience and culture, is a human phenomenon and thus ultimately what human beings make of it. The same holds true for the liberal democratic state, or for that matter any state, even a theocracy, though in an ideal theocracy human beings would be acting as genuine agents of God. If one is not prepared to accept the reality of Divine Authority, then one is ultimately left with the two options of anarchy and obedience to human authority. Few people are prepared to opt for anarchy, but almost everyone is inclined to be critical, at least occasionally, of the concrete forms that human authority takes.

The same holds true for other answers that might be given to our question about possible sources of freedom. It is certainly the case that art, science, and philosophy can be rich sources of freedom. Freedoms of many kinds have been promoted by lofty literary works, scientific discoveries, and philosophical tracts. But art, science, and philosophy are all forms of experience and culture, just as religion is, and they too depend on what human beings make of them. It is not hard to think of some artists, scientists, and philosophers who have been prepared to serve the interests of despots; and many of them have been sincerely inimical to the extension and enhancement of the freedoms of their fellows. Consider, for example, the talented and intelligent individuals who as artists, scientists, and philosophers have been prepared to go along with the social agenda promoted by each and every major form of twentieth-century totalitarianism. Of course, highly subjective evaluation may lead one to believe that religion is more threatening in this respect than art and science, or vice versa. But there is this crucial difference between religion and other forms of experience and culture: religion, justifiably or not, holds out to us the possibility that its ideas, values, and practices are ultimately derived from a transcendent authority and not merely a human one.

Philosophy, as the "love of wisdom," has done much over the centuries to enhance freedoms — both the freedoms of the philosophers themselves and the freedoms of those whom they have influenced. Even more than art and science, it has encouraged people to make use of reason in dealing with the most important questions. Philosophers will acknowledge that their predecessors and colleagues have said many foolish things — indeed many philosophers are too quick to ridicule the views of other philosophers — but they are just as likely to insist that philosophy itself, by using reason to combat superstition (and in particular, religious superstition), has been one of the greatest of all sources and manifestations of the most important freedoms. As a devoted student of philosophy, I have no qualms about singing her praises. However, I am not prepared to follow those who, like Comte, see philosophy as having replaced religion, or as at least having the capacity to do so. That is partly because I see philosophy and religion as having different gifts to offer to humanity; but it is also partly because I see philosophy and religion as being interdependent in complex ways that we shall be considering later in this study. Still, it is prudent to recall here that religion is a pre-philosophical, pre-scientific form of experience and culture, that in some sense philosophy and science grew out of it, and that it has survived and even thrived despite the calumny often directed against it by its offspring.

From where do the ideals of civilization — of which freedom, as important as it is, is but one of many — ultimately derive? Was it not perhaps religion that invented them? And if so, have not the harsher critics of religion, with their moralizing about freedom and kindred ideals, been guilty of abusing their host while eating at her table?

And if the ideals of civilization transcend religion itself, is it appropriate to disparage the form of experience and culture that once guarded them and promoted them when there was nothing else to do the job? To what or whom will we be able to turn now to guard and promote our ideal of freedom, as it finds itself under siege from determinists of many styles who have shown how easy it is to reduce "education" to indoctrination and conditioning? Who will protect the ideal from the artistic Freudians and structuralists, the scientific behaviourists and sociobiologists, the philosophical positivists and Marxists, and indeed the religious fundamentalists?

Again, if the ideals of civilization transcend religion itself, from where have they come? Are they just *there*? Did Someone put them there? Are they the products of some mysterious and unknown pre-religious form of experience and culture?[93] When we reflect on such questions, we soon realize the impossibility of answering them, for in this realm we cannot rely on archaeological excavation or radioactive dating to help us.

In any case, since this is not the proper place for religious apologetic, I shall leave it to Muller to close this phase of our investigation with a balanced appraisal of the contemporary situation: "[R]eligion still works both to inspire and to constrain, to enlighten and to obscure, to unite and to divide, to free and to enslave the spirit, to hearten and to discourage earthly purposes. A student of freedom must therefore try to make out the dominant tendencies of a given religion, in a given society, at a given time. . . . But whatever his own faith, he needs to distinguish the cause of religion from the cause of freedom."[94] We are helpfully reminded here that, however intimate the relations between religion and freedom may be in certain ways, the two are conceptually distinct. As for the question of which of the causes is nobler, that can only be answered through personal commitment and not through anything that resembles objective analysis.

4 Religious Liberty

Of the several expressions that we shall have examined in this study — "religious freedom," "liberal religion," and so on — "religious liberty" is almost certainly the most widely used in everyday discourse, so that it is not surprising that, when religion is considered in relation to freedom, issues concerning religious liberty are usually the first (and sometimes the only) issues to come to mind. While this is understandable, it is somewhat regrettable, because other important types of religious freedom are often ignored or undervalued as a result. An underlying problem is the fact that, while the terms *liberty* and *freedom* may often be treated as interchangeable, the expression "religious liberty" seems to be, for purely historical reasons, almost always associated with a particular set of religious freedoms.

In Chapter 1, I gave notice that I would be following my intuitions about ordinary language and associating religious liberty only with types or aspects of religious freedom that have an important political dimension. I also associated religious liberty there with, positively, the enjoyment of political rights and privileges and, negatively, the absence of constraints that are primarily political. Even then, you were probably struck by the ambiguity not only of such notoriously vague terms as *important* and *primarily* but of the terms *political* and *rights*. Still, I believe that a clearer analysis would not do justice to the irreducible ambiguity of the expression, so it is not much of a consolation that the expression is much less ambiguous than the expression "religious freedom."

Nevertheless, we should be heartened by the fact that "religious liberty" is associated with certain historical events, for we can expect consideration of those events to provide us with clues that will help us through some of our conceptual perplexities. We shall begin by considering some basic theory, move on to consider directly some historical matters, and conclude this part of our investigation by considering the moral justification of religious liberty.

1 The Idea of Religious Liberty

With respect to the matter of agency, a person is said to enjoy religious liberty if, given the absence of certain constraints, he can do the various "religious things" that we considered earlier, such as observe religious rites, belong to a community of religious believers, and act in public as well as in private on the basis of his religious commitment. Religious liberty admits of degrees; the more "religious things" of one's choice one can do, then, *ceteris paribus*, the more religious liberty one enjoys. Again, the less one is penalized in other spheres of social life for one's religious opinions and actions, then, *ceteris paribus*, the more religious liberty one enjoys. For example, though there is nothing particularly religious about being a corporation president, the fact that one is not prevented from being a business executive because one worships in the Roman Catholic church or the Church of Scientology indicates that one enjoys a certain degree of religious liberty. With respect to existential, psychological, and spiritual freedoms, a person is said to enjoy religious liberty if she is not prevented by certain obstacles from pursuing and attaining certain "inner" freedoms that enable her to be the fundamental kind of person that she aspires to be. But what distinguishes religious liberty from other religious freedoms would appear to be that the agent enjoys religious capacities in a specifically political context and is not restricted by specifically political constraints.

The word *political* is derived from the classical Greek term for the city-state, *polis*. The ancient Greeks were a religious people but, being an ancient people, even their greatest thinkers had not developed a sophisticated theory of the precise relationship between religious and secular authority; and the lack of such a theory eventually caused them all sorts of trouble, as we shall see later. In any case, though we now recognize religion as an aspect of the culture of our community, and though we may even expect the leaders of the state to be religious and to show respect for what certain religious authorities teach and preach, we have managed somehow to come to distinguish, at least conceptually, between religious authority and a purely political or civil authority, although even now there is considerable disagreement about how distinct these should be in *practice*. The fact that we can distinguish them conceptually is important; this philosophical and psychological capacity was not easy to come by, as the study of ancient and mediaeval history reminds us.

So, when we think of religious liberty, we may spontaneously consider rights or privileges granted to us and our fellows, or otherwise acknowledged to belong to us and our fellows, by actual political or civil authorities. Viewed from another perspective, such religious liberty is construed as the absence of the kind of obstacles that political or civil authorities could put in our way to hinder our realization of our religious aspirations. All of this is sometimes paraphrased by the slogan that religious liberty involves "freedom from state interference in religious matters." As slogans go, this one is not too bad and has even proven to be serviceable in dark times; yet it can be misleading. For one thing, almost all reasonable people expect political leaders to interfere in certain matters that can reasonably be regarded as religious, and they would be inclined to argue that in those situations the state has not violated any commitment to religious liberty. If our neighbour were about to sacrifice his daughter to one of his gods, we would expect the state to intercede and to prevent him from carrying out an activity that in an important sense of the word is a religious activity. If this neighbour were to argue that religious liberty is being denied to him, we might grant this point, but more likely we would tell him that he "has no right" to sacrifice his daughter and that the matter of religious liberty is not really at stake here because a "purely" political or civil law was about to be broken. He would understandably be perplexed by such fine distinctions.

Also, most of us believe that we have religious liberty only in a society in which the state is prepared to intercede on our behalf in order to protect our religious rights or privileges. For example, if someone is being bullied by big business because she is a Muslim or Jehovah's Witness, then even though no political figure has been directly involved in the persecution, the victim may well be seen as having been denied religious liberty, for political leaders will have failed to fulfil what most of us would consider their obligation to safeguard the woman's religious capacities. Some social theorists consider this aspect of religious liberty to be primary, as does H. G. Wood, for example, when he writes that "[Religious liberty] is primarily a demand on the State to secure to the individual citizen and to organized religious groups certain rights. In a genuinely democratic State, the government is asked to protect the responsible adult citizen in holding and professing whatever ultimate beliefs commend themselves to his conscience and reason."[1] Obviously, securing and protecting rights involves more than simply granting or acknowledging them and then refusing to intercede when private citizens violate them. But it is widely (though not universally) believed that it is the state's responsibility to do more than simply refrain from directly infringing upon an individual's (or group's) capacities. Wood, following the famous liberal philosopher John Stuart Mill, puts his point in another way: "In so far as religious liberty is a question of rights, it is wrapped up with the constitutional forms of the State and with the policies of governments. But, as Mill argues, we have to consider also the pressures exerted by Society — the problem of maintaining a social atmosphere favourable to religious liberty."[2] This point is clearly an application of a more general one we considered in Chapter 1: that the promotion of effective freedom may require providing people with realistic opportunities to fulfil their nobler aspirations.[3]

We noted early on in our inquiry that people who want freedom from religious institutions often look to state interference to secure it. It seems to me that when this freedom is secured by state intervention, it is among those things that are regularly characterized as "religious liberty." The fact that the state is being counted upon to secure the right or privilege is customarily seen as enough to provide the relevant freedom with a sufficiently important political dimension to qualify it as a type of religious liberty. The judgement in such cases about the importance of the political dimension is not arbitrary, as it reflects some people's awareness of the political context in which many historically significant rebellions against the high-handed exercise of ecclesiastical authority have taken place. Specifically, the fight against abuse of denominational authority has often been carried on in corrupt theocracies or in societies in which the nominally independent political leadership has been under the thumb of some national or international religious hierarchy. The strategy of a major tradition of religious authoritarianism has involved enlisting the military, police, taxation authorities, and other agencies of the state to promote the religious hierarchy's perceived interests. Rarely have priests and ministers attempted to do the hard work of intimidating and exploiting their co-religionists and others all by themselves.

One question here is whether religious liberty involves the enjoyment of full-fledged rights — regarded as perhaps even "natural" and trans-cultural — or simply the capacities or powers themselves. Many writers on the subject have attempted to distinguish true religious liberty from "mere" religious toleration. For example, Northcott writes that "We have to distinguish . . . between 'religious toleration' (something conceded) and 'religious liberty' (something claimed), two notions which have characteristically been intermixed in the civil and religious contentions of Britain."[4] This position is endorsed by the theologian Franklin Littell, who insists that genuine religious liberty is not simply granted by a gracious state: "Failure to perceive this fundamental difference between toleration and religious liberty continues to produce many blunders and false starts. . . ."[5] However, in her careful study of religious toleration in England in the late eighteenth and early nineteenth centuries, the historian Ursula Henriques has shown that not only is it difficult to define the precise difference between toleration and religious liberty, but no clear distinction was made between them in some of the historically most important controversies.[6] While some theorists would argue, then, that religious liberty obtains only when toleration is recognized as a right, the distinction is not as sharp as they would have us believe. There are many societies in which people who have been assured that they have such a "right" are treated much worse by their political leaders than are people in other societies who have been told by their leaders that they are the beneficiaries of "tolerance" or "toleration." Furthermore, while the primary use of the term *tolerance* is to designate a disposition,[7] this term and related terms have often had legal and constitutional significance, as in the case of the justly famous Act of Toleration of 1689. Still, we may perhaps allow that promises of religious liberty tend to be more generous than promises of religious toleration, for the latter are typically worded in terms that suggest that certain religious opinions and acts are being accepted by people who disapprove of them.

Cranston has pointed out that "The word 'liberty' has its least ambiguity in political use in times of centralized oppression. That is because the constraint or burden from which liberty is sought is clearly understood."[8] This point certainly applies to religious liberty. When a totalitarian government persecutes people for selling bibles or refusing to worship in a particular church, the denial of religious liberty is plainly apparent even to most of the people who, for reasons of expediency, will deny that they see anything immoral taking place. But restrictions are sometimes so subtle that even the most kindly and considerate observers — and sometimes even the victims themselves — cannot recognize them for the denials of religious liberty that they are, or at least are not really sure whether they constitute denials of religious liberty. The Catholic conservative Dawson bitterly commented in the thirties that "It may be harder to resist a Totalitarian State which relies on free milk and birth-control clinics than one which relies on castor oil and concentration camps."[9] But even the wise and benevolent political leader who has devoted her career to fighting against religious bigotry may find, to her surprise, that certain religious minorities reasonably believe that she has not been vigorous enough in promoting religious liberty for them. She may realize, on reflection, that members of the minorities in question suffer disabilities as a result of having certain religious obligations that members of larger and more powerful denominations do not; and when she sees that the majority is not prepared to accommodate the special needs of the minorities, she may conclude that the promise of religious liberty to religious minorities is largely rhetorical. One may think particularly of religious denominations sometimes dismissed as "cults," such as Jehovah's Witnesses, who are famous for testing the patience of members of long-established denominations. But a similar problem is faced by Christians in predominantly Muslim societies, Muslims in predominantly Hindu societies, Jews in predominantly Christian and Muslim societies, and so forth. Also, religious majorities sometimes find their religious liberty denied, either because of the secularist leanings of the society's politicians or the inept application of the principle of "separation" of spheres of religious and political authority.

While we can appreciate the longing of social theorists for a simple formula in which the ideal of religious liberty can be encapsulated, it should already be clear that nothing simple will work well. Littell, for example, writes that "Religious liberty stands on two foundations: voluntary membership and support, and secular and limited government."[10] It takes little imagination to see that this formulation is quite arbitrary. The first condition, though very important, is not the issue at stake in the majority of disputes about religious liberty; and the second condition is compatible with a government that is so secularist that its leaders cannot understand or appreciate the legitimate needs and aspirations of religious people, and so limited that it is incapable of safeguarding the legitimate capacities of religionists. Bates has noted that there are at least six categories of things that can be regarded as constituting significant denials and infringements of religious liberty: excessive pressure upon conscience; acts grossly destructive of religious interests; direct interference with the normal activities of religious groups; limitations upon the means and types of work which religious men and their organizations can carry on; direct compulsion in matters of religion; and the political use of religion.[11] Bates also draws our attention to the fact that denials and infringements of religious liberty are common not only in totalitarian and anti-religious states but in societies in which solidarity is oppressive, states with an established church or religion, and even lay or neutral states.[12]

Bates also tries hard to articulate clearly the problem that lies at the heart of the paradox of religious liberty: "The sovereign state may be peculiarly sensitive about the claim for religious liberty, since religion implies a belief in and allegiance to a higher, rival, or qualifying spiritual authority";[13] and indeed, "religious liberty may open the way to the teaching and the practice of ideas definitely contrary to the nature and policy of the sovereign state."[14] If anything, Bates has understated the problem. Despite the ingenious attempts of deep thinkers and social technicians to demarcate clearly for us the precise and separate spheres of religious and political authority, it is obvious that both forms of authority are concerned with common aspects of the individual agent's ethic or morality. Moreover, anyone who truly believes in the existence of a transcendent authority will necessarily regard the judgements of that authority (and its earthly agents) as overruling in some sense the judgements of even the most sophisticated and well-meaning secular functionaries. That, of course, is a major part of the religionist's argument in support of her appeal to politicians for religious liberty. Yet she knows full well that there are others in her society who do not share her views on who or what represents transcendent authority; and she knows that some people recognize no transcendent authority at all. Thus, she must acknowledge that in one sense political authority must be allowed, for practical purposes, to overrule the particular religious authorities of the society's constituent members and groups. For, if everyone refused to abide by the dictates of political leaders whenever those dictates conflicted with his interpretations of the demands of his transcendent authority, societies could not exist, and a primary condition of religious life would be lost.

Consider the paradox from another angle. Dawson argues that "religion is the sphere of the absolute, while business and politics belong to the sphere of the relative. Religion is the fixed pole on which human life revolves and to which all its parts must be related."[15] Dawson believes that, by having distinguished two spheres, he has shown how "Political religion is an offence alike to religion and to politics: it takes from Caesar what belongs to him of right and fills the temple with the noise and dust of the market place."[16] But how *separate* are the two spheres if, when religious and political authority come into conflict, as history shows us they inevitably do all the time, we are to regard one's judgement as absolute and the other's as merely relative?

Still another problem that we confront in trying to understand the nature of religious liberty is that religious liberty is what might be characterized as a "composite" freedom, or at least rather more so than other freedoms understood in terms of a political context. In the bill of rights appended to the Constitution of the United States, religious liberty is clearly the first freedom: the opening words of the First

Amendment enshrine it. Again, in Canada's new Charter of Rights and Freedoms, "freedom of religion" is the first freedom acknowledged. There is historical warrant for treating religious liberty as the "first" freedom, conceptually as well as chronologically. All other civil liberties are rooted in freedom of thought or freedom of the mind, and the ideas that have historically been of most importance to most people are those related to spiritual matters. Long before freethinkers roamed the face of the earth, spiritual reflection was essentially religious in character; indeed, religion was, as I have observed on several occasions, a prerational form of experience and culture. Furthermore, religious liberty directly involves the ability to do all sorts of things that are associated with other major civil liberties, such as freedom of speech and expression, freedom of assembly and association, freedom to participate in the cultural life of the community, and freedom of opportunity. Hence, it can hardly be much of an exaggeration to say that the struggle for most of the principal civil liberties we have today originated in the struggle for various aspects of religious liberty. Thus, religious liberty is not just one of many civil liberties; there is something primal about it on several planes. Perhaps the greatest evidence of this is that religious liberty is customarily associated with, and still often identified with, freedom of conscience and freedom of thought, even though conscience and thought are not in fact necessarily related to religion. We noted earlier that, rather ironically, certain forms of religious freedom are seen as encompassing one's right not to be religious at all.

A beneficial effect of the composite nature of religious liberty has been that successful struggles for religious liberty have promoted and enhanced several other civil liberties, and in particular those that represent generalized forms of the constitutive liberties that make up religious liberty. Wood notes that, "When Mill published his *Essay on Liberty* in 1859, he could point to the development of the practice of religious toleration especially among the Anglo-Saxon peoples as the only effective embodiment of the broad principles of freedom of thought, discussion and conduct for which he was contending."[17] But there is another side to this coin: because of its highly composite nature, religious liberty is often associated with only two or three of its constitutive freedoms, and when consideration of these alone comes to determine one's paradigms and criteria, other aspects of religious liberty come to be undervalued or, even worse, are disqualified outright. So, it is not unusual to hear people argue along the following lines: "Those people say that they should not have to work on their religious holiday, and they insist that they are being denied religious liberty when they are forced to work on their holiday while the rest of us have our religious holidays off. But those people are abusing the notion of religious liberty. They are allowed to pray in their own houses of worship; and no one stops them from bringing up their children in their own peculiar way. What more do they want? How much do they have a right to expect?" Although there are some interesting points raised in this type of argument, usually the speaker has an arbitrarily narrow conception of the constitutive freedoms that make up religious liberty, and usually his remarks are based more on resentment and ill will than on a philosophical insight.

As it happens, when we reconsider the several problems concerning the nature of religious liberty that have emerged thus far in our analysis, we see that narrowness of conception plays a part in all of them. Whenever people use the words, "Religious liberty is only involved when . . . ," we have to be on our guard to be sure that these people are showing proper respect for the plasticity of ordinary language, and we should also ask ourselves what reasons — and what motives — they might have for ruling out the cases that do not satisfy their preferred criterion.

2 A Brief Historical Excursus

We turn now to some historical events. As the aim here is simply to clarify our understanding of the nature of religious liberty, we shall not be undertaking the relatively thorough survey of the history of religious liberty that we associate with such distinguished historical writers as Bury and Lecky. This historical excursus will be not only short but oblique, and will attach what might seem to be unusual importance to ideas and theories at the expense of more concrete occurrences. It is not my intention to minimize the significance of such concrete matters as the joy and suffering, life and death, and achievement and failure of flesh-and-blood human beings. But my central objective in the discussion that follows is to establish that, despite what certain writers would have us believe, the development and enhancement of religious liberty have always been more the result of ideas and theories than of fortuitous circumstances. I also hope to indicate the shallowness of the widely held position that the ideal of religious liberty is a purely modern conception.

Consider these examples of the kind of historical interpretation that strikes me as misleading. First, describing the establishment of religious liberty in America, Reinhold Niebuhr writes, "Most of our founding fathers genuinely believed in freedom, but they were able to establish religious liberty in our nation largely because those who did not could see the futility of any alternative policy. In this, as in the establishment of all our democratic liberties, the providential workings in history were much more effective than the conscious contriving of men."[18] Discussing the struggle for religious liberty in an earlier period, John Gray informs us that, "In general, it is fair to say that the demand for religious toleration was in most of Europe a by-product of the political struggle between Protestant and Catholic Churches, and only in England did the connection between religious nonconformism and liberal freedoms come to be firmly established over a period of several centuries."[19] And Franklin Littell writes, "The Enlightenment brought toleration in some countries, but merely as a pragmatic realization that persecution had become counterproductive."[20] The suggestion implicit in all of these passages is that the more advanced part of the civilized world has somehow stumbled its way into religious liberty; in each case, the intellectual or theoretical contributions to this aspect of civilization have intentionally been minimized. Even Bury, who appreciates the intellectual contributions, feels impelled to add that non-intellectual factors also contributed to the growth of religious liberty, such as the decline of papal power, the decay of the Holy Roman Empire, and the development of strong monarchies.[21] In a similar vein, Bury emphasizes the fact that the Reformation only indirectly contributed to the establishment of religious liberty, for it brought about conditions that led to results "at which its leaders would have shuddered."[22]

R. G. Collingwood has sagely observed that, while the historian's work may begin by discovering the "outside" of an event ("everything belonging to it which can be described in terms of bodies and their movements"), he must always remember that the event was an action and that his main task is to "think himself into this action, to discern the thought of its agent."[23] Collingwood's advice is particularly helpful when we set out to understand something like religious liberty, to which so many people have given so much thought.

Although we have focused so far on Western religious traditions, we shall begin our historical excursus with a brief look at an aspect of the religious development of Asia. Bury suggests that King Ashoka's resolution of the problem of destructive conflict between Brahmanism and Buddhism is notable insofar as his ordinances represent the world's earliest existing edicts of toleration.[24] The cynic or historical determinist might dismiss Ashoka's Rock Edicts (third century B.C.) as representing a merely pragmatic manoeuvre by a political leader aiming to secure and consolidate his power. However, as Gustav Mensching has observed, the language of the ordinances suggests that they are animated by philosophical principles, and particularly the idea that matters concerning virtue constitute the essential core of the faiths of sects, and doctrines as such are of only instrumental importance.[25] In fact, looming in the background is a notable Buddhist tradition of tolerance. The Buddhist parable of the blind men and the elephant is well known in the West — the parable in which the blind men disagree about the nature of the animal because each of them has touched only one part of the animal. Mensching notes that

> This parable has a deep significance; it reveals the innermost reasons for Buddha's [tolerant] attitude. Every one of the blind men really does have contact with a part of the true elephant. Transposed into religious terms, the implication is that different religious views are all based on true contact with the sacred. . . . The error and the reason for engaging in strife is the fact that every one of these blind men holds his partial insight to be universally valid.[26]

This spirit of tolerance can be traced back in part to Hinduism, for as Mensching points out, "Hinduism, because of its attitude regarding different concepts of God . . . , never declared a particular view to be the only true and binding one. Hence it never regarded conversion to its own concepts as its duty. For Hinduism, religious life was always more important than dogmatic preaching."[27] Despite its terrible caste system, classical Hinduism was essentially a mystical and syncretic faith rather than a prophetic one,[28] and in this way it set the pattern to some extent for subsequent religious developments in the East. In Mensching's view, mystical religions "have tolerance in their blood," so that it should not be too surprising that, "In the religious world of the East there were, on the whole, no struggles for tolerance."[29] Though this point has been overstated, the student of Oriental history cannot find there anything comparable in magnitude, severity, organization, or duration to the systematic restriction of religious liberty that marks so much of European history. And, as Mensching has observed, this cultural difference is largely to be explained on the basis of divergent religious conceptions and divergent conceptions of religion.

The antiquity of these Asian traditions of religious liberty and toleration suggests that religious repression and persecution in a political context are not "natural" phenomena but are based on a particular type of world-view. As we noted earlier, the Jews, with their prophetic monotheism, are often regarded as the true inventors of the fanatical exclusivism that eventually gave rise to the most destructive forms of repression and persecution, of which the Jews themselves have continuously been among the most conspicuous victims. Yet historical investigation does not bear out the contention that the leaders of ancient Israel were characteristically repressive in their dealings with non-believers who came under their political influence. While modern Jewish liberalism has often been explained by the fact that Jews have for most of their history found themselves to be members of a vulnerable minority, and have been conditioned by the tragedies that have befallen their people to empathize with other victims of persecution, the fact is that Jewish liberalism is partly a function of traditional Jewish religious conceptions. As we observed in Chapter 2, there are aspects of Judaism that disincline Jews to proselytize aggressively. More importantly, the ancient Israelites, unlike the polytheists among whom they lived, were obliged to recognize that, though they were a people with a special mission, their God is the God of all peoples and expects all human creatures — and even His other creatures — to be treated with some degree of respect.[30] Moreover, Hebrew Scripture makes it plain that, while the Law was given directly to the Israelites, all human beings are to be seen as capable of having certain basic moral standards. I refer specifically to the Noachide Covenant, which has received less attention than it deserves from historians of ethics. At Genesis 9 we read: "And God blessed Noah and his sons, and said unto them, Be fruitful, and multiply, and replenish the earth. And the fear of you and the dread of you shall be upon every beast of the earth, and upon every fowl of the air, upon all that moveth upon the earth. . . . But flesh with the life thereof, which is the blood thereof, shall ye not eat. And . . . Whoso sheddeth man's blood, by man shall his blood be shed; for in the image of God made he man."[31] Hence, Jews were to be reconciled to the idea that other peoples of the world cannot be fairly judged as having "failed" to accept a world-view that was not directly made available to them, and yet are to be judged by their commitment to moral rules that any normal adult can reasonably be expected to follow on the basis of an intuitive, reflective understanding of their soundness.

Hebrew Scripture's account of the establishment of Israel's monarchy is also noteworthy here since it shows us that the ancient Israelites did, to a considerable extent, distinguish between religious and political authority. The priest and prophet Samuel was called upon by the people to make them a king, "That we also may be like all the nations; and that our king may judge us, and go out before us, and fight our battles."[32] While Samuel recognized the apostasy involved in Israel's seeking a king other than God — and requiring a temporal authority figure more imposing than someone like himself — he is portrayed in the Scripture as having been directed by God to comply with the people's demand.[33]

Bury contends that our deepest gratitude is due to the ancient Greeks as the "originators" of liberty of thought and discussion.[34] Our familiarity with the problems faced by the classical Greek sophists and philosophers, who were constantly suspected of impiety by their fellows, will enable us to detect the overstatement in Bury's position. However, as Bury indicates, it was precisely the influence of the sophists and philosophers that gave rise to the spirit of rationalism that over the centuries has been one of the primary incentives to the promotion of religious liberty. Although Bury emphasizes the influence of Socrates,[35] particularly in his defence, at his trial, of freedom of conscience and public discussion, Bury also reminds us of the influence of Pericles, a statesman Bury characterizes as a "freethinker," and one who was certainly influenced by the sceptical tendencies in Sophistic teaching.[36] As for the ancient Romans, we must not allow our familiarity with their persecution of Christians and Jews to obscure the fact that their general policy throughout the Empire was to tolerate the local religions.[37] The two great prophetic religions posed a special problem to the Romans because of the exclusivist elements in them that led their adherents to be unusually disobedient to Roman political authority; in the eyes of many Roman leaders, it was the Jews and Christians themselves who were guilty of intolerance. No matter how the contemporary historian apportions blame with respect to the deterioration of relations between the ancient Romans and the Empire's Jews and Christians, it is crucial that she recognize the extent to which the conflict between world-views was a major factor contributing to it.

We noted earlier how, in the first stages of Christianity, Christian leaders argued eloquently for toleration on philosophical as well as theological grounds. When Christianity became the dominant religion in the Empire, the arguments for toleration were discarded, but even then there was still someone like Lactantius[38] to make the case that had once been made by such influential thinkers as Justin Martyr and Tertullian.[39] We may also recall here that a key event in the Christianization of the Empire was the emperor Constantine's edict on toleration of 313. Mensching writes: "When the first Christian state emerged, there thus prevailed a situation of tolerance which had to be restored again later, in fact centuries later after long struggles, because it was soon abolished again on behalf of Christianity. Hence the idea of various religions existing tolerantly beside each other in one and the same state was actually put into practice at an early stage in church history...."⁴⁰ While Constantine may be mainly remembered by students of religious liberty as the figure who unleashed the darkest forms of Christian ecclesiastical power, one might just as well remember him for extending the policy of toleration that for so long had served the emperors and their subjects well.

Although I was willing to grant in Chapter 2 that Northcott is being only slightly extravagant when he asserts that it is futile to look for the ideas of religious liberty and toleration in the Middle Ages, the fact remains that the situation of persecuted minorities and sects would have been even worse than it was had it not been for the fact that major figures in the mediaeval church had given considerable thought to the question of what obligation the church has to those outside it. In an admirable study, E. A. Synan has shown how many mediaeval popes and other high-ranking ecclesiastics devoted much thought in particular to the church's moral responsibilities in its dealings with Jews. Of course, few, if any, complaints against mediaeval popes have been as pointed as those concerning their treatment of the Jews.⁴¹ But the mediaeval church's treatment of Jews actually varied remarkably from one generation to the next, and a major reason for the variation was the changing perspective of the church's leading thinkers. At one point, mediaeval Jews were victimized by the policies of Innocent III, who wrote in 1207 to the Count of Nevers that "[Jews, as] blasphemers of the Christian Name ought not to be coddled at the price of oppressing the Lord's servants, but rather be repressed by the servitude of which they have rendered themselves deserving when they laid sacrilegious hands on Him who had come to confer true liberty upon them, calling down His blood upon themselves and on their children too."⁴² Yet in an earlier period Jews had benefitted from Pope Gregory I's instruction to let the Jews "enjoy their lawful liberty to observe and to celebrate all their festivities, as they have enjoyed this up until now, they and their forefathers as well, worshiping through long ages past,"⁴³ and in the twelfth century, Jews were the beneficiaries of Pope Alexander III's "Constitution for the Jews," which taught that Jews "ought to suffer no prejudice," and proscribed such acts against the Jews as compulsory baptism, disruption of their religious festivals, and vandalism in Jewish cemeteries.⁴⁴ Although Christian persecution of the Jews must certainly be regarded now as one of the most important facts about life in the Middle Ages, no student of the history of religious freedoms should fail to be impressed by Gregory I's talk of the Jews' "lawful liberty," or by Alexander III's admonition that those who ignore the rights of Jews are to be "punished by the vengeance of excommunication."[45]

Many scholars share D. J. Manning's view that, "In Europe, extended arguments for religious toleration and freedom of learning were first heard during the Reformation and Renaissance"; and some will also agree with Manning that "The story of the struggle for freedom of conscience and intellectual freedom may begin with the reaction of two great Catholic humanists, More and Erasmus, to the initial stages of the Reformation."[46] It is hard to know exactly how Manning would distinguish an "extended" argument from the kinds of arguments that were offered by earlier advocates of toleration and religious liberty. Still, there is no question that the sixteenth and seventeenth centuries produced much of the most important philosophical and theological literature on toleration, and that works composed in this period eventually came to have great influence on major social institutions. But how much importance should we attach to the arguments themselves, and how much should we attach to the circumstances under which they were developed? Obviously, much importance must be attached to "circumstances" — socio-economic conditions, the state of technology, and the weakening of the papacy and the church itself, particularly as a result of their increasingly noticeable corruption.[47] And undoubtedly, men such as More and Erasmus, Luther and Calvin, and Servetus and Castellio were very much men of their time. On the other hand, we have no right to assume that, if such men had not existed, there would have been people very much like them to take their places and accomplish what they did. All one has to do is read a page or two from the writings of any of these men to realize that one has encountered a mind that has been quite as capable of influencing the outside world as being influenced *by* it. At one point in his history of rationalism, Lecky, who usually knows better, contends that "civilization makes opinions that are opposed to it simply obsolete. They perish by indifference, not by controversy."[48] The sixteenth century provides us with innumerable counter-examples to this cynical position.

We must be careful neither to overestimate nor to underestimate the contribution of early Protestantism to the growth of religious liberty. In Chapter 2, we considered the warning of such scholars as Northcott and Hayward not to assume that religious liberty and toleration arose as a direct consequence of the dissemination of the theological and social teachings of the principal Reformers. Yet, as Bury observes, certain ideas of the Reformation contributed to bringing about a new set of social and political conditions that were conducive to the growth of religious liberty.[49] Bainton has pointed out that, from the start, there were two strains in Protestant thought, that of the "persecutors" and that of the "liberals." The most celebrated Reformers — Luther, Calvin, and Zwingli — were essentially "persecutors," but the social conditions that they established enabled the "liberals" to disseminate their views effectively.[50] The Jesuit scholar Joseph Lecler has developed this point: while "not one of the founders of the Reformation tried to undo that rigid principle of the Middle Ages of one religion in one State," and indeed, "[i]n a way they even reinforced it, since they put the power to rule religion directly into the hands of the secular authority," the fact remains that "tendencies which worked for tolerance [developed] either on the outskirts of the Reformation, among the members of the mystical and spiritualizing school and among the sects (Anabaptists, Socinians, and Baptists), or among statesmen and political authors."[51] Although the theory itself was the principal contribution of the sixteenth century to the enhancement of religious liberty, even in its own day this theory had some practical, though limited, effects.[52] But the air had come to be filled with the ideas of people such as Erasmus, Sebastian Franck, Michel de l'Hospital, Jean Bodin, Montaigne, and Sebastian Castellio, and all sorts of people from all walks of life were breathing in those ideas. In the seventeenth century, the leadership in the struggle for religious liberty passed on to the Dutch and the English, and in the eighteenth, to the Americans.

Bainton, while recognizing that initially it was the "persecutors" who determined the agenda of Protestantism, notes that from the start Protestantism was in theory capable of toleration on more counts than Catholicism.[53] With its emphases on private judgement, the priesthood of all believers, and the individual's obligation to consult Scripture for himself, Protestantism promoted an individualism that, though conceptually distinct from liberalism and rationalism, provided the occasion for their more rapid development. Michael Novak has observed that "The Protestant revolt against authority in the name of individual conscience was not, in essence, an offspring of a liberal so much as of a more tightly observant spirit: ruled by the self rather than by the pope but not, to be sure, for the sake of worldly laxity. . . . What Protestant and liberal have in common is radical individualism."[54] Thus, while permitting and even encouraging the persecution of their brothers, the Reformers were laying the foundations of forms of religious liberty and religious liberalism that they would hardly have understood, much less approved. Hayward, who is highly critical of the illiberal substance of classical Protestantism, grants that "Luther's dictum that every man must do his own believing as well as his own dying has stood as a perennial charter of religious freedom despite the long history of Protestant religious intolerance."[55] And Bainton draws our attention to Protestantism's conception of the rights of error, according to which "even error has rights as a stage in the quest for truth. Error is not the goal, but honest error is nearer to the truth of religion than dishonest correctness."[56]

Without undervaluing the general contributions of Protestantism as such, we must acknowledge that the growth of religious liberty in the sixteenth century was particularly stimulated by the ideas and actions of the leaders of specific denominations; and as we have seen, Lecler singles out the Anabaptists and Socinians for special mention. Franklin Littell has observed that the Anabaptists made an important mark with their powerful attack on the union of church and state:

> The Anabaptists were in fact among the first consistently to champion religious liberty in the modern sense. They believed that no individual might rightly be compelled by the magistrate in the matter of faith, and they distinguished between political sovereignty and those controls of the church which belong to its internal discipline and integrity. . . . The Anabaptists asserted that political compulsion in religion was the denial of spiritual government and an affront to the spiritual power in the church.[57]

Just as influential in the growth of religious liberty were the Socinian Unitarians.[58] It is interesting to note that the Socinian objection to civil government's interference in religious matters was at least partly rooted in the rejection of the theological doctrine of original sin, and with it, the notion of transmitted guilt and the doctrine concerning unbaptized infants that was related to it.[59] It was from the ranks of the Unitarians that one of the greatest of all champions of religious liberty emerged, Sebastian Castellio, whose *Concerning Heretics* (1554) was important not only for its arguments but as a highly effective response to Calvin's execution of Michael Servetus the previous year. The burning of Servetus became a stimulant to much soul-searching on the part of Protestants who, having long attacked Rome for its cruelty, could no longer close their eyes to the fact that the new masters could be as corrupt and arbitrary as the old ones. We can imagine the effect that Castellio's words must have had upon the consciences of the more thoughtful Protestants of his day: "When I consider the life and teaching of Christ who, though innocent Himself, yet always pardoned the guilty and told us to pardon until seventy times seven, I do not see how we can retain the name of

Christian if we do not imitate His clemency and mercy";[60] "I hate heretics. But I speak because I see here two great dangers. And the first is that he be held for a heretic, who is not a heretic. . . . The other danger is that he who is really a heretic be punished more severely or in a manner other than that required by Christian discipline";[61] "Who would not think Christ a Moloch, or some such god, if he wished that men should be immolated to him and burned alive?";[62] and, "What more could Satan do than burn those who call upon the name of Christ?"[63]

In the seventeenth century, Holland and England produced the most eloquent and most effective promoters of religious liberty. To some extent, Dutch and English defenders of toleration were able to say the things they said because of the nature of the societies in which they lived; but we should not underestimate the extent to which high-minded thinkers contributed to making those societies what they were. With the Dutch movement for the enhancement of religious liberty we associate such famous names as Grotius and Spinoza; but we may also recall that Amsterdam in this period was at the height of its glory, largely because of its practical application of the principles of toleration advanced by its most progressive thinkers. The cultural and commercial success of the Dutch, recognized by the world to be largely due to their fair treatment of minorities, was itself a major factor contributing to the establishment of the kind of religious toleration that so many of us take for granted today. English thought on toleration during the period, much influenced by Dutch ideas, produced classic works on the subject by such writers as Richard Hooker, John Milton, and John Locke. Agitation for religious liberty culminated successfully in the 1689 Act of Toleration, which Bainton has characterized as the most significant milestone in the development of religious liberty.[64]

As Manning tells us, "Richard Hooker, Hobbes and Spinoza insisted upon the supremacy of political over ecclesiastical authority in matters relating to religious practice while arguing in favour of freedom for the Christian conscience. For them the threat to religious liberty came not from civil authority. It came from religious fanatics."[65] Milton went a step further than they did by affirming that "the Protestant church is independent of the state in matters of religious practice as well as faith."[66] If Spinoza's *Tractatus Theologico-Politicus* represents the most philosophically sophisticated version of the Dutch–English theory, it was left to the less controversial Locke to produce the version of the theory that would have the most concrete and most lasting effect.[67] Locke's writings were much admired on the continent as well as in

England, but perhaps their greatest influence was on the "founding fathers" of the United States.

The United States institutionalized religious liberty and toleration to a degree to which they had never been institutionalized before. In 1791 the founding fathers, after considerable debate, appended a bill of rights in the form of ten amendments to their new Constitution, and the first amendment opens with what may well be the most famous and influential constitutional provision for religious liberty ever devised: "Congress shall make no law respecting an establishment of religion, or prohibiting the free exercise thereof. . . . " Although this formulation has proved to be far from ideal, it made clear from the start to all concerned that American political leaders were going to work hard to avoid the evils of religious bigotry and hostility that had plagued the old world.[68] In time, American scholars, statesmen, and jurists would go on to build around the amendment an elaborate and impressive machinery to safeguard and extend the religious freedoms of individual citizens and denominations; and though this machinery has sometimes broken down, the United States continues to lead the world in this area. Institutionalized religious liberty remains, along with the enslavement of Africans, one of the two main facts of American history; most of the distinctive characteristics of American culture can be explained in large part by reference to these two institutions.

It was no coincidence that the United States came to play such an important role in establishing the practicability, morality, and prudence of a sustained policy of religious liberty and toleration. The United States was formed by the union of colonies, and while some colonies were originally dominated by Puritans, another was settled by Quakers, still another by Catholics, and so forth. Although most of the early colonists had no use for a policy of religious toleration, there were noble experiments with the policy in several of the colonies, most notably in Rhode Island, which the great Baptist leader Roger Williams had established after alienating (and being alienated by) the repressive leaders of Massachusetts. "To Roger Williams," suggests no less an authority than Bury, "belongs the glory of having founded the first modern State which was really tolerant and was based on the principle of taking the control of religious matters entirely out of the hands of the civil government."[69] Everything we know about this remarkable leader — and much was written by him as well as about him — attests to the fact that he was a man of deep religious commitment, compassion, and vision, and the success of his little experiment in New England caused people of many different backgrounds and inclinations to sit up and take notice. Like Locke, Williams had derived from the Dutch Arminians a sincere appreciation for the importance of separating political and religious authority. But unlike Locke, Williams put his ideas to work by establishing a model community; and Williams went beyond Locke in extending liberty to groups that even Locke did not consider it appropriate to tolerate. In any case, by the time that the necessity of merging the colonies into a single nation generally became apparent, not only were there models of the tolerant society for the founding fathers to work from, but there were so many different religious faiths represented on the continent — with no single denomination being dominant — that even the most bigoted of colonists could recognize the appropriateness of the new nation's having a highly institutionalized policy of religious liberty. Moreover, the United States counted among its founders such learned and progressive men as Jefferson and Madison, who sincerely endorsed the major principles of the Dutch–English theory of toleration. By the late nineteenth century, the eminent British political theorist James Bryce was able to look at America's institutionalized religious liberty as the salient characteristic of American culture and the one that most fundamentally distinguished America from the old world.[70]

We can see from our brief historical excursus that it is misleading to say, as Littell does, that religious liberty is "a very recent experiment in social adjustment."[71] Nevertheless, we must acknowledge that religious liberty is an ideal that at any given time in any given place has been realized only to a certain extent; and throughout most of the world, people enjoy far fewer rights and privileges in this domain than people do in those nations generally considered to be liberal democracies. Moreover, even the most highly civilized societies can (and do) lapse into a less civilized condition, and so a society's policy of toleration must constantly be protected. We must be especially vigilant to ensure that constitutional guarantees of religious liberty are not allowed to degenerate into manipulative rhetoric. As Bates has noted, while constitutional provisions for religious liberty are important acknowledgements of principle, in many nations they are ineffective; and many leaders throughout the world who have praised the policy of religious liberty have manifested little interest in seeing to it that the policy is more conscientiously put into practice.[72]

Even when statesmen, politicians, and jurists approach controversies involving religious liberty with the purest form of good will that their fellows can reasonably expect of them, there is a great deal of interpretation that is expected of them, and a certain degree of arbitrariness invariably enters into such interpretation. Nowhere is this more evident than in the complex cases that jurists in advanced societies often find themselves having to resolve. Hence, it is not hard to sympathize with someone like the former Chief Justice of the United States Supreme Court, Warren Burger, who prefaced his court's opinion on a typically mind-boggling high-court case with this lament:

> The Establishment and Free Exercise Clauses of the First Amendment are not the most precisely drawn portions of the Constitution. The sweep of the absolute prohibitions in the Religion Clauses may have been calculated; but the purpose was to state an objective, not write a statute. In attempting to articulate the scope of the two Religious Clauses, the Court's opinions reflect the limitations inherent in formulating general principles on a case-by-case basis. . . . The Court has struggled to find a neutral course between the two Religion Clauses, both of which are cast in absolute terms, and either of which, if expanded to a logical extreme, would tend to clash with the other. . . .[73]

We can sympathize with such a person, but still have a right to expect him to fulfil creditably the obligations that he has taken upon himself. Whatever "official" standard of religious liberty a society's intellectual, political, and judicial leaders serve up, it will have been a product of human reflection; and whenever determinations are made about the applicability of general principles to concrete cases, those too will have been products of human reflection. Alas, reflection is too often shallow and perfunctory; but when the realization of ideals is the matter at hand, as in so many dimensions of human life, there is simply no substitute for disciplined reflection.

3 The Separation Principle

My short historical excursus has been anything but thorough, and a knowledgeable reader is sure to be puzzled by the inclusion of some events and the exclusion of others; but at least we are now in a better position to appreciate some of the classical issues associated with the expression "religious liberty." Let us now build upon the basic theoretical considerations with which we began by extracting some key ideas from the concrete historical situations in which they have ordinarily been embedded. Perhaps the most accessible of these ideas is what can be termed the "separation principle," the idea that religious and political authority can and ought to be "separated."

Lecky has made the shrewd observation that, "If we take a broad view of the course of history, and examine the relations of great bodies of men, we find that religion and patriotism are the chief moral influences to which they have been subject, and that the separate modifications and mutual interaction of these two agents may almost be said to constitute the moral history of mankind."[74] Although an individual may recognize other types of authority as being even more important, such as reason, conscience, or family tradition, what communities recognize as legitimate political and religious authorities, and their devotion to those authorities, are the primary social influences affecting a person's moral conceptions; and their political and religious authorities sometimes merge, sometimes co-operate, and sometimes compete. That is one reason why religious liberty is such an important form of religious freedom: the excessively strong or excessively weak state is, because of the importance of political authority, a threat to many freedoms, but particularly those that somehow involve an equally important — and potentially rival — form of authority.

Issues concerning the actual and proper interaction between political and religious forms of authority are commonly known throughout much of the world as issues of "church and state" or "church–state relations." Most people who use such expressions use them loosely, so that by the term *church* they may mean any religious denomination (even a non-Christian one), or anything recognized by anyone as an actual or legitimate form of religious authority in his life, or even religion itself; and by the term *state* they may mean any form of political authority to which an individual or group may consider itself subject. The jurist A. E. Sutherland has pointed out that discussions of "church and state" are often complicated by the failure of the participants to recognize how the relevant conceptions have changed over the years:

> In 1215 the word "State," if it or any word like it was heard at all, carried no meaning for the hearer such as today is carried by the names "France," "Germany," "China," "Italy," "Great Britain," or the "United States." And to speak of "the Church" connotes quite different matters in our time. What Church? Respected and revered as the Roman Catholic Church is, its most devoted members must concede that the confusion of assorted Christian churches in Europe and America is inconsistent with any such position of single authority as Innocent III occupied in 1215. The thunder of interdicts no longer terrifies England. Excommunication of the Prime Minister of England as a measure of international relations now seems unlikely, no matter what the political controversy may be.[75]

It is particularly important to remember that, voluntarily or not, a person may not distinguish conceptually between political authority and religious authority. Having grown up in a certain kind of society, he may take it for granted that one's political leaders are also one's religious leaders and vice versa; or, though familiar with the distinction that other people draw between the two forms of authority, he may dismiss that distinction as muddled and philosophically unacceptable. So, some people may genuinely be unable to distinguish conceptually between "church" and "state," and others may feel obliged for ideological or theological reasons to pretend that they cannot.

However, most people, even in so-called "theocracies," seem to be able to distinguish conceptually between religious and political authority, for even if the same person in their community administers the religious rites and leads the army, people are inclined to distinguish the primarily religious aspects of his authority from the primarily political ones. They seem to be able to distinguish usefully between the same person's *role* in saving them from God's wrath and his *role* in saving them from invading armies and local criminals. Throughout history, even in so-called "theocracies," there has also been substantial division of labour, including division of labour between those who mainly do such things as preach and perform ritual sacrifices and those who are largely concerned with such things as apprehending criminals and supervising economic institutions. Of course, with respect to certain functions (such as legislating with respect to sexual and marital matters, looking after the destitute, or even preaching and supervising economic institutions), the division of labour is often unclear, if it exists at all; and in such cases the line between religious and political authority is blurred or even partly erased. The ancient Israelites probably would have been able to distinguish Moses the prophet from Moses the military leader — even if as a military leader he was successful only insofar as he was an agent of the Lord — but it would have been harder for them to distinguish Moses the prophet from Moses the judge, and it would have been extremely difficult for them to distinguish Moses the prophet from Moses the Lawgiver. Yet by the time of Samuel and Saul, the Israelites knew that what they wanted was a full-fledged king, and not just a prophet, priest, or judge who would also perform the main functions of a king.

In any case, those who have fought for religious liberty have certainly distinguished conceptually between political and religious authority, and in the process of doing so in public, they have helped others to form or clarify the distinction in their own minds, even if those others have continued to believe that religious and political authority should be *joined* or *blended* in the same individuals or institutions. But when people advocate "separation" of religious and political authority, they are invariably arguing for more than just a conceptual distinction, although drawing that distinction in a particular way is central to their argument; they are also arguing that the highest religious functions and the highest political functions should not be *combined* in the same individuals or institutions. Similarly, the typical opponent of "separation" is able to distinguish conceptually between primarily religious and primarily political functions, but he believes that the two roles are best performed by the same individuals or institutions.

Even in a society in which all people whole-heartedly recognized the same religious authority — and this situation is not uncommon in primitive societies — a good argument could be made for dividing labour up in such a way that the highest religious authority was not also the highest political authority.[76] It could be argued, for example, that it is too much to expect one person or group to perform adequately such significantly different functions as consulting God or the gods and supervising economic institutions. It could also be argued that there is a clear distinction between the realms of the sacred and the profane, and that a religious authority is demeaned or even corrupted by having to concern himself (or itself) with worldly matters. However, in societies in which there is disagreement about who or what represents legitimate religious authority, the question of separation takes on much greater significance. For in such societies, while everyone may recognize the need for a central political authority, certain people may well resent it when that authority is identical with, dominated by, or even partial to a group or institution that is other people's religious authority but not their own. One reason why they are likely to be resentful — and fearful as well — is because they have good reason to believe that, under such circumstances, their ability to live according to their own religious commitment is in constant jeopardy. They are apt to be especially resentful if they do not consider themselves to be significantly outnumbered by members of the politically dominant religious community. Still, it may not always be the case that their resentment or even their fear is warranted.

According to Bates, "Separation means in practice the placing of churches on the same basis as other private societies and the reduction to the minimum of relations between Church and State. In general separation accords with religious liberty because of the voluntary and spiritual character of religion, by contrast with the coercive and secular character of the State. The preponderance of considered experience approves separation as favorable to religious liberty."[77] Here, we have a conscientious and respected student of religious liberty speaking, and yet his remarks raise more questions than they answer. If, for example, separation means placing churches on the same basis as other private societies, why is it that governments in liberal democracies seem to be so much more careful not to interfere with churches than with other private societies? How voluntary is religion when one is subject to so many forms of religious indoctrination and conditioning, particularly in one's earliest years? What is "considered experience" in this case, and how is it that so many distinguished conservative thinkers — and some liberal ones too — have worried aloud about the threat separation poses both to religion and to political morality? Is the aim of separation really to minimize *all* relations between religious denominations and civil governments, or just certain kinds of relations, and if so, what kinds? Is the justification for separation the same in all societies, that is, in highly pluralistic societies as well as societies in which only a handful of people do not acknowledge the religious authority revered and trusted by the overwhelming majority of the citizens? For that matter, why should religion be allowed to be as "voluntary" as it is, and why is a government's allowing it to be as voluntary as possible more important than that government's obligation, say, to promote civic unity?

The fact is that, by the time Bates was writing, the reasonableness and practicability of a separation policy had already long been taken for granted by the intellectual leaders of the liberal democracies. Its wide and continuing acceptance is at least partly explicable by the respect that the success of the American approach to religious liberty has engendered; for that approach is formally based on the First Amendment, whose religious clauses can clearly be seen to constitute a version of the separation principle. There is no question that, of all the intellectual influences in this area upon the Constitution-builders of the United States, none was greater than the political philosophy of John Locke, whose 1689 *Letter Concerning Toleration* has probably had more direct influence on the institutionalization of religious liberty than any other work. However, an examination of the main ideas of this famous work reveals that the separation principle is unsatisfactory on several scores. Locke's defence of the principle proceeds by way of arguments for four theses: compulsion and conviction are incompatible; spiritual and temporal affairs must be distinguished; discipline is the business of the state and not the church; and only those threatening the state are to be denied toleration.[78] The *Letter* is filled with all sorts of errors and confusions, but we shall focus our attention here on some central weaknesses of Locke's analysis.

At the heart of Locke's theory is his demarcation of the separate spheres of civil and denominational authority. On the basis of this demarcation, he goes on to argue that civil authority has no justification for interfering in purely religious affairs, and religious societies have no justification for attempting to use purely civil institutions for their own religious purposes. Of political authority, Locke writes,

> The commonwealth seems to me to be a society of men constituted only for the procuring, preserving, and advancing their own civil interests. Civil interests I call life, liberty, health, and indolency of body; and the possession of outward things, such as money, lands, houses, furniture, and the like. It is the duty of the civil magistrate, by the impartial execution of equal laws, to secure unto all the people in general, and to every one of his subjects in particular, the just possession of these things belonging to this life.[79]

The business of a church, in Locke's view, is entirely different:

> A church, then, I take to be a voluntary society of men, joining themselves together of their own accord in order to the public worshiping of God in such manner as they judge acceptable to Him, and effectual to the salvation of their souls. I say it is a free and voluntary society. . . . No man by nature is bound unto any particular church or sect, but everyone joins voluntarily to that society in which he believes he has found that profession and worship which is truly acceptable to God. The hope of salvation, as it was the only cause of his entrance into that communion, so it can be the only reason of his stay there.[80]

Locke does not pretend that he is simply reporting to us how people ordinarily use such terms as *commonwealth* and *church*, nor does he pretend that he is merely reporting how most people conceive of the proper spheres of political and religious authority. In point of fact, however useful Locke's conceptions might conceivably be, they are quite arbitrary. As J. W. Gough points out, "Locke's solution of the age-old problem of the relationship between church and state was to repudiate the historic Catholic position entirely, and instead to adopt the characteristically Independent or nonconformist view of a church as a voluntary society, not only distinct but separate from state. The state too was a voluntary society, formed by contract; at the same time it was also a necessary society, but so, Locke believed, were churches as well."[81] However arbitrary Locke's conceptions might be, one might still be inclined to defend them on utilitarian or other general ethical grounds.

But a more serious problem for Locke is that, even with his arbitrary demarcation, he does not provide adequate justification for his claim that it is neither necessary nor appropriate for civil and denominational leaders to "meddle" in each other's affairs. As Gough notes, "Logically maintained, [Locke's] position should involve allowing both church and state equal freedom of action within their respective self-contained spheres, provided they did not violate God's law or the law of nature. In practice, however, Locke found it impossible to treat the two societies as equal. In spite of his arguments against the magistrate having any part in the sphere of religion, he could not keep them separate either, and in certain circumstances he was prepared in effect to subordinate the church to the state."[82] Consider these comments of Locke:

> You will say, by this rule [that is, political non-interference in purely religious matters], if some congregations should have a mind to sacrifice infants, or (as the primitive Christians were falsely accused) lustfully pollute themselves in promiscuous uncleanliness, or practice any other such heinous enormities, is the magistrate obliged to tolerate them because they are committed in a religious assembly? I answer, No. These things are not lawful in the ordinary course of life, nor in any private house; and therefore neither are they so in the worship of God, or in any religious meeting.[83]

When we grasp that it is ultimately the magistrate who will determine what is "lawful in the ordinary course of life," and that the magistrate may turn out in any given situation to be foolish, unjust, or bigoted, we realize that Locke's talk about separation obscures the fact that he has ultimately subordinated religious authority to political authority.

Locke's theory is often contrasted with that of Spinoza,[84] who in the process of defending religious liberty asserts that, even if the civil authority is corrupt and irrational, people must not prevent it from regulating religious rites or doing whatever else it deems necessary for maintaining the peace and well-being of the community.[85] However, Locke's position is similar to Spinoza's in certain key ways: not only does it leave supreme power in the hands of the civil authority, but it defends religious liberty only for those who practise the kind of religion with which the author is personally sympathetic.[86] One might be puzzled by how these two philosophers, whose principal objective was to promote religious liberty and general freedom of thought and conscience, could end up arguing for the primacy of civil authority. Here, it must be recalled that the state which both philosophers are defending is a state that is *ideally* as neutral as possible with respect to religious matters.

But an even more basic weakness of Locke's analysis is its failure to recognize the extent to which religious authority and political authority almost necessarily and inevitably come into conflict as a result of being major forms of authority. Both prescribe, legislate, and judge, and with respect to general ethical matters and not merely ritual and worship. Locke's conception of religion is remarkably naive: it treats the attainment of salvation as if it were some mysterious technical exercise that has little, if anything, to do with the business of living a good life.[87] Locke's contempt for modes of religious life other than those of which he approves is more obvious to contemporary readers than it was to most eighteenth-century liberals, and when one considers the limits Locke fixes to toleration in the latter part of the *Letter*, one might be inclined to agree with Morley that those limits rule out everyone except possibly Quakers.[88]

The weaknesses in Locke's position were directly transmitted to the United States Constitution, for despite the elaborate and imposing machinery that jurists have built around the First Amendment, and despite the fact that the founding fathers had more sophisticated and more generous attitudes than Locke, the fact remains that the First Amendment is essentially a version of the separation principle. Consider again its opening words: "Congress shall make no law respecting an establishment of religion, or prohibiting the free exercise thereof. . . . " Jurists have interpreted both clauses in complex and occasionally very strange ways, and that is hardly surprising, for no government can consistently deliver on such promises if they are taken literally. Although it is promised here that no law shall be made respecting an "establishment of religion," the entire American law is dominated by the ideas and values of the most powerful Christian churches, and particularly those of the more liberal Protestant churches. As for the matter of prohibiting the "free exercise" of religion, we know full well that the American Congress will not hesitate to prevent someone from sacrificing his daughter to his gods, and that Congress has, in fact, not hesitated to prevent people from fulfilling their religious obligations in much less extreme cases.

The attitude of most jurists in liberal democratic states is straightforwardly expressed by Justice Waite's opinion in the famous nineteenth-century case of *Reynolds v. United States*, in which the United States Supreme Court upheld a statute making polygamy a criminal offence even though Mormons at the time regarded polygamous marriage as a religious obligation. "So here," Waite writes, "as a law of the organization of society under the exclusive dominion of the United

States, it is provided that plural marriages shall not be allowed. Can a man excuse his practices to the contrary because of his religious belief? To permit this would be to make the professed doctrines of religious belief superior to the law of the land, and in effect to permit every citizen to become a law unto himself. Government could exist only in name under such circumstances."[89] This is a plausible utilitarian argument, but how can it not be regarded as justifying the prohibition of the free exercise of religion? And does it not indirectly endorse the policy of promoting the attitudes, doctrines, and values of a religious Establishment that, though it is not an established religion, is close enough to being one? Consider in this regard Waite's troubling comment that "Polygamy has always been odious among the Northern and Western Nations of Europe and, until the establishment of the Mormon Church, was almost exclusively a feature of the life of Asiatic and African people."[90] What are we to make of such an arbitrary ethical criterion, with its conventionalist and racist aspects; and how are we to ignore the relevant fact that every persecuted religious minority has been reviled at least in part because its practices have been "odious" to groups with political clout?[91]

The high courts of modern liberal democracies do not have to deal with cases involving questions of whether Jews or Unitarians have a right not to be burned alive. That in itself indicates a remarkable advance in Western civilization since the sixteenth century. Undoubtedly, part of this progress has been due to constitutional provisions for religious liberty and the machinery built around them. However, we may wonder how much of the progress has been a function of the direct application of the separation principle. If one surveys the relevant cases in the modern Western democracies, one finds that, despite the frequent rhetorical invocation of some version of the separation principle, specific cases are decided on an individual basis; and though legal and social precedents are often weighed, no simple formula is applied. It is worth noting that there has been substantial religious liberty even in nations in which there is an established church; the United Kingdom and Scandinavian countries come to mind. We even find a zealous promoter of religious liberty like H. G. Wood allowing that "A Church may be so intimately bound up with the life of a nation that she cannot simply decline the privilege of State recognition."[92] Thus, either the separation principle is capable of being stretched in many directions, or it is fundamentally unnecessary as a theoretical basis for the protection and enhancement of religious liberty.

There can be no question that the separation principle is historically important. Many of the thinkers and jurists who have made use of it in their arguments have been people of good will who have helped to make human society at least a little more civilized. Voltaire was a brilliant literary stylist; and Locke, who is not always thought of as a great stylist, is probably more eloquent in the first *Letter* than in any of his other major works. The most important founding fathers of the United States were masters of rhetoric; rarely have political writers been able to produce prose of the quality of *The Federalist Papers* or Jefferson's best pieces. These founding fathers — who were able to pronounce stirring words about inalienable rights while (reluctantly or not) endorsing the acceptability of the enslavement of Africans — were men of undeniable moral vision, but we must not confuse the nobility of their cause or the effectiveness of their promotional strategy with the clarity of their theory or the soundness of their argument. Nevertheless, enunciations of the separation principle have not necessarily been empty slogans or rhetorical devices, although often they have been little more. They may serve to express certain values and sentiments to which listeners and readers can relate, and they may represent, as in the case of Locke, recommendations about how corrupt or ineffective institutions might be reformed. Those who attach great importance to the separation principle undervalue the genuine conflict between two of the principal forms of authority, and in doing so they ignore the paradox of religious liberty and offer only caricatures of political and religious institutions. But they raise questions worth raising, and often their ideas and conceptions are less arbitrary than those against which they are protesting.

In no area has the genuine conflict between political and religious authority been more apparent than in that of education.[93] Is education largely a matter of, in Locke's words, "procuring, preserving, and advancing . . . civil interests"? Is it a means of attaining spiritual freedom? Religious communities educated young and old alike long before the modern nation-state existed, and it is still widely believed throughout the world that the task of educating particularly the young should be left primarily to religious agencies. In Milton Konvitz's list of leading constitutional cases concerning religious liberty in the United States, over half the cases concern education. The range of problems that have arisen in recent years alone is impressive: bus fares for parochial school pupils; release time; prayer in public schools; Bible reading in public schools; textbooks for parochial school pupils; salaries for parochial school teachers; buildings for church-related colleges; teaching of evolution in public schools; liberty of teaching in private schools;

the parochial school and compulsory school attendance laws; compulsory school attendance laws and the rights of parents.[94] Other notable conflicts between civil governments and religious denominations in the United States have arisen over such things as Sunday observance laws, religious test oaths, ecclesiastical self-government and the liberty of churches, conscription and conscientious objectors, and tax-exemption for church property.[95] And, of course, there is a religious dimension to public debates over such matters as censorship, abortion, contraception, and access to mass media of communication. Moreover, in the United States and other relatively liberal democracies, there could easily be even more conflicts between civil and denominational authority than there are now were it not for the fact that governments and religious groups have often deemed it prudent to acquiesce with respect to a particular issue. And in most parts of the world, struggles between religious and political authority revolve around much more basic issues than in the more liberal democracies. Thus, there is good reason to suspect that the distinctive spheres of religious and political authority have not yet been defined to the satisfaction of all interested parties or even all reflective and progressive thinkers.

4 The Moral Justification of Religious Liberty: Theologico-ethical Arguments and Appeals to Conscience

One of the distinctive features of defences of religious liberty that emphasize some version of the separation principle is that they indirectly undermine the status of religious liberty as a *moral* issue. According to such defences, problems arise in this area mainly because of the failure of people to *understand the nature* of religion and politics and of religious and political institutions. For someone like Locke or Jefferson, the enemies of (what they take to be) religious liberty are either curiously obtuse — in failing to understand what a civil government or religious society is in the way that they are able to understand what, say, an army or craftsmen's guild is — or execrably dishonest and manipulative — in pretending that they do not understand what a civil government or church is so that they can exploit one or both of the institutions in such a way as to promote their own interests and ideals. But since those who enunciate the separation principle are mainly concerned with *explaining* certain matters to readers and listeners, it would appear that they believe that violations of religious liberty arise primarily because even people of good will are rather *confused*.

We have seen, however, that the matter of "understanding" religious and political institutions is far more complex than a Locke or Jefferson would have us believe; even the way one understands religion and politics themselves is substantially a matter of theory and perspective. When, for example, Locke associates religion with rites and doctrines, we may want to recall Jean Holm's point that, "To concentrate on one activity, such as worship, is to ignore the fact that a religious person sees the whole of life in a religious perspective, and the rites and customs he observes, the festivals he celebrates, the code of ethics he follows, are no less aspects of his religion than worship is."[96] What is especially troubling about appeals to the separation principle is that they typically rest on half-baked theories of the nature of authority, and particularly religious authority. Indeed, many of them seem to presuppose that most people are not being entirely honest when they say that they see their religious activities as constituting the best available means to spiritual freedom and salvation.

I can understand, on one level, the desire of socio-political theorists to ground religious liberty on something that might appear to be more "objective" than ordinary moral considerations. We all know that moral judgements can be highly subjective, and that many supposedly sophisticated thinkers believe that all moral judgements are essentially subjective, and so we should not have much trouble appreciating why intellectuals, politicians, jurists, and even many religionists are easily seduced by a theory that suggests that distinguishing between the proper sphere of civil authority and the proper sphere of denominational authority is ultimately (after all the conceptual rubbish has been cleared away) as straightforward a matter as distinguishing between a knife and a fork. And however much jurists like Warren Burger may agonize over the ambiguity of the First Amendment, the fact remains that its religious clauses offer them a convenient peg on which to hang their arguments and analyses, so that they are saved from having to plunge *immediately* into the deep waters of utilitarian, deontological, perfectionist, and contractarian ethical theory. In drafting recent constitutional provisions for religious liberty, certain jurists have avoided enshrining some version of the separation principle; but, while we can appreciate the wisdom of their decision, we will find that they have ended up leaving even more scope for highly subjective interpretation. Canada's relatively new Charter of Rights and Freedoms simply guarantees citizens "freedom of religion," while the Universal Declaration of Human Rights adopted and proclaimed by the United Nations in 1948 informs us that "Everyone has the right to freedom of thought, conscience and religion; this right includes freedom to change his religion or belief, and freedom, either alone or in community with others and in public or private, to manifest his religion or belief in teaching, practice, worship and observance." We see that both of these constitutional provisions avoid not only a demarcation of the proper spheres of religious and political authority but also any reference to the matter of the establishment of religion.

Nevertheless, when we criticize religious persecution, then whether or not that persecution has a political dimension, we mean to indicate that we think that something significantly *immoral* is going on; we are implying that the people who are doing the persecuting have not simply made a technical error in their attempt to attain a satisfactory philosophical insight into the nature of political and religious institutions, but have been engaged in an activity that, on reflection, can be seen to be morally wrong. When jurists rule on concrete cases involving religious liberty, they do turn to general moral considerations at some point in their deliberations and do not confine themselves to narrow interpretation of constitutional provisions. Similarly, even people who simply profess to believe strongly in "separation of church and state" ordinarily make their judgements about concrete cases by weighing general moral considerations, and these invariably outrank the separation principle for them or, alternatively, enter into their interpretative stretching or narrowing of the principle. If, for example, someone were to announce to them that she considers it to be a violation of the separation principle when anyone other than a confirmed atheist is permitted to vote or hold elected office, they would spontaneously assume that she is either joking or manifesting some mental disorder, and they would not be likely to consider the possibility that she is simply being a more disciplined and consistent "separationist" than they are.

What, then, are the principal kinds of moral considerations that might be adduced to justify the enhancement of the various forms of religious liberty that we have noted? H. G. Wood has observed that, far from having had to rely solely on something like the separation principle, defenders of religious liberty have made a wide variety of appeals — to nature and natural rights, ethical intuition, history and tradition, the ethical postulates of science, the doctrine of creation, the need to safeguard sincerity in religion, and the gospel of redemption.[97] This list is useful though not exhaustive, and one notices the conspicuous presence on it of some theological considerations. One might rule these out as irrelevant on the ground that, being based on the theological doctrines of a particular faith (or kind of faith), they do not qualify as "general" moral considerations, since they would have no significance to a person with a different world-view. Obviously, a Marxist materialist would not be too impressed by an argument that appealed to the Biblical doctrine of creation, and we cannot expect a non-Christian to feel very comfortable with an argument that ultimately rests on an appeal to the gospel of redemption. However, we should be careful not to be too dismissive. For one thing, we must remember that, whether we like it or not, the religionist does not make as sharp a distinction between moral and theological considerations as the secularist or quasi-secularist would like him to make. The wrongness of adultery for, say, a Christian or a Muslim is not simply determined by spontaneous intuition or rational assessment; it is entailed by her religious commitment. She might grant that even someone who did not believe in the Supreme Being should be able to recognize that adultery is morally wrong, but it is very important to her that the ethical code of her religious community, and of the works she recognizes as sacred, directs her to avoid the practice. Since the age of Protagoras, Socrates, and Plato, philosophers have often gone to great lengths to try to convince their fellows that religious and moral considerations are quite distinct, and that the latter are largely "rational."[98] The fact is that morality is not purely a matter of reason — or intuition — and it actually was around in the world that existed prior to the time that the ancient Greeks "invented" systematic philosophy as we now know it. Secondly, the fact that a Marxist materialist or non-Christian might be inclined to dismiss a point as irrelevant does not necessarily mean that the point is an insufficiently "general" moral consideration. For one thing, an appeal to something like the doctrine of creation or the gospel of redemption can conceivably be defended by arguments in natural or philosophical theology, in which case, ironically, it might ultimately have to be regarded even by the secularist as more "objective" than non-theological moral appeals. Again, I can report from experience that there are Marxist materialists and other secularists who are prepared to dismiss as irrelevant not only any theologico-ethical appeal but also deontological arguments, existentialist arguments, perfectionist arguments, and so forth; and there are many non-Christians who are prepared to dismiss as irrelevant not only arguments associated with Christian theology but also utilitarian arguments, perfectionist arguments, and so on. In any case, to ask a true religionist whether he believes that adultery is wrong on religious or "general" ethical grounds is rather like asking a man whether he loves the mother who nurtured him or the wife he chose to be his partner in life because of her relationship to him or because of her personal qualities.

I shall not discuss here any theologico-ethical arguments for religious liberty, for one can get a clear enough idea of what they are like by reflecting on some of the points in the last chapter concerning religion as a source of freedom. From this we can see that Wood has in fact identified only two of the possible theologico-ethical arguments that might be adduced. One might argue instead, for example, that denying a person religious liberty prevents that person from fulfilling his obligation to *accept* God's commandments, or that it insults God by interfering with His prerogative to determine who shall receive the gift of faith, or that it interferes with the personal relationship between Creator and creature, or that it prevents the individual from attaining a deeper and more efficacious faith than he might otherwise be able to attain, and so on. For the imaginative philosophical theologian or religious ethicist, the possibilities are almost limitless. And these arguments can be very important and very effective, particularly when accompanied by the usually appropriate suggestion that religionists who do not take them seriously may be guilty of gross hypocrisy and a great sin against their God. (It is important to remember that arguments in defence of religious liberty are usually served up to *particular* individuals and groups and not to some faceless, uncommitted "general" or "universal" thinker, although sometimes they are presented to a group of people representing several different faiths.)

Also on Wood's list are references to appeals to ethical intuition and the need to safeguard sincerity in religion. Both of these are associated with the familiar appeal to conscience, which Bates tells us at one point is the "essence" of the matter: "Conscience is the essence of the matter — responsible first to God, to truth, to duty, rather than to government, to human authority in a religious body, or to opinion. Respect for conscience runs through all effort to secure religious liberty. . . . The free quality of conscience is acutely significant in the field of religion, broadly considered as man's devotion to supreme values."[99] Bates has been carried away by his own rhetoric; however important "conscience" may be in relation to religious liberty, it is not the "essence" of the matter and has in fact been dangerously overvalued by proponents of religious liberty. The term *conscience* can, of course, be understood in any number of ways, and Bates' point may be rather more innocuous than I fear. But a valuable lesson of moral philosophy is that appeals to ethical intuition, the moral sense, and conscience are usually too weak to sustain disciplined ethical dialogue and can even be used as a device for avoiding one's obligation to clarify in one's own mind why one is making particular moral judgements and why one has a right to expect other people to agree with them.

There actually have been some notable philosophers (or philosophizing theologians) who have argued at great length that conscience or the moral sense is at the core of morality. Perhaps the most famous of these is Rousseau, but we may also call to mind here most of the major British moral philosophers from Hutcheson and Shaftesbury through Hume and Mill. The dangers and limitations of ethical theories that overemphasize conscience and ethical intuition have long been recognized — sometimes even by the philosophers who have advanced them — but for present purposes we need only take note of a few simple facts. First, many people say that something is a matter of "conscience" for them only because they are too lazy to give a more helpful explanation of the basis of their judgement or because they are afraid that the shallowness and inadequacy of their reasons will be exposed. Secondly, all sorts of evils have been "justified" in the name of "conscience"; the most hateful barbarians have sometimes insisted, with the utmost sincerity, that "conscience" led them to murder, torture, and mutilate their fellows. Thirdly, many people recognize that even their own "conscience" bothers them when it does largely because they were conditioned at some point in their lives to behave in a certain way. Fourthly, many people seem to be confused about whether conscience is primarily a source of moral knowledge, primarily a force that encourages or discourages them from doing certain things, or primarily a source of guilt after the deed. Of course, many religionists have regarded conscience as somehow representing the voice of God — and have been curiously undisturbed by the fact that God seems to say so many contradictory things to different people in this unusual way — and among these believers are to be counted some saintly souls and also some authentic lunatics.[100] In any case, even many secular materialists attest to having a conscience, and some of them show by their actions that their conscience speaks to them more forcefully than does the conscience of the typical religionist.

There is another dimension to the appeal to conscience, and it involves the matter of sincerity or integrity. One of the most common arguments raised by defenders of religious liberty is the essentially psychological argument that conviction is not something that can be compelled. If faith is not a matter of grace, then it is a matter of some less mysterious condition of receptivity, but by its very nature it involves some mode of acceptance.[101] It is not too hard for an actual political authority, or a denominational hierarchy associated with it, to intimidate a human being into doing certain things, or to prevent her from doing certain others. But one cannot directly compel religious commitment as such; the closest one can get to doing this is to be able to compel the pretence of belief. Nevertheless, those who have attached great importance to this point, such as Spinoza,[102] have failed to recognize that it does not support the position that attempts to compel religious conviction are immoral or improper; rather, it supports the quite different position that attempts to compel religious conviction are foolish since they attempt to accomplish the impossible. It shows at most that a certain kind of liberty is inviolable purely as a result of natural necessity. But perhaps it does not even establish this point. Long before the rise of behaviourist psychology, people realized that there are quite effective methods of indoctrinating their fellows to believe certain things and conditioning them to behave in certain ways. People often rebelled in the past, but perhaps that was largely because methods of indoctrination and conditioning were not as effective as the methods now available.

In order for their appeal to (the primacy of) conscience to function as an argument in support of their cause, defenders of religious liberty must establish, first, that people should as a general rule be allowed to act on the basis of their religious convictions, and secondly, that people should not be subjected to extreme methods of indoctrination and conditioning that could be used to alter their world-view. I believe that a strong case could be made for both of these positions, even though the notions here of "a general rule" and "extreme methods" are vague. But I do not see how either case can be satisfactorily made simply by appealing to conscience. Sincerity is certainly an important virtue, and if Northcott is correct, the test of sincerity is the one universal New Testament test.[103] But sincerity is not the only virtue that matters; and the bottom line is that sincerity is never enough. The fact that Torquemada, the Grand Inquisitor, may have been sincere does not entail that he should have been allowed to supervise the burning of "heretics," any more than the fact that Adolf Eichmann was sincere in his commitment to the extermination of Jews in Nazi concentration camps entails that the world was right to allow him and his cohorts to carry on with their business. Again, it is not entirely clear what kinds of indoctrination and conditioning are inappropriate when civilized people find themselves faced with a dangerous, violent, deluded psychopath who sincerely believes that God has commanded him to punish loose women, homosexuals, or left-wing politicians. Of course, Torquemada and the psychopath are to be seen as exceptions to a general rule. But then it is not really sincerity or conscience that is the real issue here, for as a general rule even insincere people ought to be able to do what they want.

There is still another dimension to the appeal to conscience, and it involves the principle of individualism. We noted in our brief historical excursus that the individualism of religious reformers, even when they have not been at all liberal, has been a major incentive to their rebelliousness against established authority. And, as Bates has suggested, there is a certain kind of individualism underlying the appeal to conscience insofar as the rebel sees himself as more responsible to God, truth, or duty than to conventional conceptions or social institutions. To the extent that it represents an assertion of the primacy of the individual, the appeal to conscience is as strong or as weak as the principle of individualism itself. In modern liberal democracies, the term *individualism* is usually employed as what we have seen Cranston characterize as a "*hurrah*-word." But the "cult of the individual" has been attacked not only in totalitarian communities but in social-democratic and socialist ones as well; and even in liberal democracies, most people will admit on reflection that individualism needs to be tempered with a sense of social responsibility. The appeal to social responsibility can to some extent neutralize the appeal to conscience, even though the individual who wishes to follow the dictates of his conscience believes that he will be acting in a socially responsible way, for the appeal to social responsibility may be seen as implying on one level that it is for society more than the individual to determine in what social responsibility properly consists. So here again the appeal to conscience does not work by itself as an adequate moral justification of the enhancement of religious liberty. It always needs to be supported by rational arguments that are more concrete and more explicit. It is no mystery as to what kinds of arguments are necessary; two thousand years of moral philosophy have provided us with a useful catalogue of the types of moral argument available to us, even if it is no clearer now than it was centuries ago which types should elicit the most respect.

5   The Moral Justification of Religious Liberty: Utilitarian Arguments

One major form of moral argument is utilitarian: an action or policy is moral to the extent that it promotes the general happiness. Philosophers have long recognized that utilitarian arguments have some unattractive features: they tend to overemphasize pleasure at the expense of other aims; they seem to force us to regard as moral judgements many judgements that appear to have nothing to do with morality (such as determining which of two brands of breakfast tea one should drink); they seem to require us to do an unlimited amount of calculation every time we are about to do something, no matter how trivial, or, alternatively, they encourage us to follow certain general rules even when a concrete application of those rules may result in unhappiness; and so forth. And, of course, the concept of "the general happiness" is extremely vague. Yet it is generally felt now by scholars as well as ordinary folk that a complete assessment of the relative morality of an action or policy requires a consideration of the consequences of carrying it out.

Does the promotion of religious liberty tend "as a general rule," *ceteris paribus*, to promote the general happiness? Consider how many variables may be involved in making such a determination, and the consequent inevitability of remarkably different calculations and interpretations. We obviously need to consider the interests of religionists who aspire to enhanced liberty; but we also have to consider the interests of their fellows, some of whom perhaps stand to be badly affected by the extension of religious freedoms to others. Perhaps we have to consider posterity — a century from now or even a millennium. Utilitarian calculations can be conveniently manipulated by altering the set of variables considered, by altering the importance attached to any particular variable, and so on. Most people in liberal democracies would say that religious liberty does tend to promote the general happiness; but that has never been a universal opinion, and has often been a minority opinion.

There are probably countless considerations that could be adduced in support — or criticism — of the view, but we shall just take note of some of the more obvious ones. (1) History teaches us that many people are prepared to go to great lengths to secure and enhance their religious liberty and that of at least some of their fellows. That would seem to indicate that, despite the ideas of Ivan Karamazov's Grand Inquisitor, many people are happier when they are religiously freer. But, as the Inquisitor says, sometimes such people get more than they expected and eventually find that they and their fellows have more freedom than they can handle. Moreover, the happiness that a particular religious community derives from its enhanced freedom may be significantly neutralized by the unhappiness it derives from the enhanced freedom of religious groups of which that religious community heartily disapproves. (2) We saw in the last chapter that it is a widely held view that religious zeal can be an impetus to socially productive behaviour: if a person has a satisfying religious commitment and is able to live by it in public as well as in private, she may be more useful to her fellow citizens — and fellow human beings — than she would otherwise be.

But maybe not: we have also seen how certain religious attitudes can be a disincentive to self-assertion, and some religious communities use their newly enhanced liberty to make themselves as obnoxious as possible to those they consider "damned" or perverse. (3) The enhancement of religious liberty almost inevitably spills over into other areas, for not only has religious liberty been the fundamental form of freedom of thought, but it has generated advances in freedom of speech, freedom of association, and other civil liberties. Of course, each of these has to be evaluated in its own right. There can be no question that the growth of religious liberty has contributed, for example, to increased liberty in the area of scientific research; but there have been mixed assessments of the long-term consequences of this and other by-products of enhanced religious liberty. (4) Religious liberty establishes fertile ground for the development of a dynamic religious pluralism that brings with it healthy forms of competition among religious communities. But this is a double-edged sword, for religious pluralism has often been accompanied by the kind of sectarian conflict that destroys the unity of the state and results in violence, arbitrary discrimination, and other assorted evils.

Here, we have considered only four of many relevant utilitarian considerations, and yet even this brief list indicates major limitations of the utilitarian type of moral analysis. Arguments can be raised on both sides of each of the four issues; and calculation of how much importance to attach to each side of each issue, or to each issue itself, is apt to be extremely subjective. So, even if we ignore all other relevant considerations (and we may conceivably have ignored the most important ones), and even if we can agree on which parties' interests have to be weighed and on what sort of time frame is appropriate for our analysis, any final judgement may well be extremely arbitrary.

The limitations of the utilitarian form of moral analysis can be seen in one of the most famous of all defences of individual liberty, John Stuart Mill's *On Liberty* (1859). Mill is one of the major proponents of the utilitarian ethic, so that even though not all of his arguments in *On Liberty* are utilitarian in a narrow sense, the work as a whole complements the author's general utilitarianism. As he was writing two centuries after Locke and Spinoza, Mill was not as preoccupied as they were with issues of religious liberty, but he treats these as aspects of the general issue of liberty of thought and expression. Mill was obviously much influenced by earlier writers: Morley contends that *On Liberty* is actually little more than an enlargement of principles that had been laid down in the seventeenth century by John Milton,[104] and Bury, a great admirer of *On Liberty*, traces its central themes all the way back to Socrates.[105] Mill offers four basic arguments for the enhancement of personal liberty of thought and expression (including religious thought and expression):

> First, if any opinion is compelled to silence, that opinion may, for aught we can certainly know, be true. To deny this is to assume our own infallibility. Secondly, though the silenced opinion be an error, it may, and very commonly does, contain a portion of truth; and since the general or prevailing opinion on any subject is rarely or never the whole truth, it is only by the collision of adverse opinions that the remainder of the truth has any chance of being supplied. Thirdly, even if the received opinion be not only true, but the whole truth; unless it is suffered to be, and actually is, vigorously and earnestly contested, it will, by most of those who receive it, be held in the manner of a prejudice, with little comprehension or feeling of its rational grounds. And not only this, but, fourthly, the meaning of the doctrine itself will be in danger of being lost, or enfeebled, and deprived of its vital effect on the character and conduct: the dogma becoming a mere formal profession, inefficacious for good, but cumbering the ground, and preventing the growth of any real and heartfelt conviction, from reason or personal experience.[106]

These provocative arguments are defended by Mill at some length; and they have elicited much commentary, particularly from scholars in the English-speaking world who have assumed them to be rather more original, more influential, and more philosophically sophisticated than they are. We need only to note, first, the emphasis that Mill places on the social consequences of promoting or preventing the relevant liberties, and secondly, the gratuitousness of Mill's speculations about what those social consequences are generally likely to be. In particular, Mill underestimates the danger of allowing the dissemination of certain kinds of false ideas and ideologies, such as racism, sexism, totalitarianism, and the like. Permissiveness of this kind has contributed greatly to the development of barbarism, just as repression of civil liberties has; and people need to be very careful when they do their calculating here, whether they are assessing a particular case or a general policy, for mistakes may result in a great deal of torture, destruction, and genocide. While Mill is justified in reminding us that we are not infallible, we have to remind ourselves that we are morally obliged to distinguish good from evil and to act on the basis of our carefully considered judgements.

The limitations of an essentially utilitarian defence of religious liberty are even more obvious when one considers what Mill takes to be the central principle of his essay: "That principle is, that the sole end for which mankind are warranted, individually or collectively, in interfering with the liberty of action of any of their number, is self-protection. That the only purpose for which power can be rightfully exercised over any member of a civilized community, against his will, is to prevent harm to others."[107] Mill does not address here a fundamental practical problem concerning religious liberty that we noted in our historical sketch: the need to balance the competing demands of the forms of authority that represent the two collectivities to which the religious citizen belongs. As Wood notes, "Mill's essay was concerned almost exclusively with the liberty of individuals, but we have also to consider the relation of the State to religious groups and associations."[108] My point is not simply that Mill's main concern is not relevant to the chief problem that has bothered so many people involved in the historical struggle for religious liberty; rather, it is the stronger point that Mill's individualistic bias has led him to manipulate his utilitarian assessment in such a way that what he has ended up with is of extremely limited value to those concerned with what may well be the classical problem of religious liberty. Mill's attitude towards most traditional forms of religious authority is, in any event, disdainful; and he simply fails to understand the importance that most devout people attach to religious authority.

But an even more serious weakness in Mill's essentially utilitarian analysis is manifested in the content of Mill's principle: that interference with something like religious liberty can only be justified by the necessity of preventing harm to others. We can appreciate Mill's sensitivity to the fact that much injustice has resulted from, or been "justified" by, what is ostensibly a desire to help those who do not want to be "helped" in this way; we need only think of all the decent human beings who were burned at the stake because someone was intent on saving their souls. But even setting aside the fact that rigorous application of Mill's principle could be reasonably construed in many cases as callousness and indifference, we can see that Mill's condition of "preventing harm to others" is so vague that it can be interpreted as meaning almost anything that a persecutor wants it to mean. Indeed, if we think back to our historical survey, we see that religious persecution was not justified simply on the ground that it ultimately benefits the victim but more often on the ground that it benefits the civil society, the church, and all other communities that stand to be negatively affected by the presence of "corrupting" role models, threats to communal unity, and so on.

I indicated earlier that I believe that a strong case can be made for the position that people should be allowed as a general rule to act on the basis of their religious convictions, and also for the position that people should not be subjected to extreme methods of religious or antireligious indoctrination and conditioning. I can go further now and state that most instances of political interference in the religious affairs of individuals and groups trouble my conscience and strike me, on the basis of my own utilitarian calculations, as being contributory in the "long run" to a diminution of the "general happiness" as I understand it. But this announcement hardly constitutes an argument, especially insofar as other people who seem to have reflected on this subject as deeply as Mill and I have done have been led by their utilitarian calculations to a rather different conclusion from ours.

6 The Moral Justification of Religious Liberty: Matters of Consistency and Authenticity

Another type of moral argument focuses on the agent's obligation to consider how he himself would wish to be treated if he were in a position comparable to that in which those who stand to be affected by his actions presently find themselves. Some version of the "golden rule" has been taught by all of the world's most prominent religions. A related philosophical principle is Immanuel Kant's much discussed "categorical imperative," which he takes to be the fundamental law of pure practical reason: "So act that the maxim of your will could always hold at the same time as a principle establishing universal law."[109] Kant's principle is not quite the same as the golden rule, as it emphasizes universalizability, whereas most versions of the golden rule emphasize empathetic and sympathetic projection. Both principles ostensibly provide the agent with an understanding of his obligations or duties, and free him from the main problems associated with utilitarian moral analysis.

According to the golden-rule approach, the actual political authority that is about to restrict the religious freedom of someone or some group voluntarily or involuntarily subject to it must consider how it would feel about a comparable restriction of its own freedom. If it would deem such a restriction unwarranted or otherwise improper, then it should not follow through on its decision to restrict the religious freedom of those involved. According to the universalizability approach, the actual political authority in this situation must consider whether it would be possible for the rule it is about to apply to be universally applied. The latter approach would seem to be superior in some ways to the former. First, a political authority may be so constituted that it is not the sort of thing that is in a position to empathize or sympathize with an individual or even a group. A political authority, after all, is not necessarily a king or prince who is capable of having human feelings; it may be an amorphous, impersonal bureaucracy. We sometimes hear people say things like "Canadians feel that . . . " or "the government feels that . . . ," but such "feeling" is of a different order from that of an individual human being. Secondly, whereas application of the golden rule involves the subjective determination of whether one's feelings, values, interests, and circumstances match up with someone else's, universalizability seems to be something of a logical test and thus promises to be more "objective." Both principles emphasize the importance of consistency, but the type of consistency that each stresses is quite different. However, in any given situation, determining in what universalizability consists is ordinarily rather more problematic than determining how one would feel under comparable circumstances, so that a principle like Kant's will never rival the golden rule in popularity or utility.

But just as it may not be clear in a concrete situation to what *particular* maxim the Kantian expects us to employ the test of universalizability, it is rarely clear from appeals to the golden rule with what *particular* aspect of someone's situation we are supposed to empathize. Consider the case of a politician who is faced with the decision of whether to vote for a bill that prohibits members of a disliked religious minority from performing a rite that is for some trivial reason offensive to members of the religious majority to which he himself belongs. When he initially considers how he would feel if his own religious freedoms were curtailed by state interference, he may be inclined to vote against the bill. But then he may consider how the case in question could be significantly different from others that only appear similar to it, and he will perhaps conclude that the real issue is how he would feel if the particular kind of freedom under attack, one which he never wanted, were curtailed. He would then be able to vote for the bill without being bothered by the thought that he had violated his own version of the golden rule. Or, if he were to apply a universalizability test, he might convince himself that the real issue is not what would happen if everyone's religious liberty were arbitrarily restricted, but rather what would happen if freedom to perform such-and-such a rite were universally restricted. Analyses of this kind can be manipulated almost as easily as utilitarian analyses.

Again, consider what an ancient Israelite might have replied when chastised for forgetting, as he abused or exploited a stranger, that his people too had once been strangers in Egypt and told that he should remember what it is to be unfairly treated: "But the two situations are entirely different: when we were in Egypt we were not involved in idolatry." Or consider what a disciple of Augustine might have said when criticized for setting aside the principle of toleration that early Christians had themselves affirmed in response to Roman persecution: "How can one compare the two cases? The Romans who persecuted us were persecuting those who sought to disseminate the highest truths. Had we been in error, then they would have been justified in being severe with us, just as we are now justified in treating those in error as we do."

So, arguments based on some version of the golden rule, or on a universalizability principle, are not nearly as potent as they are often assumed to be. However, they are not merely rhetorical devices, for like utilitarian arguments, they draw the attention of the listener or reader to matters that are relevant to her judgement. This may be particularly true of appeals to the golden rule, which remind those to whom they are addressed of the danger of hypocrisy or inauthenticity. These appeals are apt to be especially effective when directed at those who want (as even some barbarians do) to regard themselves as morally superior to the overwhelming majority of their fellows. For although golden-rule arguments can be manipulated, the person who is doing the manipulating knows that once he starts to take lightly the principle underlying those arguments — and once he is prepared to accept the position that he is not obliged in any way to empathize and sympathize with others — he has ceased to be a moral agent.

This point is all the more important in religion. I know of no religion that does not encourage some form of empathy or sympathy with other human beings; and hypocrisy and callousness in a religious context qualify as forms (or marks) of idolatry and infidelity. The connection has been vividly described by Donald Evans:

> The obsessive neediness which dominates the idolater moves him to a ruthless manipulation of people. Where fidelity is strong, however, and a person perseveres in his assurance that the essentials for life are provided, other people are not caught up by him in a relentless quest for the Holy Grail. Fidelity and restraint go together. One can let others be. Obviously others may at times be obstacles or means in relation to one's particular ends, but since the ends are not absolute and are not sought because of limitless cravings, the others can be treated with restraint, with some respect for *their* ends.[110]

Bates applies this point directly to the matter of tolerance: "Sincere tolerance is quiet evidence of secure faith. . . . "[111]

We should not jump to the conclusion that whatever is perceived — even appropriately — as an arbitrary restriction of religious liberty can ultimately be explained by reference to the hypocrisy or infidelity of the political and religious leaders responsible for it. If Lecky is wrong to assume that fanaticism is at the root of most religious repression, he is at least right to observe that Voltaire and others undervalue the importance of fanaticism when they stress the association of religious persecution with hypocrisy. But, as I observed earlier, fanaticism and hypocrisy are closely related vices: while being in one sense opposed to one another — with one involving overcommitment and the other undercommitment — they both reveal an agent's failure to have achieved a healthy and socially constructive mode of commitment. And they have a way of blending with one another and being converted into one another.[112]

Even the coolness of a persecutor is not necessarily an indication of hypocrisy. For he may earnestly and correctly contend that his actions have been the result of a carefully calculated judgement. While he may acknowledge that people have suffered as a result of his judgement, he could add that his analysis has led him to the conclusion that more people would ultimately have suffered if he had not pursued the course he has followed. He may be absolutely convinced by the theologico-ethical, utilitarian, and other arguments that he is prepared to bring forward in defence of his policy, and he may even be right in believing that those arguments are strong ones. When someone like Castellio reproves a Calvin for the persecution of a Servetus, he knows that it is not likely that the party being criticized will fall to his knees in shame and horror and acknowledge what a hypocrite he has been. Strong-willed people, after all, find self-justification to be natural and uncomplicated. But Castellio could reasonably expect his tract, first, to stimulate Calvin to deepen his reflection on the matters at hand, secondly, to move Calvin's supporters to enter into dialogue with Calvin concerning those matters, and thirdly, to give additional incentive to the establishment of resistance movements. Perhaps Calvin was totally honest and absolutely committed to his religious and political principles at every stage of the Servetus affair. But we shall probably never be able to know for sure. That in itself is an argument for promoting the kinds of religious liberty that make possible a healthy religious pluralism in a society. Certainly this is one way of interpreting the theories of writers like Locke and Mill. As Reinhold Niebuhr writes, "The tendency to corruption and pretension in religion makes freedom of religion necessary in order that no religious community may have a monopoly of power and remain unchallenged by other faiths."[113] An appeal to conscience is even a weaker support for the persecutor's behaviour than it is for his victim's right to perform whatever rites and follow whatever rules of conduct she sees fit. However sincere a Calvin may be, it is not clear that he is any more sincere than a Marcus Aurelius (who persecuted Christians), an Innocent III, a Torquemada, or an Eichmann. That point certainly did not escape the attention of Sebastian Castellio or the more thoughtful and open-minded of his readers.

There are many people today who, troubled by what they perceive as the anarchy and permissiveness inherent in liberal democracy, entertain extremely authoritarian notions, and one school of conservatism even looks back fondly to the social unity and order that characterized the High Middle Ages. I think here, in particular, of the contemporary disciples of Maistre, Bonald, Cardinal Newman, and Belloc. R. N. Stromberg has suggested that Edmund Burke was a Christian because he was a political conservative and saw the church as a useful tool of political conservatism.[114] However, for many conservatives the political and theological elements of conservatism are seamlessly fused. When they look back to the "good old days" of social unity and order, they do not identify with the oppressed, exploited, and downtrodden; they identify, as romantics are often inclined to do, with the dominant personalities of their beloved Golden Age. However, most people nowadays do not think of the era of Innocent III as representing a Golden Age; and whatever dissatisfaction they may have with contemporary disorder and permissiveness, they are fairly sure that they and most of their fellows are better off here and now than they would have been in the world of Innocent III. They will probably grant that religious pluralism has to some extent contributed to the social problems of our age, but they will also insist — and rightly, I think — that it has contributed even more to genuine social progress. Indeed, the social problems of our age are more the result of the loss of faith than the plurality of faiths, and the former is not ultimately the result of the latter.

We cannot fully appreciate the value of religious liberty without considering the value of freedom itself, for religious liberty is a form of freedom. I grant that religious liberty may conflict with, and sometimes have to be subordinated to, other forms of freedom; for example, a child's right to a sound education may outweigh her parents' right to raise her in any way that they wish. But religious liberty is not simply valued as an instrument for the attainment of other objectives; it is one of the principal aspects of one of the most widely recognized ideals. Ideals themselves also conflict with one another, and there are times when freedom may have to be subordinated to, say, justice or peace. There are other times, however, when freedom may take precedence over such ideals; and even if certain ideals are in some sense absolutely higher than freedom, it does not follow that freedom is merely an instrument for the realization of those ideals.

Unlike Karamazov's Inquisitor, the overwhelming majority of people in the real world seem to believe very deeply that freedom is, at least on balance, a very important thing and a very good one. Those who restrict the freedoms of others sometimes appear to be hoarding freedom as if it were a material possession; they may feel that there is only a limited amount of freedom in the world, and that they can only have theirs at the expense of other people's. But perhaps freedom is more similar than they realize to such ideals as peace and justice, in which cases the individual's share depends largely on the extent to which the ideal has been realized by the community as a whole. This point may even apply to the ideal of material prosperity, for individuals often prosper when the community as a whole is prospering. It certainly applies to an ideal like justice, as Plato observed in the course of laying down his plans for an ideal state: "Our aim in founding the State was not the disproportionate happiness of any one class, but the greatest happiness of the whole; . . . in a State which is ordered with a view to the good of the whole we should be most likely to find justice, and in the worst-ordered State injustice. . . . "[115] Plato has often been seen as advancing the position that the leaders of the state have a right to trample upon the rights of the individual; but if one scrutinizes these lines closely, one sees that Plato would have regarded any injustice in the state as indicating that the society was not yet as well ordered as it should be.

Plato recognized, however, that there is also a sense in which a just society can only exist if the individuals who compose it are personally just, and that the principal means by which an individual promotes social justice is by putting his own soul in order.[116] For this very reason, people must be as free as possible, freer indeed than Plato himself was prepared to allow them to be. To respect a human being, it is not enough to be concerned with that person's material interests; respect for human beings requires a concern with their ability to make full use of their human capacities to put their own souls in order and to contribute to the civilizing process through which their society will increasingly become the kind of society in which the benefits of social life will filter down to all the citizens. Plato also failed to appreciate the significance of religion as faith, and he overestimated the reliability of even the most carefully selected and most highly educated leaders. And, as we observed in the last chapter, Plato did not have an adequately clear understanding of the virtue of humility; his limitations in this regard were largely a function of his inability to transcend completely the moral conceptions of his fellow citizens.

A political leader obviously must not allow citizens or subjects to do whatever they want to do, even in the name of religion. A reflective religionist can see this for himself; and he can have some insight into the peculiar paradox that arises as a result of the religious citizen's need to acknowledge two forms of authority that are "ultimate" in two entirely different senses. There is obviously no simple formula that will enable the leader or the subject to know precisely when the former has gone too far — or not gone far enough — in carrying out his duties when conflicts have arisen between the dictates of political authority and some religious authority. But the religious believer has good reason to expect political leaders to be particularly cautious when religious matters are involved. Here, the political leader must be mindful not only of his own fallibility, as writers like Locke and Mill have warned, but of the peculiar nature of religious faith itself, which for many people represents commitment of the highest, purest, and most personal kind.

5 Religious Liberalism

The terms *liberty* and *liberalism* are derived from a common root, so one might well be tempted to assume that, when people talk about "religious liberalism," they are simply talking about any substantial commitment to the promotion of religious liberty. However, given the way in which terminology has evolved, we must be careful not to assume too close an association between "religious liberty" and "religious liberalism." Many people who think that religious liberty is basically a good thing that ought to be promoted do not wish to be regarded as advocates of religious liberalism; some of them even feel that many of those who call themselves "religious liberals" are enemies of religious liberty, or at least end up undermining religious liberty in the process of promoting their own special brand of "liberal religion." Thus, Hayward has noted, for example, that "to say that one is a liberal because one believes in free inquiry and tolerance of differences is to fail to distinguish oneself from a large number of orthodox Christians and Jews, not to mention many existentialists."[1] We have seen how *liberty*, like *freedom*, can be a highly ambiguous term in certain contexts; and *liberalism* also is often an ambiguous word. One notable problem here is that, when liberalism is considered in relation to religion, one may be thinking primarily of a certain "liberal" conception of religion itself (in contrast with, say, orthodox, conservative, traditionalist, or fundamentalist conceptions) or one may be thinking more of a "liberal" political view of the value of religious liberty. But, when people talk about "religious liberalism," they are usually thinking of the former more than the latter, although they may uncritically assume that the two necessarily accompany one another. Hence, as Hayward has suggested, someone who calls himself a "religious liberal" is usually telling us more than that he favours the major kinds of religious liberty we considered in the last chapter; he wants us to recognize that he sees religion itself in a certain light, regardless of any political considerations. Hayward has suggested that we distinguish the "classical substance of liberal faith" from "liberalism as a method of free inquiry," and to prevent confusion he refers to the former as "sectarian liberalism."[2] Whatever the value of this label, there is clearly a need to distinguish *conceptually* between the kind of liberalism manifested in efforts to promote religious liberty and the kind manifested in efforts to promote a certain conception of religion itself. These two kinds of liberalism may be related in complex ways, but they do not necessarily accompany one another. And, of course, additional confusion arises as a result of the fact that references to "religious liberalism" — both positive and negative ones — are often emotive and rhetorical, and made without any disciplined effort to distinguish among various kinds or aspects of liberalism that may be relevant to religion. Two of the most important general kinds of liberalism are political liberalism and religious liberalism, and even setting aside for the moment the fact that there are competing political liberalisms and competing religious liberalisms, we can see that a political liberal may have reasons for favouring religious liberty that have little, if anything, to do with the "liberal" conceptions of religion associated with religious liberalism. Again, even if most political liberals are religious liberals and vice versa, being liberal in one way does not necessarily entail being liberal in others.

I have indicated in several places that my intuitions about ordinary linguistic usage have led me to believe that, when people speak about "religious liberty," they normally have in mind types or aspects of religious freedom that have an important political dimension. Similar intuitions have led me to believe that, when people talk about "religious liberalism," they are normally referring to a commitment to a certain kind of conception of what religion is and, accordingly, of how religious attitudes, institutions, and communities should be developed or reshaped so as to accommodate and promote particular forms of personal and group freedom. Different though it may be from other general kinds of liberalism, such as political and economic, religious liberalism still has much in common with these and, if we are to understand it and its relation to religious freedom in general, we need to consider it as a kind of liberalism.

1   Liberalism

Most serious writers on the subject of liberalism agree that such terms as *liberal* and *liberalism* are generally quite ambiguous and that their vagueness contributes to making them vulnerable to exploitation by bigots of various sorts who have less interest in their descriptive significance than in their potential emotive force. There is also much agreement among scholars that *liberalism* and the relevant use of *liberal* may be traced back to early nineteenth-century Spain, where a party of *Liberales* in the Cortes advocated constitutional government and opposed various forms of authoritarianism.[3] Later, the terms were taken over elsewhere to designate a government, party, policy, or opinion that favoured freedom as opposed to authoritarianism.[4] Thus, *liberalism* might appear to refer to a phenomenon — or range of phenomena — that originated in the nineteenth century. But most scholars recognize that, though the term *liberalism* is not even two hundred years old, the spirit of liberalism goes back to the time of the ancients. John Gray believes that we should distinguish between the "prehistory" of liberalism and the "modern liberal movement."[5] However, there is notable disagreement as to when this "modern" movement may best be said to have begun. Salvadori tells us that "the liberal movement was born, and acquired strength, in nations belonging to the branch of Western civilization deeply affected by the sixteenth-century spiritual upheaval which reached its climax in the Reformation."[6] The famous twentieth-century liberal John Dewey sees his seventeenth-century predecessor Locke as "the author, one may say, of the philosophy of Liberalism in its classic sense."[7] Gray attaches much importance to how the system of thought of classical liberalism was "raised up" in the Scottish Enlightenment of the eighteenth century.[8] And, while Manning attacks Cranston for overstating the point, he allows that "There is no such thing as 'universal liberalism' in the sense that the ideology possesses a definable and unchanging essence everywhere and at every level of its expression,"[9] and that "the essence of liberalism cannot be found in the work of a founding father, in the work of an author who wrote at what is deemed to be the pinnacle of its development, or in a position to reflect upon its whole past."[10]

Most definitions of *liberalism* refer at some point to freedom, but almost all of the theorists who offer these definitions seem to feel that it is not enough merely to say that liberalism is simply a matter of being substantially committed to the promotion of freedom. They apparently recognize that, while the label of "liberal" may sometimes seem to be applied in a random manner, it tends to be associated with people, ideas, institutions, and policies concerned with *particular* freedoms. Also, liberalism has come to be associated with ideals other than freedom (and in concrete situations some of these may actually come into conflict with freedom). This association of liberalism with values other than freedom poses problems for both defenders and critics of liberalism, who cannot always agree among themselves — much less with each other — on which values are essential to liberalism and which have only come to be associated with it as a result of historical or cultural accident. In Anthony Arblaster's view, "There has never been much disagreement as to what the principal 'official' values of liberalism are. Pre-eminent among them is freedom or liberty. And with freedom are connected certain other values, such as tolerance and privacy, which are in essence deductions from, or extensions of, the idea of freedom. . . . Reason or rationality in some sense, is . . . important to liberalism, and with it we should associate the identification sometimes made between liberalism and the spirit of science."[11] However, not all theorists share Arblaster's perception that, say, privacy and scientism are "official" values of liberalism; and most theorists would express surprise at other values that Arblaster has left off his list. For example, Gray sees liberalism as having four primary "elements": individualist, egalitarian, universalist ("affirming the moral unity of the human species"), and meliorist ("in its affirmation of the corrigibility and improvability of all social institutions and political arrangements").[12]

According to Gray, one of the key notions of the liberal tradition is the idea of the autonomous individual, the individual who is not ruled by others and rules himself.[13] Many theorists take the central principle of liberalism to be a commitment to the right of members of the community to act, within reasonable limits, according to their own judgements and decisions. Among these is Salvadori, who also sees the liberal position as involving commitment to four other major principles: respect for reasonableness, individualism, belief in equality ("and what makes it meaningful at the material as well as the moral level"), and appreciation of the importance of tolerance.[14] Other theorists, while acknowledging the importance of the aforementioned values, see liberalism as essentially reactive and, specifically, reactive to authoritarianism, or the arbitrary exercise of authority (either the exercise of illegitimate authority or the abusive exercise of legitimate authority). Some theorists actually see liberalism as an attack on the principle of authority as such, and particularly on the principle of moral and religious authority. Religious critics of liberalism have sometimes perceived it as an attack on religion itself; thus, for Dawson, liberalism is essentially a transitional phase between religious culture and secular culture, a "half-way house" that lives on the spiritual capital it has inherited from the former while preparing the ground for the barbarisms that will inevitably result from the ascension of the latter.[15] Yet even someone like J. S. Schapiro, who seeks to provide a balanced appraisal of liberalism, is prepared to grant that liberalism has traditionally embodied certain secularist tendencies: "In general, liberals have been rationalists. As a consequence they have developed what may be called a secular attitude toward religion. To achieve complete religious freedom required the secularization of public life. Everywhere, liberals generally have advocated separation of church and state; secular, public education; civil marriage; and laws permitting divorce."[16] Here, Schapiro is not thinking so much of religious liberalism as of the political liberalism that approves of the growth of religious liberty. But as Schapiro realizes, this political outlook may both influence and be influenced by one's way of conceiving of the "true essence" of religion.

The association of liberalism with democratic principles is not as close as has often been supposed. Morley has observed that John Stuart Mill, probably the thinker most commonly associated with classical British liberalism, "had no more partiality for mob rule than De Maistre or Goethe or Carlyle."[17] The same point could be made with respect to other figures traditionally associated with liberalism, such as Locke, Spinoza, Milton, Voltaire, and T. H. Green. Indeed, one of the main themes of most liberal theory is the primacy of individual rights over the arbitrary will of the majority.[18] Given their concern with the individualism related to personal autonomy, we can see that it was almost inevitable that the principal liberal theorists would have mixed feelings about democracy. We must also remember that, whatever mainstream liberalism involves today, and that is far from clear, it has reached its present state only after having gone through various phases of development (or deterioration). By Schapiro's reckoning, liberalism had its beginnings as a *movement* in the Renaissance, Reformation, and Scientific Revolution: the Renaissance shifted human interest from the next world to this one; the Reformation's emphasis on private judgement in interpretation of Scripture promoted individualism; and the scientific method freed inquirers from reliance on dogma and superstition.[19] As a *system of thought*, liberalism received definite expression in the Age of Reason and the Enlightenment;[20] and the nineteenth century brought the *classical* liberalism represented by France's 1830 revolution and Britain's Reform Bill of 1832. According to Schapiro, "Classical liberalism developed policies, ideas, and attitudes which harmonized with the class interests of the bourgeoisie, and at the same time advanced greatly the cause of human freedom. In the new order all men were free and equal in the sense that all had equal civil rights. But all men did not have equal political rights."[21] Only later did *democratic* liberalism develop.[22]

In any case, it would be wrong to think of liberalism as purely, essentially, or even primarily concerned with political matters. Liberalism in all of its phases has been concerned with the promotion of basic freedoms; and political freedom, though of both intrinsic and instrumental value, has never been perceived as the most basic of these. Many of the figures from liberalism's "prehistory" who exercised the greatest influence on its development — such as Socrates, Abelard, Erasmus, and Descartes — were at most only indirectly concerned with political matters.[23] Liberalism has always ultimately been concerned with such "spiritual" matters as human dignity, self-realization, and civilization. Hence, it is not surprising that, from its "prehistory" to the modern day, liberal theory has concentrated much of its attention on issues concerning religious liberty and religious freedom in general. Liberalism has obviously had much to say about political interference in religious affairs; but it has also had much to say about religion itself. In fact, many of the most important figures associated with liberal theory have been significant contributors to the philosophy of religion. One may consider, for example, Locke, the French Encyclopedists, Lessing, Thomas Paine, Hume, and Kant. Such thinkers have aimed to emancipate their fellows not only from political despotism but from the dogmas and superstitions that enslave their minds; dogmas and superstitions make it easier for political adventurers to exploit their subjects, but political despotism is ultimately reprehensible precisely because of what it does to the minds and souls of human beings and to the communities that depend for their well-being on the reflection of people who are capable of making full use of their intellectual and creative powers.

Salvadori has pointed to another interesting aspect of liberalism: its association with more informal notions of what is involved in being a "liberal" person.

> From ancient to modern times, to be liberal has meant to be generous, broad-minded, compassionate, altruistically inclined, somewhat tolerant of different views and of new ideas, fashions, customs and trends; to prefer compromise to intransigence; possibly but not necessarily to be forward-looking in the sense of being in sympathy with change. It has meant acting on the basis of a concept which is also an attitude and which, if widely diffused, becomes the foundation of a way of life: to live and let live.[24]

Eighteenth-century dictionaries define being *liberal* as a matter of being generous and bountiful in a way associated with dignity and gentility.[25] Contemporary dictionaries associate it with being open-minded, unprejudiced, and tolerant.[26]

In recent years, economic liberty has come to occupy a much greater share of liberal theorists' attention. It has become increasingly obvious to proponents of liberalism that, whatever rights the economically disadvantaged may enjoy in theory, their real opportunities are severely limited by their material condition. Hence, liberalism has come to be associated more and more with arguments in favour of the use of governmental power to redistribute wealth more fairly and to ameliorate the economic situation (and indirectly the spiritual condition) of the underprivileged. Interestingly, the classical defence of capitalism was provided by thinkers firmly rooted in the liberal tradition, such as Adam Smith. When we reflect on this last point, we realize that not much is to be gained by contrasting liberalism with conservatism. For, although many thinkers who would identify themselves as ideological "conservatives" have been openly critical of what they perceive as the excessive egalitarianism, progressivism, tolerance, anti-authoritarianism, and secularism of their "liberal" rivals, most of them are committed in principle to the promotion of the same individualism and respect for personal freedom that are at the heart of the liberal's agenda. Disagreements between liberals and conservatives are, more often than not, disagreements about tactics and strategies, and often the very same position can be appropriately characterized as either liberal or conservative. In any case, the connections between one or another form of economic liberalism and the kind of liberalism that concerns us here, religious liberalism, might well seem to be tenuous at best. But even though economic liberalism, political liberalism, and religious liberalism do not necessarily come together to form a neat package, the fact remains that many of the concerns that animate liberal theory in one sphere also ultimately animate it in other spheres.

When we consider the various ideas associated with religious liberalism, we shall see in fact that religious liberalism is in certain ways appropriately named, not only because of the importance that it attaches to the promotion of freedom as such, but because of its association with many of the values that have for one reason or another become connected with liberalism in general. And though religious liberalism does not necessarily require political liberalism, or vice versa, it is no coincidence that the two often fit together so comfortably.

At various points in our inquiry we have seen how, in the search for clear distinctions that will make the business of thinking and judging easier and more efficient, even usually cautious thinkers are sometimes given to proposing or endorsing shallow and misleading definitions and formulations. Thus, Schapiro remarks in one place that "The fundamental postulate of liberalism has been the moral worth, the absolute value, and the essential dignity of the human personality."[27] Many, if not most, people who do not consider themselves to be liberals would be quite willing to endorse this principle; and I am far from being convinced that all or even most liberals hold some version of this principle. More importantly, when asked to explain in what their liberalism consists, most liberals would not use this kind of language. Sooner or later, the liberal theorist will explicate his theory by reference to freedom. *Freedom*, as we saw in Chapter 1, may be a vague term but it is certainly not entirely devoid of content. The same applies to *liberalism*, which, in addition, focuses our attention on particular freedoms and draws our attention to possible relations between freedom and other values. Obviously, there has been considerable disagreement among proponents of liberalism as to what exactly freedom is, what freedoms are most important, and what the other values are that most complement freedom or most obviously follow from it or are most likely to promote it. Thus, with respect to, for example, egalitarianism or democratic principles, some liberal theorists have had what others regard as far too much (or far too little) to say. And, while one liberal theorist may regard respect for scientific method as central to liberalism, another may think that it has little, if anything, to do with liberalism. However, when we consider a list of the various freedoms and other values that have been associated with liberalism by reflective people over a long period of time, we can see that one is not helpfully characterized as a liberal if one is not strongly committed to many, if not most, of the items on that list. Here is a basic list which our investigation thus far has produced: freedom, liberty, the promotion of freedom, free inquiry, religious freedom, religious liberty, political freedom, economic freedom, tolerance, respect for privacy, individualism, egalitarianism, belief in the moral unity of the human species, belief in the corrigibility and improvability of social and political institutions, reasonableness and rationality, scientific method, resistance to the arbitrary exercise of authority, respect for the value of secularizing certain aspects of public life, democratic principles, belief in the primacy of individual rights over the arbitrary will of the majority, civil rights, political rights, human dignity, self-realization, civilization, emancipation from dogma and superstition, generosity, compassion, respect for the value of compromise, open-mindedness, and concern for the fair distribution of wealth and the amelioration of the condition of the underprivileged.

2   The Idea of Religious Liberalism

One might characterize as religious liberalism any sustained commitment to promoting the agenda of liberalism through religion. Among those who appropriately regard themselves as liberals, some are religious and others are not; and those who see a religious commitment like their own as representing a significant means to promoting the values of liberalism could reasonably be regarded as proponents of a religious liberalism. Most of these people do not regard religion as a mere instrument for the promotion of liberal values; they tend to see the agendas of their religion and their liberalism as consistent and complementary. They believe that the reasonableness of the liberal agenda is a good ground for holding the sort of religious opinions they hold, and at the same time they believe that someone with a religious world-view like theirs is obliged to live by and promote the values of liberalism.

Most discussions of religious liberalism are based on a perception of it as a commitment to a particular kind of religious world-view — some "liberal" religious faith — and secondarily as whatever goes along with such a commitment in the way of behavioural practice and communal institutions. Usually, when one thinks of a religious liberal, one does not merely think of someone who happens to be both religious and liberal or even of someone who sees religion as a significant means of promoting liberal values; rather, one tends to think of someone who is committed to a liberal religious world-view and seeks to promote commitment to that world-view and to other liberal religious world-views.

Some people are led to a religious world-view, at least in part, by their liberal values; they come to regard a certain kind of religious faith as the completion or refinement of a liberal outlook. Other people are led to liberal values by their religious world-view; all world-views have an axiological or ethical component and, as one's religious faith becomes more liberal, the values that go along with it will become more liberal. In many cases it is difficult to know whether a liberal's religion or her values came first chronologically; and, in any event, the chronological order does not indicate which of the two the liberal religionist *ultimately* regards as more basic or more important. Such a person normally comes to regard the agenda of her religion and her liberalism as consistent and complementary.

There is, however, another dimension to religious liberalism. Like all "isms" it is a continuing stimulus to polemic, on the part of both those who approve of it and those who disapprove of it. Almost all critics of religious liberalism and also many proponents of religious liberalism believe that in its earliest phases religion (or any particular natural religion) was significantly different from how the contemporary liberal religionist now wants us to conceive it; thus, the critic of religious liberalism is apt to regard it as representing a betrayal of traditional religious faith, while some defenders of religious liberalism regard it as an improvement upon traditional forms of religious commitment. There are also some religious liberals who sincerely believe that religion (or their particular religion) was in its pristine form very much like the religious faith by which they now live; they will argue that religion (or their particular religion) was corrupted over the years by self-serving or incompetent leaders who obscured the liberal values at the heart of it.

Religious liberalism involves both a religious way of thinking about liberalism and a liberal way of thinking about religion. With respect to the former, we may call to mind the irreplaceable contribution that religious thinkers have made to the promotion of liberal causes; but as our concern is with religious freedom, we shall focus now on the liberal religionist's conception of religion and its concomitant elements in the realm of communal institutions. And in fact it is the liberal religionist's conception of religion (or a particular religion) that the expression "religious liberalism" normally calls to mind.

According to J. F. Hayward, sectarian liberalism exhibits three main characteristics: "(1) religion is defined as a human achievement rather than a divine gift; (2) man is defined as naturally equipped to achieve all that is necessary for his well-being, including religion as one such achievement; (3) the function of freedom is to release the natural goodness of man which will lead all free men to live in spontaneous harmony and cooperation."[28] But Hayward goes further. He tells us that sectarian liberalism is "rationalistic through and through, giving to man reason and tolerance";[29] moreover, "The sectarian liberal delights in an essentially permissive approach to the behavior of religious groups. He is suspicious of the leadership of denominational authorities."[30] Even from these few lines, we can see that, if Hayward's characterization of religious liberalism is reasonably accurate, religious liberalism is committed to the promotion of many of the freedoms and other values that reflective people have long associated with liberalism in general: freedom, tolerance, belief in the moral unity of the human species, reasonableness and rationality, resistance to the arbitrary exercise of authority, and so forth.

While Hayward is concerned with religious liberalism in general, there can be no question that he has in mind a particular paradigm of religious liberalism, a kind of American Protestant liberalism that has its roots in a theology that developed in the United States in the early nineteenth century.[31] Liberalism has been a particularly important tradition in Protestantism — owing largely to the traditional Protestant emphases on private judgement[32] and the priesthood of all believers[33] — and religious liberalism is sometimes thought of as being primarily a movement within Protestantism.[34] Hayward himself recognizes that religious liberalism has been significantly manifested in other traditions, such as Roman Catholicism and Judaism, and he believes, rightly, that there are important features shared by Protestant liberalism and non-Protestant religious liberalism. Even so, it is not easy to capture in a few lines the essence of religious liberalism as such; and even many Protestants will be troubled by the importance that Hayward's description attaches to certain factors at the expense of others. Indeed, there are substantial differences between mainstream American Protestant liberalism and, say, late nineteenth-century German Protestant liberalism or recent Canadian Protestant liberalism, and it is not clear that a simple formulation can do justice to all the nuances. Moreover, even in the United States, there are various forms of Protestant liberalism, and a formulation like Hayward's probably does not do justice to the theological differences between, say, liberal Baptists, liberal Methodists, and liberal Episcopalians. The upshot of all this is that there are numerous religious liberals who will protest against Hayward's association of sectarian liberalism with something like "permissiveness" or the notion that religion is not a divine gift. There are many other religious conceptions that are compatible with such liberal values as tolerance and resistance to the arbitrary exercise of authority, and these have as much right to qualify as liberal religious conceptions as do those that have their roots in early nineteenth-century American theology or any other historical movement.

Consider, for example, recent Roman Catholic liberalism. There are some who would regard the expression "Catholic liberalism" as self-contradictory or at least an oxymoron. It is not hard to see why; as Novak says, "The term 'liberal' is consistently used in the literature of the papacy, even today, as a pejorative."[35] Still, Roman Catholics and non-Catholics alike are able to look at the views of a distinguished Catholic theologian like Karl Rahner and see in them something akin to the views of major Protestant liberals. For example, Rahner writes, "The Church's life is sustained not only by the initiative, orders or instructions of ecclesiastical authority, but also, though it is still under the direction of the Hierarchy, by the charisms of the Holy Spirit, who can breathe upon whomsoever he will in the Church — even the poor, the children, those who are 'least in the Kingdom of God' — and infuse his own impulses into the Church in ways that no one can foretell."[36] Rahner is far from advocating any "permissiveness," and he is certainly not denying that religion is in a sense a divine gift. Yet it is not hard to see why so many people feel comfortable characterizing the above position of Rahner's as an expression of religious liberalism.

Consider, again, a certain aspect of "classical" German Protestant liberalism. No figure in the history of theology has been more closely associated with Protestant liberalism than Friedrich Schleiermacher, who, in contrast to another major influence on German Protestant liberalism, Kant, emphasizes *feeling*. As B.M.G. Reardon tells us, Schleiermacher, in contrast to Kant, "introduced into religious reflexion a different spirit and gave it a new ethos. For him religion is a condition of the heart. Its essence is *feeling*. Without a deep emotional impulse it cannot be sustained in its true character and becomes either rationalism or moralism."[37] We should be careful not to overestimate the differences between a Kant and a Schleiermacher, for as A.P.F. Sell points out, "Whether reason or the pious feeling is to the fore, man remains the key to the system. The starting-point is variously my own reason, my own grasp of the moral law, or my own feeling of absolute dependence. . . . "[38] It is worth noting, however, that Schleiermacher, who is undeniably a religious liberal who emphasizes individual experience, is very different from Hayward's paradigm of the sectarian liberal who is "rationalistic through and through." It is a curious formulation of the essence of religious liberalism that would force us to disqualify one of the dominant figures in the history of religious liberalism.

The problem here does not lie with Hayward's formulation, which is in fact better than most we are likely to encounter. The problem is a much deeper one, having to do with the nature of liberalism itself. Putting a somewhat positive gloss on the problem, Reardon writes, "No two liberal thinkers are ever quite in agreement. But such personal freedom in choosing the way of faith is of the liberal ethos, and liberals would firmly deny that the constraint of a precise dogmatic system in religious belief is something that the modern world is likely ever again to find tolerable."[39] With their concerns for tolerance, individualism, avoidance of dogmatism, and so forth, religious liberals may well take pride in the fact that they seem not to be stuck with a rigid formula of the kind that they associate with various forms of orthodoxy and fundamentalism. But is this necessarily a good thing? Most critics of religious liberalism do not think so, and even many religious liberals have been moved to entertain grave doubts.

The fact is that most religious liberals have, at one time or another, been very suspicious of other people who have characterized themselves as "religious liberals." They resent such people going about proclaiming that they represent a "liberal" religious viewpoint on certain controversial matters. "These are not *true* religious liberals," they will muse to themselves. But if religious liberals cannot agree upon a relatively fixed formulation of the essence of religious liberalism, how can they expect people to be able to tell the difference between true religious liberalism and the counterfeit variety? Furthermore, religious liberalism is apt to be less attractive to people if they are forced to conclude that it is purely reactive (against orthodoxy, abuse of authority, and so on) and has little to offer in the way of positive direction.

Some promoters of religious liberalism have endeavoured to provide such direction, and one remarkable example is the educational theorist Adelaide Teague Case. Case recognizes that "Liberalism is in its essential nature a progressive movement, always changing, always in flux; its conclusions are never fixed or static; it has no unalterable 'deposit of faith' to teach. It does not desire uniformity of opinion."[40] Yet as an educational theorist concerned with promoting liberal religious ideas among the youth of America, Case feels the need to provide her fellow educators with something more concrete in the way of educational guidelines than the abstract recommendations to promote freedom and reason and encourage tolerance. So, while her main inspiration is obviously the educational progressivism of John Dewey, she has taken the trouble to consult the writings of numerous prominent liberal theologians and religious leaders and has arrived at a summary of the "distinctive positions of liberal Christianity and their implied educational objectives."[41] What Case ends up with is so detailed and in places so dogmatic that it reads as if it were a parody of an extremely dated Roman Catholic Catechism. For one thing, Case sees what she takes to be "liberal Christianity" as having distinctive positions on at least ten major subjects: the Bible, theological dogmas, the historic Jesus, social welfare, the reconstruction of society, the political state, international and inter-racial problems, human nature, the educational process, and the Church. Drawing on the views of her own chosen authorities, such as Shailer Mathews, Harry Emerson Fosdick, George Hodges, and Lyman Abbott, she goes on to advance dozens of positions "of liberal Christianity" that she sincerely believes should animate not only the religious instruction of young Americans but the moral vision of her society. Many of the positions that she enumerates are certainly held by most people who would characterize themselves as "religious liberals"; but many religious liberals would refuse to endorse the majority of Case's positions, and few, if any, religious liberals would accept all of her positions.

It is interesting to note which authorities Case has chosen to consult and which she has opted to ignore. Writing in 1924, when ecumenism was not the craze it later came to be, Case has no qualms about ignoring Roman Catholic thought — even at its most "modernistic" — and she feels that she has little to learn from even the most liberal of non-Christian religious writers. What is perhaps more striking is Case's lack of concern with anything and everything in the major European traditions of religious liberalism. A "good American" with an old-fashioned respect for the uniquely American way of looking at things, she quotes with reverence the gems of wisdom of a Mathews or Fosdick and shows little interest in the more seminal ideas of such renowned liberal religionists as Ritschl, Herrmann, Schleiermacher, and Harnack. It almost goes without saying that she appears to be blissfully ignorant of how liberal Christianity ended up in the America of 1924 with its "distinctive positions."

Let us focus for the moment on one of the ten subjects that Case addresses: liberal Christianity's distinctive positions on the Bible. It is generally known that people who call themselves "religious liberals" disapprove of certain traditional ways of approaching the Bible and are wholly unsympathetic to the conception of the "inerrancy" of Scripture that has been promoted by Protestant fundamentalists. As James Barr has remarked, though most fundamentalists have little understanding of religious liberalism, they feel that they know enough about the liberal attitude towards Scripture to be justified in pronouncing the words "religious liberalism" with contempt and disgust:

> The most striking characteristic of the fundamentalist picture of other theologies is its failure to discriminate, perhaps its inability to do so. All of them come to the same thing. There is, no doubt, Schleiermacher, and there is Ritschl; in modern times there is Tillich, and then there is Bultmann, and there are many others. Indeed, conservatives suppose that the very variety between different non-conservative theologies is a reason why one should stick to a conservative position: at least it is (they think) only one, while the others are many. But this variety makes no real difference to them: from the viewpoint of fundamentalism, they all come to the same thing. They do not expressly begin from the authority of scripture, understood and defined as inerrancy, and thus they can all be classed together.... It is a psychological necessity of membership in the fundamentalist organizations that one should be convinced that everyone

outside is completely "liberal" in theology, or at least that he has no stable defences against the adoption of a totally liberal position.[42]

But do religious liberals themselves always discriminate sufficiently with respect to the various non-fundamentalist positions that one might adopt towards the interpretation of Scripture? How many contemporary religious liberals would endorse Case's statement, for example, that "Liberalism encourages historical method in Biblical criticism and accepts without equivocation the results of scientific inquiry"?[43] When Case asserts that "Historical and scientific study has led liberals to discard the 'authority of the Bible' in the usually accepted sense," how many contemporary religious liberals would understand precisely what Case means by "the usually accepted sense"?[44] Is a religious liberalism genuinely obliged, as Case thinks, to "lay much less stress on the miracles of both Old and New Testament than has been the custom in the past"?[45] Would the typical religious liberal of our own day feel that Case has done a helpful job of distinguishing religious liberalism from rival commitments when she asserts that "A most striking point in the writings of liberals is the fact that they are enormously interested in the life and teachings of Jesus"?[46] There are places in her discussion where Case acknowledges significant philosophical and theological differences between liberal Christians,[47] but in her attempt to delineate as precisely as possible the distinctive positions of liberal Christianity, she often makes it seem as dogmatic as the orthodox types of religious faith against which it so often protests.

Nevertheless, I have acknowledged that many of the positions that Case enumerates are held by most people who would characterize themselves, and be classified by others, as "religious liberals." Even if they would not be endorsed as *positions* in Case's sense of the word, they would be regarded as "attitudes" reflecting the "spirit" of religious liberalism. Liberal Christians of many different types and backgrounds would accept Case's association of liberal Christianity with, for example, the idea that creedal statements should not be the test of a person's standing as a Christian,[48] or the opposition to barriers erected in the interest of ecclesiastical orthodoxy.[49] And yet, curiously enough, Case gives little attention to the question of what general philosophical principles, if any, underlie the various positions she enumerates; the closest she comes to identifying one of those principles is in her frequent references, in the spirit of Dewey's philosophy, to liberalism's emphasis on "progress."

A.P.F. Sell realizes that, with respect to religion, "the terms 'liberal' and 'conservative' are so highly ambiguous that any attempt at stipulative definition is hazardous in the extreme."⁵⁰ However, following the philosopher Henry Aiken, Sell takes a stab at indicating what lies at the heart of the various disputes between religious liberals and their critics:

> "From the time of Kant onwards," writes Professor Aiken, "it is the thinking subject himself who establishes the standards of objectivity." Can there be any commerce between this standpoint and that which seeks to think God's thoughts after him? This question underlies much of the modern theological discussion of such issues as transcendence and immanence, the authority of the bible, evolutionary thought and ethical Christianity. The question is thrown into relief in the debate between theological conservatives and liberals.⁵¹

Most religious liberals have been sensitive to the historicity of religious phenomena; but along with their awareness of the importance of historicity there often goes a kind of individualism that borders on radical subjectivism. This dimension of much religious liberalism has been discussed by D. E. Miller in his highly personal defence of liberal Christianity. Along with Case and others, Miller believes that "Liberal Christians have understood that Christianity must evolve and adapt itself — or at least its expression — from age to age."⁵² But Miller sees this understanding as having deep philosophical roots. While deploring many forms of the fashionable relativism of the day,⁵³ Miller approves of the liberal Christian's "troubled commitment . . . the way of commitment beyond belief, faith without an objectifying assurance."⁵⁴ Using language similar to that of one of the most influential of twentieth-century religious liberals, Paul Tillich, Miller argues that Christianity can be both true and yet a product of human creativity, and that we can grasp this point if we recognize the difference between the "substance" of religious faith and the symbolic and metaphorical "form" that theological expression necessarily takes.⁵⁵ But Miller sees the subjectivistic aspect of much liberal Christianity going further: "Rather than starting with God, postulating divine initiative, many liberal Christians begin with the human predicament and emphasize *man's search* for God"; and, according to this approach, of which Miller himself approves, "God is synonymous with the search for human wholeness, for confidence in the ultimate meaningfulness of human existence."⁵⁶ Most religious liberals would probably find Miller's choice of language too radical; but Miller has usefully drawn our attention, as Aiken and Sell have, to the possible connections between the religious liberal's conception of religious freedom and the humanistic and individualistic attitudes that derive from subjectivistic notions.

From where did religious liberals acquire these subjectivistic notions? Obviously, people from all walks of life have been able to entertain such notions on one or another level of complexity; and religionists have been substantially influenced by the teachings of theologians and other religious leaders. However, I suggest that there is a more profound answer to the question that will also explain to us how religious liberalism came to be so concerned with respect for reason, reasonableness, and rationality, and that we look here to the influence of philosophers.

One way of approaching the concept of religious liberalism is to return to the considerations raised in Chapters 2 and 3. We saw there that religion is in many important ways a hindrance to freedom and yet in others a fertile and perhaps irreplaceable *source* of freedom. The religious liberal is concerned with freedom. She is usually (though not always) concerned with promoting religious liberty. But she is always concerned with something else: encouraging her fellow human beings to think of religion itself in a way that will minimize its significance as a hindrance to freedom and enhance its status as a source of freedom. In the last analysis she may want to conclude that religion (or Christianity or Judaism or whatever her particular religion happens to be) by its very nature seeks to promote liberal values, and that the only reason why religion historically has been a hindrance to freedom is because it has been corrupted by the orthodox, the fundamentalist, the conservative, and all of the other self-serving or incompetent types who have so often found themselves in positions of actual authority. But on reflection she may be prepared to conclude that progress is possible in religion as it is in other forms of experience and culture, and that as human communities become wiser and more civilized, they are in a better and better position to recognize the need for constantly refining and reforming religious attitudes and institutions in such a way as to promote freedoms and other liberal values.

From what source can the impetus to religious reform arise? We might be tempted to assume that there are many possible sources, insofar as, at the present stage of the development of civilization, we take for granted that religion is but one of many facets of life on earth, and that while religious experience and culture influence other aspects of life and nature, they are in turn influenced by those other aspects of life and nature. But what besides religion can generate the *values* necessary for altering the conception of religion itself? Ultimately, only a form of experience and culture can generate values; however important natural events may be in shaping our values, they can only do so by way of the medium of thought or consciousness. As important as politics and economics are, these also depend on the valuation generated through some form of experience and culture. What, then, are the forms of experience and culture to which we can trace the incentive to reform our conception of religion, our religious conceptions, and our religious institutions? The ones that come to mind are art, history, philosophy, and science.[57] But art, history, and science can only play this role insofar as they have been infused with some religious or philosophical vision or, alternatively, insofar as their products have been subjected to some religious or philosophical interpretation. That leaves two possible sources, philosophy and religion. Since philosophy is an epiphenomenon of religion, that is, a form of experience and culture that grew out of religion and eventually attained some degree of independence and distinctness in relation to its source, we can say that in a sense the impetus to religious reform can only come from religion itself. However, since philosophy did, in the age of the ancient Greeks, attain a substantial degree of independence and distinctness from its parent form, and since philosophy, like its parent, can generate full-blown world-views that include value-systems and that can be the objects of faith or commitment, we can also say that there is another sense in which philosophy can reasonably be regarded as a primary impetus to religious reform. And, as we shall now see, a survey of the development of philosophy suggests that philosophy is, among other things, the attempt to liberalize religion.

3 Philosophy and Liberal Religion

We cannot address here the interesting question of how philosophy was born from the spirit of religion, and some comments from the distinguished classical scholar F. M. Cornford will have to suffice for our purposes:

> There is a real continuity between the earliest rational speculation and the religious representation that lay behind it; and this is no mere matter of superficial analogies, such as the allegorical equation of the elements with the Gods of popular belief. Philosophy inherited from religion certain great conceptions — for instance, the ideas of "God," "Soul," "Destiny," "Law" — which continued to circumscribe the movements of rational thought and to determine their main directions. Religion

expresses itself in poetical symbols and in terms of mythical personalities; philosophy prefers the language of dry abstraction, and speaks of *substance, cause, matter,* and so forth. But the outward difference only disguises an inward and substantial affinity between these two successive products of the same consciousness. The modes of thought that attain to clear definition and explicit statement in philosophy were already implicit in the unreasoned intuitions of mythology.[58]

Cornford goes on to make a point that is more directly relevant to our concerns: "The work of philosophy . . . appears as the elucidation and clarifying of religious, or even pre-religious, material."[59] This state of affairs, Cornford observes, goes back to the beginnings of Greek philosophy, for even in the doctrines of Thales about nature, soul, and God, the primary datum is inherited from religion.[60]

As its very name indicates, philosophy as we now understand it was largely the invention of the ancient Greeks. If we study the works of earlier Middle Eastern and Asian cultures, we certainly find something akin to the rational reflection manifested in the works of the classical Greek philosophers; and there is a sense in which such reflection qualifies as philosophy in the most honorific sense of the term. But the Greeks established philosophy as the systematic form of inquiry involving the weighing of alternative answers to the "eternal" questions, and subsequently a large part of the most intensive and disciplined reflection on those questions has been made at least indirectly with reference to the intellectual agenda established by the classical Greeks. In considering philosophy as a sustained effort to liberalize religion, we may thus regard the activity of the pre-Sophistic Greek cosmologists as the first major phase of the effort. What is of particular interest is that these early philosophers, though not recognized by their fellows as religious authorities in any institutional sense, freely and boldly took it upon themselves to speculate on religious subjects, to interpret the material of religion on the basis of their rational reflection, and to pass their conclusions on to other inquirers. Consider these representative pre-Sophistic fragments:[61] "Aethiopians have gods with snub noses and black hair, Thracians have gods with gray eyes and red hair" (Xenophanes, 16); "A man's character is his guardian divinity" (Heraclitus, 119); "[God] has no human head fitted on to his body, nor does a pair of wings branch out from his back; he has no feet, nor hairy parts. He is purely mind, holy and ineffable, flashing through the whole world with swift thoughts" (Empedocles, 134). In their efforts to elucidate and clarify religious material, these philosophers inevitably encouraged their fellows to reflect for themselves on religious subjects, to use reason to weigh competing religious conceptions, and to isolate abstract metaphysical and ethical principles from the mythological context in which they were previously embedded.

The second phase of the philosophical liberalization of religion is represented by the Sophistic movement, which went beyond the earlier philosophy in this respect in several different ways. Most importantly, the Sophists introduced a radical humanism based on an even more radical epistemological, metaphysical, and ethical subjectivism: "Man is the measure of all things: of things that are, that they are; of things that are not, that they are not" (Protagoras, 1). One effect of this radical humanism was to emphasize the significance of religion as a form of culture; another was to free ethical and political inquiry to some extent from its dependence on appeals to the wisdom of institutional religious authority. Moreover, by cultivating the form of argument known as *eristic*, the Sophists revealed to their fellows the extent to which reason can be successfully employed to undermine unsophisticated religious conceptions.

The third phase is represented by Plato, the greatest and most influential of all philosophers, who, though reactionary in certain important respects, established personal philosophical reason once and for all as a potential source of the highest wisdom, freed Sophistic humanism of its extreme and destructive relativism, and instituted the first genuine philosophical "system" as a rival to the traditional religious world-views of the ancients. Although Plato attacks religious liberty in Book X of the *Laws*, and asserts there that God rather than man is the measure of all things,[62] he goes to great pains in his works, and perhaps most impressively in his early Socratic dialogue, the *Euthyphro*, to show that appeals to religious authority are nowhere near as effective as appeals to reason in the resolution of the most basic practical problems. The fourth phase is represented by Plato's student, Aristotle, who lays the foundations for systematic scientific investigation and in his *Metaphysics* reduces major religious conceptions to heuristic scientific conceptions.

Did these ancient Greek philosophers consciously set out to liberalize religion, or was the liberalization of religion a by-product of their disinterested pursuit of wisdom? This is obviously not an easy question to answer. Not only does it involve considerable speculation, but it is not entirely clear that the ancient Greek philosophers would have been capable of forming in their minds a conception of "liberalizing religion" or even a conception of religion as such. Nevertheless, as these men were deep thinkers who were probably constantly mindful of the superiority of their own reflection to that of the institutional religious authorities, political operators, and superstitious and ignorant masses, it is not implausible that they had a real sense of the impact that their new talk about the gods and related subjects might have on the future development of their culture and of humanity. I doubt whether any among them was a full-fledged secularist; even Protagoras, despite some agnostic utterances, recognized the pragmatic value of religion as a form of experience and culture. Yet their philosophical vision — which lay at the heart of their highly personal religious orientation — clearly involved a commitment to certain liberal values that they sought to promote not only in their own lives but for those among their fellow citizens whom they thought capable of appreciating and living by those values. Although liberal ideals were not as clearly defined for them as those ideals came to be for certain later inquirers, we may seriously entertain the possibility that the earliest philosophers aspired to increased freedom (particularly freedom of inquiry and expression) for themselves and others, that they sought to encourage resistance to what they perceived as the arbitrary exercise of both religious and political authority, and that they aimed to promote reasonableness and to combat religious superstition and dogmatism.

As philosophy subsequently developed, and as it became more and more removed (in time, content, and style) from the particular religious form of experience and culture that gave birth to it, some philosophers began to conceive of philosophy as a rival and ideal successor to religion. Now, we may think of philosophy as being, among other things, the attempt to attain spiritual freedom through the exercise of reason. For most philosophers, such spiritual freedom is to be associated in some sense with religion; but in the opinion of other philosophers, philosophy has established that such spiritual freedom is not necessarily related to what has been traditionally regarded as religion, and in the view of certain radical philosophers, religion is itself an intolerable obstacle to spiritual freedom. So we must acknowledge the existence of a type of philosophy that does not aim at the liberalization of religion but aims rather at the liberalization of personal commitment to the point where religious conceptions are expendable.

One might regard the efforts of Hellenistic philosophers and the more liberal mediaeval philosophers as representing significant phases of the philosophical liberalization of religion. With respect to mediaeval philosophy, one may recall that the ascent of Christianity eventually brought with it the illiberal attitudes and institutions that we considered in relation to religious liberty in Chapter 4. However reactionary the socio-religious teachings of people like Abelard and Thomas Aquinas may now seem, we should not forget how much more liberal such thinkers were than the anti-intellectual bigots among whom they lived. But the fifth main phase of philosophical liberalization of religion is represented by the master thinkers of the Renaissance, such as Erasmus, Pico della Mirandola, and Francis Bacon. The importance of Erasmus in particular can hardly be overestimated; as Bainton says, "A vein of rationalism runs from Erasmus through Castellio to Locke,"[63] and Erasmus' passionate defences of religious liberty, tolerance, and reasonableness, and his repudiation of superstition, dogmatism, and abuse of ecclesiastical authority are almost as fresh today as they were when penned centuries ago by the great Dutch humanist. The contributions of the Reformation to the promotion of religious liberty and to the general liberalization of religion cannot be regarded for the most part as philosophical; however, on the basis of our earlier consideration of the rise of Protestantism, we can see how the spread of Protestantism made possible the rapid growth of freedom of philosophical inquiry, which in turn led to new forms of religious liberalism.

The sixth phase is represented by the Age of Reason and its extension, the Enlightenment, with which we associate philosophers extremely well known for their influence in promoting more liberal religious conceptions. Among these are Descartes, Spinoza, Locke, Adam Smith, Hume, and Kant, and the semi-philosophical men of letters who popularized and occasionally refined their ideas, such as Voltaire, the French Encyclopedists, and Lessing. The seventh phase is represented by the Hegelians and particularly those among them actively involved in the development of the "science of religion" and the "higher criticism." The eighth phase is represented by the nineteenth-century positivism inspired by Darwinism and other scientific currents of the day. The ninth phase is the classical liberalism of John Stuart Mill and related thinkers, and the tenth phase is represented by the pragmatism of William James and F.C.S. Schiller and related voluntaristic theories such as the fictionalism of Hans Vaihinger and the vitalism of Bergson and Blondel. The eleventh phase of the philosophical liberalization of religion is that of the Christian and Jewish existentialism rooted in the insights of Pascal, Kierkegaard, Nietzsche, and Husserl.

This outline is, I admit, rough and not very informative. And I do not wish to be seen as denying the influence of non-philosophical theory — especially theological theory — on religious liberalism. Nor am I denying that natural and historical occurrences have at times, independently of theory, facilitated the growth of religious liberalism.

Again, I have not meant to suggest that the philosophical contribution to religious liberalism has proceeded smoothly and in a straight upward path from Xenophanes and Thales to twentieth-century religious existentialism. I do believe, however, that the insights of philosophers are at the heart of all conscious efforts to liberalize people's conception of religion and specific religious ideas and institutions. So it is no coincidence that from Aristophanes' attack on philosophy in the *Clouds* through the anti-philosophical diatribes of the Patristic period to the anti-intellectualism of religious bigots in our own day, philosophy has been one of the main targets of ridicule and attack by promoters of religious orthodoxy, dogmatism, and fundamentalism. On the rare occasions when the orthodox have looked favourably upon certain philosophers, it has invariably been because they have (rightly or wrongly) seen those philosophers as apologists for their own views and their own influence.

The role played here by philosophers is significant on several scores. First, it is now clear that we should not assume that advances in religious liberalism have been largely the result of either fortuitous circumstances or hidden determining factors. Religious liberalism has not been primarily a by-product of the resolution of economic conflicts, wars, or political re-alignments; nor has it been the direct result of empirical discoveries. Secondly, the connection between freedom and reason is nowhere more pronounced than in liberal religious movements. The philosophers' appeal to reason for metaphysical wisdom and scientific knowledge, for guidance in practical affairs, and for the resolution of conflicts between proponents of competing world-views or principles provides the philosophers' disciple with a proven and imposing alternative to reliance on the judgement of religious authorities. The religious liberal's emphasis on reason, reasonableness, and rationality is essentially the philosopher's. Even when a religious liberal points to some non-rational source of wisdom and guidance, such as conscience or the moral sense, her belief in such a faculty has at least indirectly been made possible by a tradition of philosophical theory represented by such thinkers as Hutcheson and Rousseau.

Thirdly, the religious liberal's views on the importance of personal autonomy, freedom of inquiry, individualism, the primacy of individual rights, self-realization, and emancipation from dogma are all based at least in part on a philosophical awareness of the importance of subjectivity. We took note earlier of Aiken's comment that since the time of Kant it has been the thinking subject who establishes the standards of objectivity. In point of fact, sensitivity to the subjective dimension of judgement has characterized philosophy from its beginnings. It is particularly evident in the writings of certain philosophers, such as Protagoras, Descartes, Hume, Kant, the pragmatists, and the existentialists. But even when we find philosophers discoursing at length about eternal truths and timeless realities, we cannot fail to be consistently impressed by the importance that any philosopher attaches to his personal vision, perspective, or *Weltanschauung*.

Fourthly, in our effort to understand the essence of religious liberalism, it is useful to consider the extent to which liberal religion is basically philosophical religion. Its promoters deliberately play down all those elements of religious experience and culture that have little or nothing to do with philosophical concerns, though they are normally led by prudential considerations and their respect for the liberal values of tolerance, generosity, willingness to compromise, and open-mindedness to acknowledge that such non-philosophical elements may be retained in some diluted form. Such elements include belief in the literal truth of the historical accounts provided by sacred works, rites and sacraments, and concern for things of the "other world" and the "next life." Such elements are retained in some form as a sop to the traditionalistic, the naive, and the irredeemably ignorant and superstitious, and the religious liberal reconciles herself to them by looking upon them as quaint and aesthetically pleasing. The promoters of liberal religion tend to be suspicious of anything related to cult. They generally associate the "meaning" of religious faith — and their reference to meaning is often an allusion to function — with creed and code, both understood philosophically. The philosophical religion that is left after all this pruning consists fundamentally of an abstract metaphysic and an abstract ethic, that is, of very general theories of Reality and Morality or of the ground of Being and the ground of Action. Twentieth-century religionists who have been scandalized and offended by "new" efforts by religious liberals at "demythologization" have failed to appreciate how this project goes all the way back to the pre-Sophistic cosmologists who encouraged their fellows to isolate abstract metaphysical and ethical principles from their mythological context. With all of this demythologization has gone the de-ritualization, de-eschatologization, and de-tribalization of religious faith. In short, what religious liberalism gives us is the philosophization of religious faith. Yet while the word *philosophy* strikes fear into the hearts of most plain folk, religious liberals insist, and apparently quite sincerely, that, in having urged a return to the "essential core" of religion, they have tried to bring their fellows back to the "simple" faith advocated by the founders, prophets, and saints of every religious tradition.

Consider, as a case in point, the liberalization of Judaism. In the minds of many people — Jews and Gentiles alike — Judaism and liberalism go hand in hand. The attraction of Jews to political liberalism has undoubtedly been partly a function of the fact that in most societies Jews have constituted a small minority amidst a sea of hostile neighbours; clearly, Jews have depended more than most other people on the benignity of political leaders sincerely committed to the protection and extension of religious liberty. As I suggested earlier, there are also theological reasons why Jews have attached as much importance as they have to various kinds of freedom. But with respect to religious liberalism as such, though Jews have made substantial contributions, the primary incentive to make reforms has come from philosophy. Hence, despite the significant differences between Judaism and Christianity, the development of Jewish liberalism has been strikingly similar to that of Protestant liberalism and even to some extent to that of Roman Catholic liberalism. Consider, for example, the contribution made by one of the central figures in the liberalization of Judaism, Hermann Cohen. According to Emil Fackenheim,

> Of liberal or Reform Judaism the profoundest exponent thus far has been the German-Jewish philosopher Hermann Cohen (1842–1918). Superficially this movement within Judaism may seem to be nothing more than an attempt to keep up with modern times. At its most profound, however, it springs from the conflict between the claim of past authority, that of a revealed canon included, and the modern claim of the free, "autonomous" moral and religious conscience. No modern thinker sides more emphatically than Cohen with the claim of conscience against authority, that of a divinely revealed Tenach included. Yet he finds that very claim not merely endorsed in the Tenach but proclaimed with a radicalism that dwarfs the radicals of modernity. . . . Hence it is from the ancient "sources of Judaism" that the modern Jew — nay, modern man as a whole — must learn "the religion of reason."[64]

But why did Cohen read Ezekiel 18:31 and related passages of Hebrew Scripture in the way he did? Why was he able to find in Hebrew Scripture what countless generations of orthodox Jewish scholars were unable to find there? One quite plausible answer is that Cohen read his Jewish sources with the spectacles of the Kant scholar, for Hermann Cohen was unquestionably one of the greatest Kantians and Kant scholars of his time. We have noted Kant's influence on the growth of Protestant liberalism; it is ironic that this curious little man whose remarks about Jews are for the most part shallow and disparaging also exerted a parallel influence on the growth of Jewish liberalism. In fact, in the view of the historian Heinz Moshe Graupe, "The impact Kant had upon Jews and Judaism was unquestionably more profound and decisive than his influence on non-Jewish Germany and Europe"[65] despite the celebrated thinker's "peculiarly ambivalent relationship to Jews and Judaism."[66]

The influence of philosophy upon the growth of liberal Judaism can be traced back much further. One may call to mind, for example, the importance of Moses Mendelssohn, one of the major figures of the Enlightenment, a philosopher and student of philosophy, a man who conversed with Kant and Lessing, and a pivotal figure in the modern history of the Jewish people. As did other figures of the German Enlightenment, Mendelssohn sought to rationalize and thereby generalize matters of religious faith;[67] in distinguishing within Judaism two separate components, the natural religion of reason and the Jewish Law, he sought to promote a compromise between universal modernity and Jewish tradition, but most of his young Jewish disciples undervalued the specifically Jewish dimension and became little more than symbols of apostasy and assimilation.[68] This story goes back even further, for as Fackenheim points out, "it is erroneous to believe that the advent of pluralism in Judaism coincides with the advent of modernity. This is shown by the fact of protest movements against the dominant rabbinic-Halachic Judaism, in premodern as well as modern times. Perhaps the most powerful of these is Kabbalistic Judaism."[69] Kabbalistic Judaism was much influenced by Neoplatonism, but there was an even more powerful protest movement against rabbinic orthodoxy that, significantly, someone like Fackenheim would probably not even recognize as a protest movement. I refer to the Aristotelian propaganda of Maimonides, who despite the suspicion of many orthodox contemporaries that he was a dangerous heretic, emerged in later centuries as the most eminently respectable of orthodox intellectuals. The mediaeval rabbis who ran to the Catholic hierarchy to have Maimonides' teaching suppressed were not the wisest or most generous of souls, but they were at least good enough students of Jewish history to know about the corrupting influences of Hellenism, and they did not allow Maimonides' personal orthodoxy to obscure the fact that his attachment to Aristotelian philosophy had led him to take a rather patronizing attitude towards the garden variety of Talmudic scholar and to have grave doubts about the reasonableness of some favourite rabbinic teachings. There are sections near the end of Maimonides' *Guide for the Perplexed* and in his introduction to tractate *Sanhedrin* that are in their own way as subversive to Jewish orthodoxy as anything that Mendelssohn and Cohen were able to come up with, especially as Aristotelianism is so much subtler and more profound than Kantianism; but modern orthodox rabbis have prudently recognized that more is to be lost than gained by portraying Maimonides in the disdainful way in which they increasingly portray Mendelssohn or Cohen, as an apologist for apostasy and assimilation.

The extent to which philosophical standards have been employed to determine attitudes towards religion is well illustrated by Morley's remarks that "Our comfort and the delight of the religious imagination are no better than forms of self-indulgence, when they are secured at the cost of that love of truth on which, more than anything else, the increase of light and happiness among men must depend. We have to fight and do life-long battle against the forces of darkness, and anything that turns the edge of reason fatally blunts the surest and most potent of our weapons."[70] Even those who, like myself, are inclined to agree with Morley need to remind themselves from time to time that there have been countless good people in this world, promoters of light and happiness among their fellow creatures, who have not been convinced that reason is either the surest and most potent weapon against the forces of darkness or the most important source of truth. But whatever one may think of philosophy, something akin to James Barr's comments about the Christian tradition probably applies to most major religious traditions: "We do not have to be liberals: but we have to recognize that the liberal quest is in principle a fully legitimate form of Christian obedience within the church, and one that has deep roots within the older Christian theological tradition and even within the Bible itself."[71]

4 Criticisms of Religious Liberalism

Religious liberalism has been subject to a variety of criticisms, and even some of its most passionate proponents have worried aloud about the frequency with which certain aspects of it have been misinterpreted or misapplied. The most serious, most common, and most telling criticism of religious liberalism is that it inevitably leads to the dilution of religious commitment. Almost as important is the criticism that the liberal religion that religious liberalism has invented is as dogmatic and as arbitrary as the rival conceptions of religion that it condemns on this very ground. Related to this criticism is the argument that religious liberalism ignores important historical and theological truths.

The thesis that religious liberalism inevitably leads to the dilution of religious commitment has many dimensions and comes in different forms. Indeed, I offered one version of the thesis only a few pages ago when I asserted that the "philosophization" of religious faith involves playing down its non-philosophical elements. Let us consider some other versions of the thesis. One influential version is the view that, regardless of what they pretend, liberals in general do not respect authority and do not take Revelation seriously. This view has been advanced by many distinguished Roman Catholic writers; it appears over and over again, for example, in the works of John Henry Newman. Yves Simon says that "The liberal revolt against authority . . . represents a monstrous spurning of the most invaluable gift that the divine generosity could make to man, the revelation of the secrets of the divine life."[72] Dawson writes that, "Against the Liberal doctrines of the divine right of majorities and the unrestricted freedom of opinion the Church has always maintained the principles of authority and hierarchy and a high conception of the prerogatives of the State."[73] Novak, explaining the Catholic hierarchy's traditional disapproval of liberalism, notes that "The Catholic tradition held that liberalism as a *moral* doctrine too lightly valued authority and tradition in religion, and yielded too much to individual conscience, which after all is prey to whim, the spirit of the age, and unreliable contrariety."[74]

Another version of the thesis emphasizes the inevitability of religious liberalism's interfering with the zeal — and consistency — of religionists. According to the historian Henriques, "It is a truism that to obtain the virtues of moderation it may be necessary to sacrifice some of the virtues and advantages of zeal, and a further truism that practical moderation may entail a sacrifice of logic. For toleration tends to attract to its banner those who feel that they can go through life without some of the certainties that others find indispensable and therefore call good."[75] Henriques herself does not declare that the price of liberalism is too high, but other writers have wondered aloud about this price, including, significantly enough, many thinkers highly sympathetic to religious liberalism. Hayward, for example, laments that "Liberals are often excessively afraid of dogmatism, especially if they are but lately escaped from some orthodox denomination. They do not like to enter into even a loving controversy over religion. . . . They are so suspicious of many beliefs that they begin to suspect and distrust belief itself."[76] "It may be that many of the liberals are so empty spiritually that they envy one who is full and, in the name of continued unfulfilled search, they unconsciously disparage his fullness and thus comfort themselves for their own spiritual failures."77 Morley, in a similar vein, observes that "Indolence and timidity have united to popularise among us a flaccid latitudinarianism, which thinks itself a benign tolerance for the opinions of others. It is in truth only a pretentious form of being without settled opinions of our own, and without any desire to settle them."78

Perhaps the most eloquent statement of the problem is that of Lecky, who ends his monumental survey of the history of rationalism on a curious note by regretting the extent to which rationalism, despite all of its positive achievements, has contributed to the decline of spirituality and the growth of a shallow materialism:

> The destruction of the belief in witchcraft and of religious persecution, the decay of those ghastly notions concerning future punishments, which for centuries diseased the imaginations and embittered the character of mankind, the emancipation of suffering nationalities, the abolition of the belief in the guilt of error, which paralysed the intellectual, and of the asceticism which paralysed the material, progress of mankind, may be justly regarded as among the greatest triumphs of civilisation; but when we look back to the cheerful alacrity with which, in some former ages, men sacrificed all their material and intellectual interests to what they believed to be right, and we realise the unclouded assurance that was their reward, it is impossible to deny that we have lost something in our progress.79

Early on in this chapter we took note of Dawson's characterization of liberalism as a "half-way house" between religious culture and secular culture that inevitably deteriorates into the latter. D. E. Miller, though a defender of liberal Christianity, admits that "My fear is that in the absence of a vital liberal theology, many members of liberal congregations are on their way toward creating a class of formerly religious but now secular humanists. I am not opposed to humanism except when I sense that its proponents know more what they are against than what they are for."80 A related concern for Miller is the relation of liberalism to relativism. "The danger in liberalism is that the Christian message may become a mirror reflection of the spirit of the age. This is an ever-present problem for liberal Christians to confront."81 So worried is Miller about the "relativizing of the Christian paradigm"82 that at one point he wonders aloud about whether perhaps the time is right for a revitalized natural law.83 However, it is not clear how a device such as natural law could be neatly incorporated into a conception of religion that has so subjectivistic an orientation.

We noted in earlier chapters that a traditional argument against religious liberty has been that it prevents communal unity. It has been argued that religious liberalism itself, in promoting radical individualism and pluralism, weakens our commitment to our fellows and makes true community more difficult. As Barr says, fundamentalists see the very variety of non-conservative theologies as a reason why people should stick to a conservative position.[84] But Macquarrie, who is certainly no fundamentalist, grants that "if there is a unity that swallows up freedom, there is also a diversity that breaks up unity rather than contributing to it. The member lives to itself in a false autonomy, eventually destroying itself and perhaps the whole body with it."[85] The problem here is psychological as well as social, for as the psychologist Rychlak tells us, "It is not always psychologically harmful to relinquish our range of personal freedom in favor of following the intentions of other identities whom we assess positively."[86] Here, we need to consider the personal as well as social value of loyalty, trust, fellowship, respect for legitimate authority, the willingness to sacrifice for others, and the willingness to love.

One might, of course, argue that the dilution of religious commitment is in itself desirable, and that religious liberalism has performed a service to humanity in contributing such dilution. This argument could be advanced not only by the positivistic or radical humanistic critic of religion but by someone who feels that, while religion is basically a positive force for civilization, it has often been either too intense or too dominant a form of experience. A pro-religious thinker may want to argue that religious liberalism does not dilute the core elements of religious faith but rather helps to convert the overcommitment of fanaticism into a healthy balanced commitment.[87] A secularist, while regretting the survival of even the liberal type of religion, will usually grant that liberal religion is preferable to orthodox religion. Some people will see religious liberalism's status as a "half-way house" between traditional religious culture and secular culture in a rather more positive light than a traditionalist like Dawson does; and, while most defenders of liberal religion will insist that it is not destined to deteriorate into secularism, there are actually critics of religion who will argue that it is to the credit of liberal religion that it is a stage on the road to the secularization of culture.

Therefore, in assessing the significance of the dilution of commitment that may follow upon the liberalization of religion, one must pass judgement on the value of both religious zeal and religious commitment in general. While Lecky feels that we have lost something in the liberalization process, he still holds that on the whole humanity has made progress as a result of rationalism. The zeal that animates the saint must be weighed against the zeal that animates the sinner; and, in the view of the liberal religionist, liberal religion preserves enough in the way of spiritual incentive while reducing the chances of faith turning fanatical. Furthermore, for the religious liberal, religious commitment does not have to do the job of moralizing on its own, for it can be made to co-operate with practical reason. As for the question of the value of religion itself, that is something that will be debated until the end of time, but it is noteworthy that religion in some form or other has not only survived in the most advanced civilizations but has proved to be highly and widely valued even among the most admirable people.

An argument of a very different kind that has been directed against religious liberalism is that it is even more dogmatic than the supposedly dogmatic systems that it seeks to have reformed or replaced. This attack is two-pronged, for it levels the charge of hypocrisy as well as that of excessive dogmatism. Foakes-Jackson, himself a Protestant, writes,

> What is now called Liberal Protestantism is far from encouraging freedom in thought. It relaxes the obligation to subscribe to creeds and to accept all Scripture as the literal law of God, but has little or no sympathy with what it considers to be superstition. The most intolerant men I have known have been clergymen of outstanding ability who are as ready to jettison the leading articles of the Creed, as they would, if they had the power, be to punish those who want to believe a little more than the formularies of the church to which they belong seem in their eyes to warrant.[88]

It is not clear how much importance to attach to this mixture of personal testimony, speculation, and value-judgement, but the main theme here appears regularly in the works of troubled liberals as well as orthodox critics of liberalism. We find the hostile J. G. Machen remarking that 'The movement designated as 'liberalism' is regarded as 'liberal' only by its friends; to its opponents it seems to involve a narrow ignoring of many relevant facts."[89] But we also find the defender of liberalism, Hayward, warning that, while liberals cannot simply rally their forces under the banner of denial, "corporate religious affirmation seems to move toward creedalism and threatens to bind the individual's freedom of decision."[90] In fact, "For all their vaunted freedom and scope of religious concern, liberals are quite capable of settling into a groove of unconscious orthodoxy, enjoying the like-mindedness of people who are all too like-minded and not seizing but avoiding every opportunity to challenge one another on life's most critical issues."[91] The leaders of liberal churches have shown all too often that they can be as high-handed, manipulative, and obstinate as the leaders of those churches that they are constantly condemning as illiberal; and they exacerbate such situations with their special brand of self-righteousness and self-satisfaction.

Related to this argument, and normally combined with it, is the criticism that religious liberals ignore important historical and theological facts. This argument usually involves more than simply asserting that one disagrees with religious liberals, or that religious liberals have been led by their methods to false conclusions. It tends to imply that there is something wilful and perhaps even dishonest about the way in which the religious liberals discard relevant facts because those facts conflict with their arbitrary conceptions and their project of theologico-political reform. This has been a major theme of neo-orthodox, "post-liberal" theology. "The burden of the neo-orthodox case against liberalism has been that it has evacuated the gospel of its necessary *offence*," Reardon points out;[92] for "the failure of liberalism, religiously speaking, was, as the post-liberals see it, its inability to contemplate either the actual condition of man or the doctrine of God which the remedy for such a condition inherently demands. The danger to which it was exposed, and in certain instances succumbed, was that of transforming Christianity into a high-minded ethical humanism, a point of view admirable indeed for those — the few — with the moral resources to sustain it, but unavailing for the masses helplessly caught up in the fearful travail of the present century."[93] Stromberg feels that the neo-orthodox revival of the twentieth century may well have fallen in danger of glorifying the irrational; but he appreciates the neo-orthodox thinkers' dissatisfaction with the "meek submission of liberal Christianity to science and secularism."[94] Moreover, it is significant that religious liberalism has been seen by many critics to be an essentially academic and bourgeois movement,[95] and thus to involve the narrowness of perspective that academic and bourgeois interests promote or even require.

Stromberg, who is not at all hostile to religious liberalism, notes that historical investigations of the kind recommended by religious liberals do not always support liberal religious conceptions. For example, "The ethical Jesus of religious liberalism, so vital to deism and moralistic Christianity, does not seem to be historical, as Albert Schweitzer, Johannes Weiss, and others have shown. . . . The 'eschatological' or 'apocalyptic' Jesus emerges instead — hardly the teacher of secular morality."[96] The reactionary Machen is particularly severe in his appraisal of religious liberalism's handling of what he takes to be facts. "The modern liberal does not really hold to the authority of Jesus";[97] "It is not Jesus, then, who is the real authority, but the modern principle by which the selection within Jesus' recorded teaching has been made. Certain isolated ethical principles of the Sermon on the Mount are accepted, not at all because they are teachings of Jesus, but because they agree with modern ideas."[98] And Sell, who aims at providing a balanced appraisal of religious liberalism, suggests with respect to the highly influential Ritschl that his "incipient subjectivism led him to pay much more attention to some Christian facts than to others — a circumstance which has resulted in the charge levelled by conservative theologians from his day to ours that Ritschl has only a seriously attenuated gospel to offer."[99]

However pertinent these various criticisms of religious liberalism may be — and, as we have seen, even religious liberals themselves are sometimes prepared to acknowledge their relevance — the fact remains that, when all is said and done, religious liberalism may still be more attractive than any of its alternatives. For one thing, while the orthodox may insist that people should believe this and that, people cannot always believe the things that their religious leaders expect them to believe. Unfortunately, the orthodox have often pursued strategies of defending and promoting their faith that have encouraged people to *pretend* that they believe the "right" things; and, of course, even orthodox leaders have been given to pretence and hypocrisy. That in itself is an argument in favour of religious liberalism, which does, after all, recognize actual individual differences. Again, one does not do an effective job of disposing of religious pluralism when one simply dismisses rival religious viewpoints as "foolish" or "shallow"; and the arguments that religionists have used to convince members of rival denominations of their errors have generally not been very impressive. It is hardly surprising that millions upon millions of Christians have refused to accept the contention of non-Christians that they are simply "mistaken" about their most basic beliefs; and the same holds true for members of the smallest and most obscure religious denominations and intradenominational groups and, for that matter, for secularists of all stripes.

Thus, despite his reservations about various aspects of his own commitment, the religious liberal, who as a liberal values compromise, may ultimately be moved to defend his position as a mean between two extremes. Miller writes:

> The alternatives to liberalism are limited. About evangelism I have already intimated a great deal. Liberation theology is another vital expression of Christianity. But however well placed liberation theology is

in its Latin America [sic] setting, it is questionable whether it is equally applicable to the North American and European contexts. . . . With a burgeoning population of evangelicals on one side and radical secularists on the other, the *mediating position* — I would say, the *temperate alternative* — of liberalism is being lost.[100]

Yet we cannot blame either the traditional religionist or the secularist for wondering whether what might seem to the religious liberal to be a temperate alternative based on compromise is not really a bizarre combination of elements that fundamentally conflict. There may seem to be a paradox here similar to the one that we saw arise with respect to religious liberty. Regardless of what prudence and social harmony require, there is something odd about expecting a religious person to regard some secular political authority as higher than his chosen religious authority; and similarly, it is hard to understand how religion is improved by being made weaker.

5   Liberal Religion and Spiritual Freedom

The most passionate critics of religious liberalism do not only believe that religious liberalism teaches what is false and socially destructive; they believe further that religious liberalism harms the individual, for it makes it harder or even impossible for her to be "saved." Religious liberals are rarely disturbed by the eschatological notions of such critics. However, they are apt to be rather touchy when the critics add that religious liberals deprive people of their *freedom*; for when the critics argue in this way, they are meeting the religious liberal on her own terms. Of course, it is not easy for them to make their case by reference to political freedoms or even most religious freedoms. But it is here that they are most often given to bold pronouncements about "spiritual freedom."

Simultaneously mocking and condemning the religious liberal, Machen informs us that "The grace of God is rejected by modern liberalism. And the result is slavery — the slavery of the law, the wretched bondage by which man undertakes the impossible task of establishing his own righteousness as a ground of acceptance with God. It may seem strange at first sight that 'liberalism,' of which the very name means freedom, should in reality be wretched slavery. But the phenomenon is not really so strange. Emancipation from the blessed will of God always involves bondage to some worse taskmaster."[101]   And Dawson, who sees liberalism as inevitably degenerating into secularism, writes that "A secularist culture can only exist, so to speak, in the dark. It is a prison in which the human spirit confines itself when it is shut out of the wider world of reality.... The recovery of spiritual vision gives man back his spiritual freedom. And hence the freedom of the Church is in the faith of the Church and the freedom of man is in the knowledge of God."[102]

The liberal religionist may respond to such charges in several ways. First, she may insist that her critics here have misunderstood her position. She may contend that, in contrast with the caricatures presented, she in fact does not reject the grace of God and does not endeavour to rob people of their spiritual vision. She may contend further that her critics have not produced adequate evidence to justify their claim that religious liberalism inevitably deteriorates into secularism, atheism, and materialism. A second line of response could concentrate on the possible emptiness of her critics' references to "spiritual freedom." She might go further and, dismissing her critics' references as instances of sophistical rhetoric, demand that they spell out in precise detail what they think they mean by "spiritual freedom." More often than not, her critics will not have an easy time with this task. They may give an eschatological explanation of spiritual freedom, but the eschatological notions of most religious faiths are notoriously — and quite intentionally — vague, and when eschatological speculations do become very precise and detailed, they begin to sound rather childish. Furthermore, even if the critics produced an elegant and profound eschatological explanation of spiritual freedom, the religious liberal could still reply that she is unconvinced that such freedom is possible or even desirable, and she might still maintain that she does not understand exactly what the critics *mean*. Conceptions of spiritual freedom can only be satisfactorily explicated — or understood — from within the context of a particular world-view. This may be true to some extent of conceptions of all kinds of freedom, but it is certainly true of conceptions of spiritual freedom. If her critics offer a purely pragmatic moral or psychological explanation of spiritual freedom, then the religious liberal can rightly contend that they are talking in the way that religious liberals do.

There is a third possible response available to the religious liberal. She may argue that the notion of spiritual freedom is largely a liberal religious notion and that it has been liberal religious thinkers who have done most of the work of refining and elaborating upon the concept and making it central to religion. She may contend further that, though they appeal to spiritual freedom whenever they find it convenient to do so, the orthodox have generally obscured the phenomenon by burying it under a heap of dogmas, rites, and superstitions. It will not do for the traditionalists to emphasize in response that direct or indirect references to spiritual freedom can be found in works of sacred literature, for the liberal religionist can respond that those sacred works have been a major inspiration to her own way of thinking, indeed more of an inspiration to *her* thought than to her critics' thought. Accordingly, she may dismiss as slanderous misinterpretation the claim of her critics that she and her fellow liberals ordinarily do not take sacred literature seriously.

Let us explore one aspect of this third possible response. In drawing attention to the importance of spiritual freedom, and the difference between spiritual freedom and political and economic liberty, Dawson remarks that "It is one of the great classical commonplaces of religion and of ancient philosophy that the two are not the same: that a man may possess citizenship and wealth and yet be without spiritual freedom and that a man may be poor and a slave, like Epictetus, and yet enjoy the good of spiritual freedom."[103] Dawson's interpretation here of the teaching of the ancient philosophers is questionable; Plato and particularly Aristotle have grave doubts about the extent to which a slave can be spiritually free. But Dawson's comment is more generally misleading because of what he leaves out of his account. As part of a sustained attack on liberalism, Dawson associates something that he takes to be at the heart of religion — and specifically of his own favoured form of traditional Christianity — with a force, classical philosophy, that perhaps more than any other contributed to the liberalization of religion that he deplores. When the classical (and subsequent) philosophers have discoursed at length on the subject of spiritual freedom, they have usually done so in the general context of their project of compensating for the failure of orthodox religious teaching to provide an adequate account of what such spiritual freedom truly involves.

When Dawson points to the need for a revival of traditional religious commitment, he has in mind, as I have indicated, his own favoured form of traditional Christianity. Dawson belongs to the highly distinctive English apologetical tradition of Cardinal Newman, Chesterton, and Belloc, and along with these thinkers, Dawson believes that the only significant form of civilization is "European" civilization, which is to be *identified* with Christian civilization.[104] However, thinkers in Dawson's tradition also admire those good Europeans, the pre-Christian classical Greeks, even though much that the ancient Greek philosophers taught is antithetical to, and subversive of, orthodox Christian teaching. Of course, many New Testament ideas reflect Greek philosophical conceptions; but, if Christianity combined insights of Judaism and Greek thought, it was very selective about which particular insights from those two traditions it was going to bring into its grand synthesis. Certain Christian conceptions are distinctly Platonic, just as certain Christian conceptions are distinctly Hebraic; but much of Christianity is absolutely anti-Platonic and anti-Jewish. The fact is that, while the major Greek philosophers and most orthodox Christian teachers have both attacked materialism and emphasized the things of the spirit, philosophical conceptions of spiritual freedom — including those of the major Greek philosophers — have been rather more sophisticated than most orthodox Christian conceptions of spiritual freedom.

Whether the liberal religionist will be offended or encouraged by Dawson's appeal to the wisdom of the ancient philosophers, he will not have much trouble seeing that, with respect to the matter of spiritual freedom, "Athens" and "Jerusalem" have less to do with one another than might be assumed. The greatest of comic poets, Aristophanes, knew nothing about Judaism and Christianity; the latter did not even exist at the time Aristophanes wrote the *Clouds*, his famous indictment of the corrupting influences of philosophers. But Aristophanes, with his keen understanding of cultural dynamics, was perceptive in recognizing how the teachings of the Sophists and of Socrates himself represented a threat to the prevailing religious orthodoxy. And Plato, despite his feeble attempts to sound orthodox at *Republic* 427 and Book x of the *Laws*, was very much the disciple of Socrates, at least in this realm. Now, the Socrates we meet in the *Clouds* has been broadly caricatured by his friend, who knew Socrates well enough to know that he was no cosmologist, did not run a school, and did not accept money for his teachings. Aristophanes knew, in short, that Socrates was not the Sophist that he was portraying him as, and if the classicist James Mantinband is right, therein lies the fun of the *Clouds*.[105] But Mantinband overstates the point when he suggests that the Socrates of the *Clouds* is nothing like the real Socrates.[106] It is no coincidence that, when the Athenians finally condemned Socrates for impiety and corrupting the youth, they adopted the very charges that Aristophanes had directed against him. At the end of the *Clouds*, the naive protagonist, Strepsiades, attacks Socrates and his disciples with words that are extraordinarily bitter for a comedy: "You have insulted all the blessed Gods in Heaven / and peered into the crevices of the Lady Moon! / Strike, don't spare a single one of them, they deserve it, / especially because they have blasphemed the Gods!"[107] Plato was much offended by Aristophanes' caricature of his beloved teacher,[108] whom he portrays in the *Apology* as the most genuinely religious figure of his day. There is good reason to believe that Socrates was indeed a very religious man, but Plato probably overestimated the extent to which Socrates' religion was orthodox. Even in the *Apology,* Plato portrays Socrates as someone who had no desire to be like ordinary men and recognized that in fact he was not like ordinary men.[109] If it was not quite true that Socrates was inventing new gods and denying the existence of the old ones,[110] and if his final announcement of his confidence in the justice of the gods showed him to be rather more sincere in religious matters than the hypocrites who had condemned him,[111] the fact remains that Socrates had his own personal vision of what spiritual freedom involves.

Socrates was a great martyr not only in the cause of religious liberty but in the cause of religious liberalism as well. Yet in assessing the events that had befallen him as a result of his unorthodoxy and rebelliousness, Socrates ultimately determined that he was about to attain a spiritual freedom that his philosophical inquiries alone had not been able to bring him. According to Plato's portrayal, Socrates did not know in the end where, if anywhere, he was going after death, but he sincerely believed that he was coming to a good end.[112] Of special importance, he saw himself as being *freed* in various ways: from the hypocrisy of his fellows,[113] from dreams,[114] from troubles.[115]

His greatest student, Plato, went on to advance some of the most remarkable ideas about what spiritual freedom consists in, both in this life and in the next; and, if Plato's vision was different from anything that came before it, so also it was different from anything that came after it. Since Plato's time, countless philosophers and other liberal religionists have arrived at their own conceptions of what spiritual freedom involves, and some of them have shared those conceptions with their fellows. Few have spoken with more conviction than Spinoza, who in the last part of his *Ethics* describes the way that leads to freedom for all those who seek true salvation and, repudiating the religious orthodoxies of his own day and age, declares that "Blessedness is not the reward of virtue but is virtue itself. . . . "[116]

6. Freedom and Authority

We set out in this study to consider some of the more important relations between religion and freedom and, as we have now covered a great deal of philosophical ground, and some theological, social-scientific, and historical ground too, it is a good time to take stock of what we have collected along the way. So, let us remind ourselves of how we have reached the point at which we now find ourselves.

There are many reasons why one might be troubled about the state of spirituality in the modern world. Despite extraordinary advances in recent centuries in technology, scientific knowledge, social institutions, and the fine arts, we still find ourselves looking back to the glory of societies long gone, and many of us are often seized by a nostalgia for ages, places, and world-views that we have never directly known. Our century has produced atrocities that are unprecedented in scale, if not quality; even the barbarians of earlier times might have been horrified by the mass murders, the techniques of torture and destruction, and the systematized exploitation that have marked recent generations. Perhaps they would also have been puzzled by the emptiness of so much of the high and popular culture of so-called "advanced" civilizations. It is no wonder, then, that some people have been moved to lament the decline of religious zeal, while others have bitterly rejected religious traditions that they regard as the source of the shallowness of modern spirituality. Nor is it surprising that some people have looked upon the absence of freedom as the key problem of our age, while others have blamed the loss of respect for authority for having unleashed what they take to be unprecedented permissiveness and nihilism.

However, we were prepared to consider the possibility of a genuine alternative to both reactionary religious authoritarianism and secularist materialism and, with philosophy as our guide, we went on to explore ideas related to various expressions that we have encountered in everyday language: "religious freedom," "religious liberty," "religious liberalism," "liberal religion," and so on. We did so with the objective of clarifying our own conceptions of the relations of religion and freedom so as to be able to improve the quality of our own lives and have something concrete to offer those among our fellows who are confused about the place of spirituality in a world that they perceive as having been increasingly despoiled of authentic faith, hope, and love.

1 Resolving the Paradoxes

We have sought practical wisdom, but when we survey what we have collected in the course of our intellectual journey, what we find is a collection of paradoxes. We started out by considering the basic concepts of religion, freedom, and religious freedom, and we quickly found that not only have serious inquirers failed to agree with respect to these concepts, but that some of their ideas are actually diametrically opposed. Armed with some rather vague notions about religion and freedom, we then went on to consider whether religion is primarily a hindrance to freedom or a source of freedom, and we found that, while it appears that only personal judgement can resolve this issue in one's mind, there are good reasons for believing either way. In the course of that phase of our investigation we found that many of the practical problems about the relation of religion and freedom have revolved around questions concerning the relation of religious and political institutions. However, when we set out to clarify in our minds the nature of "religious liberty," we found more paradoxes. For example, we found enemies of authoritarianism defending the unlimited authority of the state, and we found people defending religious freedom while simultaneously asserting that political leaders should not "recognize" religious groups. Most importantly, we found that many thoughtful, high-minded people expect us to be able to regard political authority as higher than our religious authority for practical purposes even though it must obviously be regarded as lower in theory. So we surmised that the real problem may lie with our religious conceptions themselves. But when we considered religious liberalism and liberal religion, we found that on the one hand they seem to lead to the dilution of religious commitment and an ethical humanism bordering on secularism, while on the other hand they seem to be as dogmatic and arbitrary as the modes of religious faith that they dismiss as illiberal. Finally, when we considered the concept of spiritual freedom, we found that there is good reason to expect that every reflective person — liberal or otherwise — has his own highly personal way of conceiving of such freedom, and that it is far from clear whether liberalism promotes the most important forms of spiritual freedom or prevents us from attaining them.

Some people think of paradoxes as genuine self-contradictions, but historically the term *paradox* has more often been applied to positions that only appear to be internally inconsistent. Reflection should help us to resolve or unravel paradoxes or at least make them somewhat less daunting. How, then, does one go about resolving a paradox? That would seem to depend in part on the nature of the paradox under consideration; we may suspect that there is a great difference between the formal paradoxes of mathematics and logical theory and the more informal paradoxes that one encounters in discussions of ethical, political, and cultural subjects. However, there can never be a simple or wholly satisfying resolution of a genuine paradox; if the resolution has been simple and wholly satisfying, then the tension we have been confronting was not properly given the name of *paradox*.

With respect to the paradoxes that have emerged in our investigation, the proper method of resolving them is to work at the establishment of a balance between conflicting conceptions. To do such balancing, we must recognize first that, although the conceptions may in a sense be absolutely in conflict, we can interpret them in such a way that they are reconcilable perspectives of the same phenomenon or reconcilable elements within a stable synthesis. Interpreting them in this way may well involve diluting their content. For one thing, it may involve changing *all* to *most*, *many* to *some*, *usually* to *often*, *wholly* to *partly*, and so on. But it may require rather more than that.

Words like *diluting* and *perspective* may suggest that such a methodology is already biased in favour of liberalism against orthodoxy; and compromise itself is certainly a standard liberal value. Thus, the religious liberal, faced with "white" orthodoxy and "black" secularism, may be the champion of "grey," and anyone who shows a willingness to dilute conceptions so as to make them reconcilable may be giving away the secret that in his heart of hearts he too is committed to "greyness." But perhaps what is required here is a blending of "white" orthodoxy with "black" liberalism, which, "grey" though it may be, cannot fairly be associated with liberalism alone. Perhaps what the required "dilution" involves is freeing both orthodoxy and liberalism from accretions which have become attached to them through arbitrary and unhelpful interpretation. The traditionalist may declare that he refuses to compromise where his basic principles are concerned; but even the liberal, as we have seen, could say the same, and is indeed obliged to say the same.

Unless he is extremely powerful — and willing to be tyrannical, even at the risk of revealing his religious hypocrisy — the traditionalist has no choice but to compromise, and his real obligation is to compromise in a thoughtful, morally correct manner. At the same time, the liberal has no right to assume that he is such an expert on compromise that he instinctively has a better understanding than the traditionalist does of what constitutes a fair and responsible compromise. A sensible liberal will have freed himself of the delusion that he has no dogmatic and arbitrary conceptions of his own.

Our paradoxes have manifested themselves on two planes: the social, institutional level and the personal, theoretical level. There is obviously a connection between the two: societies are made up of individuals, and social institutions are based on the ideas put forward by individuals. Still, the distinction is worth making. We are concerned with the types of social institutions that will promote those kinds of religious freedom that are worth regarding as substantial realizations of an ideal. At the same time, we must not only look to social institutions to make us better; we have to look to ourselves to do part of the job of improving ourselves and helping others to better themselves. On the social level, we need to consider how political institutions and ecclesiastical and other religious institutions might be reformed, or at least perceived in a new light, so as to accommodate the major demands of the competing interest groups (political leaders and religious leaders; denominations; intradenominational groups)[1] and promote in society desirable forms of religious freedom. The reform (or new understanding) of political and religious institutions would ideally be based on a substantial consensus among serious inquirers who have given careful consideration to the matters at hand.

In the successive phases of our investigation we have gradually come to recognize more clearly the various kinds of interest groups (and individuals) that come into conflict over matters involving both religion and freedom. We have also come to understand more clearly the principal kinds of demands that lie at the heart of the conflicts. And we have taken note of some of the more serious consequences of the failure of the competitors to work towards a fair, balanced, and effective resolution of their conflicts. Obviously, each particular conflict must be considered on the basis of its unique aspects as well as the general aspects of all conflicts involving religious freedom. That is why people like you and me are normally not in a position to advise particular political leaders and the leaders of a particular religious denomination, or members of competing orthodox and liberal groups within a particular denomination, precisely as to where they should do their compromising. We are rarely in a position to know what matters most to them as opposed to what they feel may ultimately be sacrificed for the sake of compromise.

What is clearly needed on the social level is the institutionalization of better procedures for resolving conflicts over religious freedom. The institutions that have traditionally done the job best have probably been courts, such as high civil courts that rule on constitutional issues and ecclesiastical and other denominational courts that rule on conflicts between intradenominational groups. But institutions of this kind are significantly limited. When civil courts rule on conflicts between "church" and "state," the fact is that no matter how fair-minded the judges may be — and, as we saw in Chapter 4, they have not always been fair-minded — they have ultimately acted as agents of the state. This has always troubled me and, in addressing the issue of religious liberty some years ago, I argued, in opposition to the Lockean and Spinozistic assumptions of most jurists and philosophers in liberal democracies, that religious leaders should have a real share in the decision-making power in such cases.[2] I continue to support this position even though I have been informed in casual conversation by certain self-professed political "experts" that it is unrealistic to believe that the institutionalization of the appropriate procedures could be implemented. Again, while ecclesiastical and other denominational courts have often done a creditable job of resolving intradenominational conflicts, they have almost invariably been dominated by the leaders of the denomination and have thus inevitably leaned, or at least appeared to lean, in the direction of the interests of the prevailing orthodoxy (which, as we have seen, may be a "liberal" orthodoxy). As it happens, over the centuries several informal methods for resolving intradenominational conflicts have also emerged;[3] but the persistence of bitter conflicts within almost every major denomination suggests that these procedures need to be improved.

At the core of any successful procedure of this type we are sure to find dialogue; for when talk stops, conflicts can only be "resolved" by the use of force, which in fact rarely resolves anything permanently or effectively and almost never resolves anything fairly. Even angry dialogue is usually better than no dialogue at all. True dialogue is a matter of talking *with* people and not just *at* them; true dialogue involves communication, communication involves listening, and listening requires attentiveness to the significance of the sounds entering one's ears. But dialogue also requires one to have something worth saying, something that one may reasonably regard as being of interest to one's partners in the dialogue. This is especially important in the case of procedures for resolving conflicts. Although the willingness to enter into dialogue with antagonists is in itself an admirable thing, a mark of good will and good sense, too many procedures for resolving conflicts fail because, when the competing parties sit down at the bargaining table, they suddenly find that they have nothing of interest to say to one another.

I raised the philosophical considerations that I did in earlier chapters partly with the hope that they may be of interest and value to people who find themselves, or will some day find themselves, faced with the task of contributing to procedures for resolving concrete disputes involving religious freedom. Institutionalized procedures of this type, like all social institutions, are only effective and valuable in proportion to the competence and integrity of the individuals who participate in them, and participants can only do their job well if they have sound theoretical conceptions with which to work. But I am not convinced that the theory I have offered here so far has been adequate for practical purposes, for the paradoxical character of so many elements in that theory troubles me greatly. So I shall now approach the constellation of problems that we have been considering from one more angle, admittedly a rather oblique one, in the hope that this final perspective will help us to see beyond some of the paradoxes.

2   The Marks of Legitimate Authority

Early on in our investigation, we took note of the basic importance of the concept of authority in any effort to understand religious freedom. I suggested then that we would not be far off the mark if we concluded from historical studies that the major struggles for religious freedom have been attempts to shake off constraints established and justified in the name of authority. I suggested that a familiar pattern emerges: people have wanted to do certain things and be certain types of people, and then along has come someone "in authority" or some group or institution professing to be "authoritative," to stand in their way. Recognizing the exercise of actual political or denominational authority to be the most significant limitation to their religious freedom, people have sometimes accepted it with gratitude and humility, sometimes merely tolerated it, and at times rebelled against it. Our subsequent philosophical, theological, social-scientific, and historical considerations have tended to bear out our initial hypothesis about the significance of conceptions of authority in relation to conceptions of religious freedom. Even when we have considered spiritual freedom, whatever it may be, we have noted the threat posed to it by the external constraint represented by the exercise of authority, and particularly by the exercise of illegitimate authority and the abusive exercise of legitimate authority. Throughout our investigation, we have focused on two main types of authority, political and denominational. We have also given some attention, in passing, to various forms of academic and professional authority. We have not, however, given any attention to what may be, as I suggested in Chapter 1, the most important form of authority in the long run, parental authority. This last form of authority is one to which we shall be giving considerable attention in this final phase of our inquiry.

Although we considered the basic concept of authority in some detail in Chapter 1, we did not systematically explore the question of the sources from which legitimate or ideal authority is derived. In the course of considering religion as a hindrance to freedom and a source of freedom, religious liberty, and religious liberalism, we touched here and there upon ideas about what legitimates certain kinds of authority, but we have not as yet exploited the insights gained there to help us to see beyond the paradoxes of religious freedom. We recognized from the start that disputes over religious freedom have involved different kinds of critical attitudes towards actual authority. Many have arisen as a result of the perception that there is an intolerable gap between actual and legitimate authority; some have arisen because of the belief that particular leaders are incapable of adequately carrying out their responsibilities; some have arisen because people have become convinced that what is legitimately authoritative in one sphere is not legitimately authoritative in another; and so on. We noted that some have even arisen because of the increased popularity of radical anti-authoritarian ideas of the kind associated with anarchy. But just as there are very few hermits, so there are very few anarchists; most people believe that significant happiness and self-realization are only possible in a community, and that some form of communal authority is a condition of communal survival. Most people believe further that, with respect to the most advanced forms of community, political societies and religious communities, authority is a condition not only of survival but of civilization, and that without substantial civility, there can be no protection of personal freedoms.

Even in the most democratic political societies and the most liberal religious denominations, there is exercise of, and respect for, the authority of some individual or group, though that authority may not be fully recognized for what it is. We must realize that, for the most part, anti-authoritarianism is not opposition to the institution of authority as such. As Novak has helpfully noted with respect to liberalism,

> The root meaning of "liberal" is "liberated from," and so there inheres in the liberal attitude a complex relation to authority. The liberal tradition, for example, has a certain authority of its own, together with a pantheon of great liberators; so one cannot say that liberals lack all respect for authority, status, and prestige. To be liberal, however, generally implies that one questions authority, values dissent, appreciates early what seems at first to be heresy, moves rather more quickly to favor what is new, and enjoys challenging regnant standards.[4]

Political and religious institutions involve authority by their very nature; authority is at the heart of these institutions. Without exercise of, and respect for, authority, there would be no phenomena that could properly be characterized as "political" or "religious." Even personal autonomy in matters of thought and action is only possible because one has been indoctrinated and conditioned in the earliest stages of life with ideas and values accepted on the basis of authority; one may go on to repudiate those ideas and values to some extent, but such repudiation is only possible because of the education one has received from those one has taken to be authorities. And education of large groups has largely been under the influence of political and religious authorities, so that we can now appreciate all the more the point made by Lecky about the influence of political and religious identification: "If we take a broad view of the course of history, and examine the relations of great bodies of men, we find that religion and patriotism are the chief moral influences to which they have been subject...."[5]

But although most people are born into the "great bodies" we know as "nations," "societies," "cultures," "peoples," "churches," and so forth, they are not entirely aware of the fact until their world-view has already been substantially formed. That world-view is initially shaped mainly by people who themselves are aware of their membership in "great bodies" but who also bring something personal — indeed intimate — to the upbringing they provide for the child. These are normally, of course, the child's natural parents, who have a unique physical and emotional bond with the child. We die alone, at least in a sense, but we are not born alone; we are delivered from the womb of someone who carried us and sustained us and suffered many forms of discomfort and inconvenience to bring us into the world, and who is ordinarily prepared to sacrifice still more for us. Our mothers and fathers are our first gods, and in a way perhaps our last ones too, for they are the primary prototypes from which we form our conceptions of supreme, transcendent reality. The family, and particularly the nuclear family, is the primary community into which a person is born; it is the first community of which he is aware, and his conception of its structure and function shapes his views on all other communities to which he comes to realize he belongs, or into which he voluntarily enters. When the natural parents cannot, will not, or are not permitted to do the job of "parenting," the task must be assigned to someone else. Plato was so obsessed by the power exercised by parents in the raising of children, and by the remarkable bond that exists between parent and child — and particularly natural parent and child — that he saw the establishment of an ideal state as requiring that the children of the leadership class be taken away from their mothers at birth and raised by professional nurses.[6] Plato was right to be obsessed here, but his recommendations were not altogether wise.

Another philosopher deeply impressed by the importance of parental authority is R. G. Collingwood, who, as we saw in Chapter 3, feels that no science of community, social or non-social, must ever forget that "A man is born a red and wrinkled lump of flesh having no will of its own at all, absolutely at the mercy of the parents by whose conspiracy he has been brought into existence."[7] Children, Collingwood reminds us, do not join the family of their own free will but rather are "drafted" into it; and children must be looked after if they are to survive.[8] But parents, or those who play the role of parents, do ideally (and usually) look forward to the time when the children in their charge will be physically and mentally mature enough to live on their own and even to raise their own families.[9] Now, although the parents want their children to grow up to have personalities of their own, they have brought children into the world (or at least taken on the role of "parenting") because they feel that they have something significant to offer in the way of bringing up a child; they feel that they are capable of contributing in this way not only to the welfare of one person but to that of the community that they hope and believe this person will enrich. The growing child requires order in his life. As Collingwood says, "A child visibly thrives when a regular life is provided for it and imposed upon it; and visibly pines when that provision is lacking. A child noticeably craves order and regularity in everything to do with its life; enjoys it when it is forthcoming, and clamours for it when it is not."[10] It almost goes without saying that a very young child looks up to those who are raising him as representing the highest authority in his world. As he becomes older and wiser, he becomes more and more impressed by the extent to which his personality and world-view have been influenced by the ideas and values of his parents (as well as, we might add, by the genetic inheritance from natural parents). Hence, it is absolutely necessary for the good of their children, their community, and humanity that those entrusted with the power of bringing up children, those who are authorities in this most fundamental way, take their responsibilities as seriously as possible. Among other things, family life prepares an individual to accept various forms of authority; for, as the typical nuclear family is the individual's prototype of all communities, parental authority is his prototype of all forms of authority.

Yet our relationship with our parents is unique; there is no other emotional bond quite like that between parent and child. Our parents love us in a very special way; they are prepared to sacrifice for us, often even to die for us. But why should one accept the authority of priest, holy man, politician, teacher, and journalist? What interest do such people have in our welfare? What makes them "higher" or "better" than us? What can they do that we cannot, and what do they know that we do not? For one thing, we must accept certain authorities as actual and too difficult to depose, and even if we distinguish in theory between legitimate and illegitimate actual authority, we can see that for important practical purposes any entrenched authority has a sort of "practical legitimacy." Without endorsing the principle that "might makes right," we can appreciate the significant extent to which the behaviour of even the most creative and most rebellious of our fellows is determined by the various powers that be. Although the very young child is not yet aware of it, he soon comes to realize that, in addition to being born into a family, he has been born into various communities whose leaders exert an influence upon him (and usually upon his parents) by means of several kinds of sanctions. Later, he may come to realize that these leaders also exert a more subtle influence through their powers of indoctrination and conditioning. These leaders may have actual authority in any number of cultural communities: linguistic, economic, ethnic, and so forth. Traditionally, however, the most important communities into which people are born are political and religious communities.

The practical sort of "legitimacy" that some actual authorities have — that is, having actual power and being seen as too difficult to depose — can be viewed negatively in terms of fear and repression or from a more neutral perspective in terms of social necessity. Much depends on the individual case and the particular leaders and subjects involved.

However, it might be said that, whenever one's acceptance of actual authority is to some extent involuntary, one necessarily feels somewhat repressed and is obedient at least partly because of fear of punishment, which may involve anything from execution, incarceration, and excommunication to ostracism and ridicule. On the other hand, common sense suggests that anarchy is not a desirable state of affairs, and that for the most part even a corrupt authority is better than no authority at all with respect to those forms of communal life that are absolutely necessary. This position was notably developed not only by Hobbes[11] but by the liberal Spinoza, who was prepared to endorse Hobbes' view that the sovereign's right is to be understood in terms of his power.[12]

Hobbes, in fact, sees God's authority in this light. This theme appears in several places in his *Leviathan*, as for example when he writes, "God is King of all the Earth by his Power."[13] Hobbes is sufficiently familiar with Scripture to know that God is not only powerful but just, wise, and merciful. However, he chooses to be more impressed by the extent to which a being with unlimited power to enforce obedience can stimulate the awe necessary for the stability of political and religious community. In any case, for those who believe in Him, God is the only god, and if one refuses to accept His authority, one will be severely punished for one's idolatry; so it is safer to reflect on how fortunate we are to have God running the universe than on how our freedom is limited by God's demands. And, significantly, our earliest attitudes towards parental authority are not very different. We start out in life with a virtually limitless trust in our parents; we have no good reason to doubt their claim that they are not only fair-minded and knowledgeable but wholly committed to what is in our best interest. However, we sometimes are more impressed by their power to enforce obedience than by their personal qualities. Even the most gentle and permissive parents are occasionally given to intimidating and punishing their young children, and some parents use violent methods to enforce obedience. The child grows to realize that her parents are not the saints and sages she was once led to believe, but even after she has developed a personality and a world-view "of her own," she is left with some of the most basic ideas, values, and attitudes of her parents, and indeed still maintains a respect for their judgement that outweighs her respect for that of people that reason suggests to her are much wiser and nobler.

So, acceptance of the "practical legitimacy" of certain actual authorities in the political and religious spheres parallels to a great extent the "practical legitimacy" of God and, in particular, one's parents. However, to those who believe in Him, God is, after all, the

Supreme Being, so whatever reservations one might have about His commands at some level of one's consciousness, it is rather easier to develop a positive attitude towards His leadership than that of mere mortals. Even though one begins to sense fairly early in life that one's parents are not necessarily the best and brightest people in the world, one can never lose sight of the fact of one's special, intimate relationship with them; however questionable my parents' values and methods may be, they are, after all, *my* parents' values and methods. But no comparable attitude is possible towards actual political and religious authorities. Whatever "practical legitimacy" such people and institutions have in our eyes is a function of their position rather than any *personal* qualities or intimate relationship with us.

However, rarely is our acceptance of actual political and religious authorities exclusively a matter of acknowledging such "practical legitimacy." Whether in the case of living authorities or more obviously in the case of a community's earlier "fathers," members of the community may see, as they are indeed encouraged to see, personal qualities of those leaders that have rendered them suitable for leadership. The idea that living authorities play something of a paternal role is reflected in much political and theological rhetoric. Political leaders tend to encourage the attitude that the *polis* is a large family of which they are the "father figures." Roman Catholic and Anglican priests are called by the name of "father," and the pope of Rome is now referred to even by many non-Catholic journalists and broadcasters as "the holy father." Of course, political constitutions are justified by reference to the wisdom and integrity of the "founding fathers" of societies, while members of religious communities are encouraged to accept traditions on the basis of the experiences, testimonies, prophecies, and teachings of the "fathers of the church" or other patriarchal figures. References to these patriarchal figures are often combined with references to God the Father, as when the Jews speak of "our God and God of our fathers." Such father figures are obviously not merely functionaries whose power and influence are to be grudgingly accepted. Rather, the acceptability of the political and religious commitments themselves is to be seen as involving a personal loyalty to one's ancestors; one's faith is the faith of one's fathers, living still. Lessing beautifully exploits this fact in *Nathan the Wise* to support religious tolerance; he has the wise Jew, Nathan, ask the relatively open-minded Muslim, Saladin, "How can I place less faith in my forefathers than you in yours? or the reverse? Can I desire of you to load your ancestors with lies, so that you contradict not mine?" Lessing's Nathan knows that he does not have to defend his faith with deep theological arguments, and that in any case doing so before Saladin would not be prudent. But here is a point on which he and Saladin can both agree: that religious faith involves trust, and that we are naturally inclined to trust "those whose flesh and blood we are . . . those who from our childhood have lavished on us proofs of love, who ne'er deceived us, unless 'twere wholesome for us so."[14]

Feminist political ideologists and theologians have raised troubling questions about all of this patriarchal talk. In fact, some of the most important qualities that we admire in our political and religious authorities — living, dead, and mythical — are qualities that are more reasonably associated with a traditional "mother figure" than a traditional "father figure." And, of course, the traditional assignment of roles to both figures has been quite arbitrary. But the point that interests us here is how the lustre of political and religious authorities is derived partly from the light of parental authorities. Since political and religious authorities generally are not so intimately related to people as to elicit the kind and degree of loyalty and affection that parents normally do, they usually attempt to convince members of their community that loyalty to them, loyalty to the community, loyalty to ancestors, and loyalty to loved ones are all indissolubly linked. But they also work hard at persuading those subject to their authority that they and the earlier authorities with whom they seek to be associated have outstanding personal qualities that make them reliable and effective leaders.

Having listened to too much political rhetoric for one lifetime, most of us know all too well the general form of the slogans used by political leaders and the public relations specialists who promote them: "I have the skills and the experience"; "I have your interests at heart"; "I am an enemy of the people who have exploited you"; "I know how to communicate with people"; "I am a true patriot"; "I have significant credentials"; and so on. We also know that those who reach positions of glory and power in religious denominations usually do so by means of a denominational politicking not all that different from the kind one encounters in secular domains. All of the puffery that is involved in politicking has the basic functions of getting people into positions of power and keeping them in those positions once they have achieved them. Undoubtedly, a certain amount of narcissism enters the picture at some point too.

Liberalism, as we have noted, disrupts the routine somewhat, for the liberal, with his anti-authoritarian inclinations, often believes in the necessity of questioning and testing actual authorities. Thinkers like Hobbes and Spinoza, who exercised so much influence on the development of liberalism in the Age of Reason and the Enlightenment, were particularly interested in the question of why and in what sense the Scriptural prophets are to be trusted. It is no coincidence that we associate this whole period in intellectual history with the dramatic rise in popularity of the theory that some personal faculty, ordinarily reason or conscience, is more authoritative in its own way than any external authority. But, as Hobbes and Spinoza observed, Hebrew Scripture itself indicates clearly that few abilities are more crucial than the ability to distinguish between true and false prophecy, and it offers something in the way of guidelines. Hobbes points out in Chapter 32 of *Leviathan* that the primary statement of those guidelines is at Deuteronomy 13, and he offers the following helpful exegesis: "[W]hat certainty is there of knowing the will of God, by other way than that of Reason? To which I answer out of the Holy Scripture, that there be two marks, by which together, not asunder, a true Prophet is to be known. One is the doing of miracles; the other is the not teaching any other Religion than that which is already established. Asunder (I say) neither of these is sufficient." Another relevant passage of Hebrew Scripture is Deuteronomy 18:20–22; at Deuteronomy 18:22 we read that, "When a prophet speaketh in the name of the Lord, if the thing follow not, nor come to pass, that is the thing which the Lord hath not spoken, but the prophet hath spoken it presumptuously; thou shalt not be afraid of him." We can see on reflection why Hobbes regards this particular guideline as "unuseful." In any case, we see from Hebrew Scripture (and the New Testament as well) that those people widely regarded over the centuries as prophets did not have an easy time convincing people in their own age of the legitimacy of their authority. Every so often, a Moses, Elijah, or Jesus was able to offer an extraordinary demonstration of his qualifications, but even then he was soon reminded that people are terribly fickle and that even the most spectacular wonders are not always enough to sustain their firm allegiance.

People do not customarily expect political authorities or even most religious authorities to perform miracles. Nevertheless, the guidelines we find in Deuteronomy are suggestive. For one thing, even if he is not advertising himself as a full-fledged prophet, people expect someone who claims to be worthy of being regarded as an authority to be able, so to speak, to "deliver the goods," especially when he has been given an opportunity to prove himself. They expect such a person to stand out from the crowd in some significant way. At the same time, they expect him to be faithful to the primary traditions of the community, and particularly to the basic moral principles underlying the communal world-view. That does not mean that they expect him to be "orthodox"; they may indeed agree with him that the self-professed "traditionalists" have obscured the essential core of the community's defining world-view, but he must be able to combine his radical conceptions in a stable synthesis with certain conceptions with which his fellows feel comfortable.

Still, as we see from Hebrew Scripture and the New Testament, even the abilities to perform the most amazing miracles and make consistently accurate predictions concerning the most important events to involve the community, combined with absolute fidelity to the most important ethical traditions of the community and unquestionable personal integrity, have not been enough to convince people of the legitimacy of one's authority. And in spheres in which the performance of miracles is not requisite — and in an age when most people do not believe in miracles — the test of true authority is inevitably all the more subjective. Moreover, from ancient times to the present day, people have constantly been willing to give their allegiance to false prophets and idols, even when in the presence of true prophets. Bury concludes his *History of Freedom of Thought* with the recommendation (and admonition) that "It should be a part of education to explain to children, as soon as they are old enough to understand, when it is reasonable, and when it is not, to accept what they are told, on authority."[15] Unfortunately, those adults entrusted with educating children (whether those adults be parents, statesmen, clerics, teachers, journalists, broadcasters, or whatever) are often not sure themselves, and when they *are* sure, they are often wrong.

Moreover, once one gets into the business of rationally assessing actual, professed, and potential authorities, it is inevitable that subjectivity will enter into one's interpretation. If we were able to interview a relatively thoughtful idolater from Scriptural times, he might justify his decision to follow a false prophet with observations like these: "How was I to know that the whole thing was a fraud? The fellow was clever, spoke beautifully, and did some amazing things. To me they looked like miracles. Besides, he quoted from traditional texts and did some good deeds too; and anyway, aren't the miracles more important than the quotations?" Such comments could easily be adapted for use in our own era.

Subjectivity is not in itself a bad thing. It is the personal nature of commitment that, perhaps more than anything else, makes human self-realization more than a mechanical affair; subjectivity is, in other words, the key to one's existential situation.[16] However, as we saw in our historical reflections, problems inevitably arise, both for individuals and communities, when the commitment of one group and the authorities accepted by one group are imposed on all groups within the community. While it is regrettable in one sense that some people follow false prophets and highly questionable authorities, such people are at least following *their* accepted prophets and authorities; but when people within a community do not work hard enough at distinguishing between those fit to lead and those unfit, they greatly increase the likelihood of the wrong people taking control of the community's affairs.

As for the rational assessment of actual, professed, and potential authorities, it must be regarded as being, on the whole, beneficial. However, one reason why God's authority and the authority of one's parents are so imposing is that they are pre-rational for us; rational appreciation of the positive qualities of such authority is, so to speak, "after the fact." But when our approval of leaders is essentially a function of rational assessment, they can never elicit the same degree of loyalty, awe, and affection. However, we shall turn in a moment to a non-rational factor that has figured greatly in judgements about the legitimacy of political and religious authority.

If we are to resolve the paradoxes of religious freedom, we must understand the kinds of political and religious authority with which people can feel comfortable, that is, the kinds that they will not regard as threats to their religious freedoms. Almost everyone, including the typical liberal critic of authoritarianism, agrees that some form of authority is necessary in both political and religious communities, and that the major personal freedoms are only possible in a stable community with sound leadership. Although critics of paternalism have rightly argued that there is no good reason why an adult should be treated in the way a child is treated, no one is so wise that he can manage to live a full life without the companionship, co-operation, and guidance of his fellows in a carefully conceived system of social organization. It is obviously desirable that those to whom we look up as authorities be more than mere functionaries and that they possess personal qualities that can be reasonably regarded as marks of the legitimacy of authority. For, if we have no confidence in actual authorities, we cannot regard ourselves as truly free, in the realm of either politics or religion. And when political leaders and religious leaders clash, or when leaders of intradenominational groups clash, it is important that we are able to determine which particular leaders are most trustworthy, regardless of their formal function.

3   Charismatic Authority

Most of us are familiar, maybe too familiar, with the term *charisma*, though few are familiar with the terms *charism* and *charismata*. That is significant, as is the fact that remarkably few people appreciate the traditional religious significance of this now popular term. Indeed, when we come to appreciate the dilution of the force of this term, we better understand the related phenomena of the loss of faith and the loss of respect for authority, which, important as they are now, are eternal human problems.

Cutting through complex etymological, historical, and theological issues, we may say that once upon a time charisma was thought of as a matter of being divinely inspired; a charism was considered to be a very special quality or capacity of a person which, being as imposing as it is, must be a direct gift from God. As the theologian Schütz tells us, the term *charisma* plays a significant role in the theology of the apostle Paul, who associates it with authority;[17] and, when we consider the significance that charismatic authority had for people many centuries ago, we realize that charismatic authority was for them essentially irrational.[18] If their acceptance of the authority of a charismatic individual was itself irrational — as was the charismatic authority itself — then it was also highly personal, indeed intimate, much as was their acceptance of the authority of God Himself or their parents.

Nowadays, people are in the habit of attributing charisma to all sorts of people; only occasionally, however, do they attribute it to religious leaders, and even more rarely do they appreciate the term's historical connection with religious conceptions. In fact, it is striking that those historical figures who would once have been regarded as being the principal paradigms of the charismatic individual had qualities that would nowadays ordinarily disqualify them from being regarded as charismatic. For example, we read at Exodus 4:10–13: "And Moses said unto the Lord, O my Lord, I am not eloquent, neither heretofore, nor since thou hast spoken unto thy servant; but I am slow of speech, and of a slow tongue. And the Lord said unto him, Who hath made man's mouth? or who maketh the dumb, or deaf, or the seeing, or the blind? have not I the Lord? Now therefore go, and I will be with thy mouth, and teach thee what thou shalt say. And he said, O my Lord, send, I pray thee, by the hand of him whom thou wilt send." So the greatest of the Hebrew prophets, a man whom "the Lord knew face to face,"[19] went off to do God's will with the help of his brother, Aaron, who was not a stutterer. However, when the role of Moses is portrayed in Hollywood motion pictures, Moses rarely is depicted as a stutterer; movie directors feel that audiences will not stand for a stuttering Moses — any more than they will stand for a stuttering broadcaster, lecturer, or spokesman — so the directors correct what they consider to be one of God's little mistakes. And Socrates, the archetypal philosopher, who considered himself divinely inspired and was regarded as such by his followers,[20] impressed most people of his time as much by his ugliness, poverty, and lack of elegance and sophistication as by his wit, wisdom, and spirituality. Today, a figure so absurd-looking and unkempt would find it virtually impossible to be taken seriously by academic scholars, much less ordinary citizens, and that is certainly not because we now appreciate beauty and refinement more than the ancient Greeks did.

However, not only do people nowadays still regard many individuals as charismatic, but they continue to associate charisma with authority. They are prepared to listen attentively to what such "charismatic" individuals have to say, regardless of how trivial, and they are increasingly fascinated with their private lives, regardless of how empty. These "charismatic" individuals exercise an influence in their communities that is wholly out of proportion to their personal qualities. People want to be like them; people model themselves after them. People want to associate with them and be associated with them. People watch them on their televisions and read about them in their magazines. People are prepared to pay large sums of money to be entertained by, inspired by, or even just exposed to them, as a consequence of which these individuals are obscenely wealthy in terms of material possessions. People quote them, imitate them, dress like them, and sooner or later begin to think like them, at least to the extent that an "unimportant" person can think along the same lines as an "important" one. People see them as being particularly gifted in various ways, and they regard them as the creatures that really matter in this world.

I refer, of course, to the "celebrities" who occupy so much of the conscious (and probably unconscious) thought of so many of our fellow human beings. I refer to celebrities from every domain of cultural activity — from the worlds of politics, arts and entertainment, sports, business, the professions, "scholarship," technology, terrorism, organized crime, religion, and so on. Some of these people are genuinely gifted. Few stutter or are ridiculously ugly and impoverished with respect to material goods. I am convinced, perhaps unjustifiably, that even fewer are divinely inspired.

If such celebrities are not divinely inspired, then how is it that they have come to be so widely regarded as charismatic, and how is it that they have managed to come to be looked upon by so many people as authorities, even with respect to matters far removed from the specific domains in which their unusual gifts may lie? This is a fair question and an important one, and I am not sure that I can give an entirely satisfactory answer to it. However, I shall venture a few suggestions. My first suggestion is that the historic struggle for the extension of fundamental freedoms, with its anti-authoritarian rhetoric, has, for all the great good it has done, intensified some remarkable confusions in people's minds. On the one hand, almost all people recognize the practical need for authority figures, living as well as mythical or from the past; moreover, even if people like Nietzsche and Karamazov's Grand Inquisitor have overstated the point, most people have a craving for leadership. They need surrogate parents to whom to look up at every stage of their lives; they never entirely outgrow that need. In Kant's words, it is so comfortable to be a minor and to have people giving you guidance and direction. This is true not only in the political and religious spheres, but in other areas as well. On the other hand, people also resent interference with their freedoms, and they especially resent people who hold themselves up as being wiser and better than they are. That is why they are so often attracted to leaders and authorities that they perceive as being so much like themselves. And so people have increasingly come to make a psychological compromise whereby they look up to people who appear to be superior to them in certain ways but are also, in ways that are at least as important, distinctly no better than they are. Although this psychological compromise is certainly characteristic of most modern thought and culture, it was recognized by the most perceptive of the ancients. Plato understood it particularly clearly, and his contempt for it animates much of his criticism of democracy.[21] Many of the Hebrew prophets seem to me to have understood it. However, in our own generation, after many centuries of anti-authoritarian rhetoric, the attitude has become more and more entrenched. It is now akin to the *ressentiment* against which Nietzsche is constantly warning superior people.[22]

A related point concerns the increasing influence of "public relations." Of course, public relations is not a new business. Once again, Plato understood it quite well, and his awareness of it was at the heart of his hostility to the Sophists, who, denying the existence of absolute reality, truth, and goodness, busied themselves with "appearances," and made themselves comfortable and prominent in the "higher" circles by showing disciples how to be "successful" through cultivating certain styles of talking, arguing, and even thinking. The greatest moral and religious teachers, and many not as great, have learned from bitter experience how difficult it can be to compete with the imposter, with the false prophet and pseudo-authority who cozens and misleads the masses, and particularly the most sophisticated among the masses, with his sophistical talk and high style. With the aid of self-serving sycophants, such an imposter becomes the master of shadows and illusions; he learns to package and process false charisma and to promote it at the expense of anything even remotely resembling the authentic article. Need I add that the "success" of such a person is illusory? Yet such a person does much harm to individuals, and he slows down the process of civilization, and may even temporarily reverse it.

It takes little imagination to realize that our own age is, more than any that has preceded it, an age of "hype." False charisma has come to infect even the most spiritual domains, the worlds of religion, education, art, and high culture. When we look at the so-called "real world," it may sometimes seem that authentic power is only in the hands of operators, schemers, manipulators, and charlatans. So many people seem to be fascinated and awed by worthless celebrities — by crooked politicians, callous bureaucrats, hypocritical clerics, and venal professionals. Young people emulate their parents in looking up to professional athletes who earn in a week the salary that a dedicated social worker, nurse, or musician earns in a year. The airwaves are awash in a sea of babble directed at the public by people almost ironically characterized as "personalities": terrorist "freedom fighters," professorial "experts," popular psychologists, and ignorant, self-important "newsmen" and talk-show hosts. Everyone seems to be hawking something, including her "personality." Mindless Hollywood starlets have unlimited access to the mass media of communication, while the most thoughtful and compassionate people, people with genuine integrity, are dismissed as bores and pedants. Even in the world of learning and scholarship, appearance increasingly matters more than substance. Scholars are judged more and more by whom they know rather than what they know, and by where they come from rather than what they have to say. Civilization is choking on false charisma and phoney credentials.

I have one more suggestion. False charismatic authority has so easily supplanted true charismatic authority partly because of the diminution of faith itself. There is a troubling pattern to the descent: the diminution of faith leads to an inability to appreciate the true worth that ideally legitimates authority, and the half-hearted respect for false charismatic authority contributes to the further diminution of faith. Even people who consider themselves to be religious find it harder and harder to take seriously the notion that someone can literally be divinely inspired. And so they are increasingly prepared to settle for less and, as we have seen, that is just what they get.

But what if there are people who are genuinely charismatic, who are actually divinely inspired? What if there are people out there in the world who are truly fit to be our political, religious, and other cultural authorities? What if there are people who really ought to be trusted and followed, people whose words we should heed and whose example we should follow? If there really are such people, then we cannot afford to ignore them, any more than the Israelites could afford to ignore a Moses or the Greeks could afford to ignore a Socrates.

If such people exist, there is reason to hope that we can get beyond the paradoxes of religious freedom. For, if such people become our authorities, then we will not feel unfree when we accept their leadership and guidance. Ideally, with them at the helm of political and religious communities, there would be no more squabbles over power, fights over shadows, among self-serving incompetents who do not know what to do with whatever actual authority they already enjoy. Power would then be in the hands of people with genuine humility, people who would inspire in others a genuine humility. Spiritual freedom would be possible. We would really matter to the people to whom we look up, and we would be able to look up to them whole-heartedly, with genuine respect and affection, and with confidence and hope.

But where are we to find such people? Who today can perform miracles and wonders? Who will come to the defence of the noblest traditions of our community and all of humanity's communities? Who can make us look upon their political, religious, or other cultural authority as something akin to the authority with which we associate the Divine and the noblest aspirations of the parents who brought us into the world and nurtured us, sacrificed for us, and hoped for our sake?

Frankly, I don't know. I suppose that we just have to keep our eyes open and keep looking for clues. In the absence of philosophical wisdom, I offer a story, a true story. Imagine the author in a queue with hundreds of other people in Duffy Square in the heart of Manhattan, with taxis and other cars whizzing by and pedestrians running frantically in all directions. The people in the queue are waiting to purchase theatre tickets at a discount, and most of them appear to be in good spirits; they are smiling, conversing with one another and, in some cases, making amusing gestures. In the midst of all of this hubbub and razzle-dazzle, an isolated figure, a man who might be anywhere from thirty to sixty years of age, makes his way to the heart of the square. He is dirty, unkempt, and apparently confused; as he is holding a paper bag with a bottle in it, the people in the queue probably reasonably assume that he must be drunk. This isolated figure has momentarily disrupted the levity of the people in the queue, for even those who pretend not to see him have suddenly become quiet. What can be going on in their minds? Do they feel sorry for him? Are they disgusted by him? Do they feel partly responsible for the situation of such a person? Are they afraid of him? The distraction has proved to be only momentary, and spirits are revived. But then the isolated figure stumbles and falls to the ground, striking his head against a bench. The people in the queue are now very uncomfortable. After a few minutes, another isolated figure appears. A woman of about twenty years of age has left the queue and walked over to the man; though dressed in fine clothes, this slight young woman reaches out to the man and lifts him off the ground, brushes some of the dirt off him, leans his head against a tree, smiles at him, and exchanges a few words with him. Then she resumes her place in the queue and, with the grace and lack of self-consciousness of a prima ballerina, she carries on with her life.

Meanwhile, the author, who has long taken for granted his inability to do anything concretely useful in a difficult situation, is given to reflecting on what might now be going on in the minds of the various people who have watched this little episode of urban drama. What can all of these theatre-lovers make of the young woman's solitary response? Was the young woman silly and naive for not minding her own business? Could she really have believed that she was accomplishing something significant? Was she trying to impress her friends or relatives in the queue? Was she trying to make the other people in the queue look bad? Did the man on the ground remind her of someone she once knew? Is she some sort of self-righteous religious fanatic? Is she just a good person? There are some people in the queue who will have been more stimulated and enlightened by that little dramatic episode than by the Broadway show they will soon be seeing.

There is little point here in being sentimental. Hundreds of episodes of this kind take place every day and in all parts of the world. If one has studied even a little psychology, sociology, or philosophy, then it is easy to be unimpressed by a simple act of charity, especially when it seems to have cost the agent so little. If we are troubled a bit by our own consistent failure to perform such acts, then we can look at those who perform them from a Machiavellian perspective, or a Nietzschean one, or a Freudian one. Cynicism is very much in fashion, now as always; thanks to a lot of high-powered intellects, we have come to "see" that few things are as easily explained away as virtue and civility. Yet maybe these high-powered intellects are wrong; maybe the behaviour of people like that young woman that day in Duffy Square should not be explained away but should be studied sympathetically, appreciated, admired, and used as a model for our own self-improvement. That young woman gave evidence of the fact that she was a leader, that she can take the moral and practical initiative. She showed herself to be a guardian of the best in the moral traditions of her own communities and the human community. She provided some of her fellow human beings with an effective lesson in moral education, one that outstripped anything that could be offered by a typical preacher or moral philosopher. For all we know, the woman may be no better than the rest of us, or even a good deal worse. But on the basis of the little that we have seen of her, there is some reason to believe that this woman may be a very significant human being, the sort of person who keeps civilization moving ahead. Is she not perhaps the kind of person we need, not only in queues, but in a position of authority? And, assuming for the moment that this woman is what she appeared to be on that summer day in Manhattan, can we not conclude that the world would be a much better place if our prime ministers, bishops, and mass media "personalities" were more like this woman than they are?

Dare we entertain the notion that there is even something miraculous about a deed like hers? Can a wholly "unknown" figure like her be truly charismatic? And if not in her case, can we not at least regard as miraculous certain acts of heroism, sacrifice, and martyrdom that we too often take for granted and forget? In the midst of the worst outbursts of barbarism, there are always individuals who take a firm stand against evil; and in light of the numerous incentives for them to be like almost everyone else — to mind their own business and concentrate on their own private interests — these people miraculously do what is right instead of what is prudent, what is noble instead of what is conventionally approved. These people may be the ideal authorities; to be spiritually free may be, among other things, to be free from the influence of the "hype" and false charisma that prevent us from fully appreciating the true worth of such people, these inspired workers of miracles, individuals meant to lead.

The concept of miracle is a complex one that has elicited considerable philosophical discussion. By the time of Spinoza and Hume, philosophers were given to taking miracles lightly. Testimony about miracles is not nearly as impressive as bearing witness to them, and in any case, with recent advances in technology, tales of the miraculous have lost much of their glamour. In an era when men and women fly around in outer space, "special effects" hands at motion picture studios can part waters or turn them into blood. However, even in Scriptural times, the greatest wonders of all were the *moral* wonders, although they were generally not recognized in those days for their true importance. Even the ignorant of Scriptural times could be impressed by the parting of a sea, but it would have taken more understanding to appreciate the full importance of a prophet's willingness to confront an angry God with the words, "Turn from thy fierce wrath, and repent of this evil against thy people."[23]

4   Authority and Love

Early on in our investigation I criticized the Roman Catholic apologist Yves Simon for justifying arbitrary paternalism with his comment that "One who is ruled for his own good or for the common good is a free man."[24] Countless violations of human dignity have been "justified" by such a principle. However, in the same place, Simon makes a valid and helpful point: "Authority cannot be in any way identified with coercion, which is only one of its possible instruments. As a matter of fact, persuasion is used by authority much more often than coercion. No social life would be possible if authority should have all its decisions enforced by coercive procedures."[25] The very term *paternalism* rarely inspires wholly negative feelings; even people who have been abused by their parents often retain a somewhat mysterious affection for them. The influence that our parents exert upon us, even long after their death, cannot ordinarily be characterized as simply "coercive." We want to please our parents; we want them to be proud of us. Even after they have finished with this life, we still often wonder in a given situation what it is that they might have hoped we would do. A behaviourist might argue that the coercive procedures are merely more subtle here; but a behaviourist who argued in this way would be pretentious, shallow, and stupid. What is really subtle in this domain is the relation between authority and love.

The term *love* has been so debased by pop singers, Hollywood screenwriters, advertising agents, and popular psychologists that I am hesitant to employ it, especially in a book that will be of interest mainly to academic scholars. But I need it, so I am going to use it anyway. Consider how people have quite consistently been prepared to make sacrifices on account of love that even fear, torture, and the force of rational argument could not compel them to make. When someone makes the greatest sacrifices that a person can make in this life in order to protect the interests of a loved one, people will say, "It was an act of love," as if there were nothing else to be said. Maybe there is in fact nothing else to be said. However, what interests us here is simply the relation of authority to love. Obviously, those we love exert a unique kind of influence upon our judgement and behaviour. So powerful can that influence be that we are sometimes inclined to apologize for it: "I have no choice in the matter; you see, I love these people very much, and I wouldn't do anything to hurt them." Such phrases are very significant: they suggest that a loved one's power to "enforce obedience" is so great that it may even seem to be an obstacle to personal autonomy. There may be some truth to Nietzsche's suggestion that everyone for whom we feel affection is a kind of "nook" that draws us away from our personal schemes.[26] But having loving relationships is a central part of life. One of the most famous photographs in the history of philosophy is a charming picture of Nietzsche with his tiny mother. After Nietzsche went mad, it was his mother who looked after him; after she died, his sister took over and proceeded to do considerable damage to both Nietzsche and his reputation.

If loved ones can effectively enforce obedience, then perhaps the behaviourist is not so shallow after all. But a loved one does not use force at all, nor does she expect us to "obey" her "commands." Such terminology is inappropriate to the characterization of manifestations of love. Thus, when a person apologizes for the influence of loved ones by asserting "I have no choice in the matter," he is misleading us and perhaps deceiving himself in the process. There certainly is a sense in which he does have a choice in the matter; and if there is also a sense in which he does not have a choice in the matter, it has nothing to do with coercion, force, or obedience. A commitment to another human being is like a commitment to a world-view, in this sense at least: both require some degree of personal acceptance, and such acceptance follows upon a certain amount of scrutiny of one's existential "situation." One may be said to have been to some extent indoctrinated to think and conditioned to behave in the way one's parents determined one to do, but that has little, if anything, to do with one's *love* for one's parents.

It should not be surprising that the sacred works of the Western traditions constantly associate Divine authority with love. Consider Christianity. Even those whose Christianity is of the most primitive sort recognize the importance of God's love for them. A primary focus of the gospel accounts of the life of Jesus is on Jesus' love for humanity and his great sacrifice for humanity: "For this is my blood of the new testament, which is shed for many for the remission of sins."[27] But the love must be reciprocal. It is not enough even to love one's neighbour; the first and foremost commandment is love of God. Nowhere is Jesus more severe than in his judgement on his persecutors: "But I know you, that ye have not the love of God in you."[28] "Thou shalt love the Lord thy God with all thy heart, and with all thy soul, and with all thy mind. This is the first and great commandment."[29] There are places in the New Testament where the association of God with love is metaphysical, as at 2 Corinthians 13:11 where Paul speaks of the God of love and peace, or even more strikingly at 1 John 4:8 where we read, "He that loveth not knoweth not God; for God is love." Acceptance of Divine authority is not a matter of fear or necessity; it is a matter of reciprocal love.

God's love for His people and for all humanity is vividly described by the Hebrew prophets. One may consider in this regard, for example, the book of Hosea, or Jeremiah 31:3: "The Lord hath appeared of old unto me, saying, Yea, I have loved thee with an everlasting love; therefore with lovingkindness have I drawn thee." At the core of Judaism is the commandment that we have already seen echoed by Jesus: "And thou shalt love the Lord thy God with all thine heart, and with all thy soul, and with all thy might. And these words, which I command thee this day, shall be in thine heart."[30] It is only in such a context that we can understand the Fatherhood/Motherhood of God and the brotherhood/sisterhood of our fellow human beings. The highest exemplification of the personality of God is not in the God who judges but is not to be judged; it is in the God who loves and is to be loved. Ultimately, the authority of God is based on God's love for His creatures and their reciprocal love for God.

Some philosophers have been greatly perplexed by the Scriptural injunction to love God. Kant, for example, is so confused about it that he concludes that what it must mean is that we should like doing God's commandments.[31] What Kant fails to realize is that one's attitude towards God's commandments is conditioned by one's attitude towards God. If one conceives of God as a terrifying bully or despot who is making one's life miserable, then no matter how hard one tries, one cannot feel spiritually free, and one cannot like doing God's commandments. These matters were better understood by Spinoza, who emphasizes throughout the last part of his *Ethics* that true freedom can only be attained through the intellectual *love* of God, and not fear of God. In a letter to Blyenbergh, Spinoza writes:

> Therefore since the pious have incalculably more perfection than the ungodly, their virtue cannot be compared with that of the ungodly because the ungodly lack the love of God which springs from the knowledge of Him, and whereby alone we, according to our human understanding, are said to be the servants of God. Indeed, since they know not God, they are no more than a tool in the hand of the master which serves unconsciously, and perishes in the service; on the other hand, the pious serve consciously, and become more perfect by their service.[32]

And in defending himself from the charge that he is an enemy of religion, Spinoza asks, "Does that man, I pray, cast aside all religion who declares that God must be recognized as the Highest Good, and that He must be loved as such with a free spirit? and that in this alone does our highest felicity and supreme liberty consist?"[33] In the same letter he adds: "I have expressly said that the sum [and substance] of the divine law . . . and its supreme injunction are to love God as the highest good; that is, not from fear of some punishment (for love cannot spring from fear) nor for love of some other object, by which we hope to be gratified, for then we should not so much love God Himself as that which we desire."[34] Spinoza has his own special conception of the love of God as essentially intellectual, but his more basic points are of general interest.

In fact, Spinoza's association of love of God with knowledge of God is instructive in its own right. What sense, after all, are we to make of an injunction to love God or, for that matter, to love anyone? How can love be commanded when, as most of us know from experience, affection is not something that one can turn on and off like water from a tap? The answer may lie in one's continuing obligation to make an effort to understand and appreciate those qualities of God — or one's neighbour — that merit our affection and provide a firm foundation for our trust. Compare one's love for a parent. In the first phase of one's relationship with one's parents, one's love is largely a matter of dependence; Schleiermacher's famous expression, "absolute dependence," comes to mind. As one matures and becomes more sophisticated and somewhat philosophical in one's reflections, one develops mixed feelings towards parents and their authority. One is able to love one's parents more deeply insofar as one has a better understanding of both their frailties and disappointments and their positive qualities, as well as of the sacrifices that they have been prepared to make to protect and further one's interests; yet one's love is apt to be tempered by an increasing realization of the extent to which one's parents have consciously and unconsciously established limits to one's personal autonomy, and will continue to do so. Mature love can only be achieved by the overcoming of resentment. Parents often are given to saying such things to their children as "Trust me; when you are older, you will see that what I am requiring you to do now is for your own good." Though parents sometimes use such words to deceive their children, or are deceived themselves, they are usually speaking honestly, so that it is crucial that children be able to summon up enough trust and good will to be open to a more mature understanding and appreciation of the significance of parental authority. The attitude towards transcendent authority may be understood along similar lines. Early in life one tends to associate the authority of a personal God with that Being's power as such; even then one does not simply fear God, for one is taught to think of God also in terms of such qualities as wisdom and mercy. However, it is usually the idea of her absolute dependence on God the King that is most prominent in the young child's consciousness. As one matures, and one becomes increasingly aware of the suffering to which mortals seem almost to have been condemned, resentment towards transcendent authority inevitably enters the picture. One may toy with the possibility of blaming God for one's miseries and frustrations; one may consider rejecting God. When they are vulnerable in this way, as they continue to be at many crucial points in their lives, religious people need to regard it as their obligation to remain open to an understanding and appreciation of God, and of all the good things that have happened to them in this life, and of the possibility of future joys and accomplishments.

Scripture provides us with many vivid pictures of what such openness involves, but none is more powerful than that of Job, a righteous man beset by one terrible misfortune after another, sitting among the ashes. "Then said his wife unto him, Dost thou still retain thine integrity? curse God, and die. But he said unto her, Thou speakest as one of the foolish women speaketh. What? shall we receive good at the hand of God, and shall we not receive evil? In all this did not Job sin with his lips."[35]

Permissiveness towards blasphemy is one of the outstanding characteristics of much contemporary culture. In the communist world, blasphemy has been institutionalized; materialist ideologists have made war on transcendent Spirit. In North America and Western Europe, where many people pride themselves on having religious freedom, blasphemy routinely appears on the airwaves, in periodicals, and in casual conversation. Since such blasphemy is treated jocularly by those who indulge in it and tolerate it, it is even more offensive in its own way than the calculated blasphemy of Marxists. Blasphemy, with its contempt for spirituality, is a sign of the obstinate refusal to be open to an understanding and appreciation of spiritual things. Parallel to it is the encouragement that popular psychologists give to young people to mistrust the authority of their parents, and to blame their parents for all of their neuroses and incapacities in life. But to where can people turn if they cannot turn to a transcendent Spirit or even to their own loved ones? "Trust *us*," answer the false prophets.

There are people who have tried hard to love God, their kin, and their neighbours, and have consistently failed. They have not even been capable of the existential resignation commended to them by a Pascal. It is not always easy for someone whose parents have truly done wrong by him to see beyond the wounds they have left; and there have been people in this world who have suffered far worse than Job, and have not been gifted with Job's patience. We cannot reasonably expect their attitude towards authority to be as "loving" as that of others. And perhaps there are false prophets who can at least bring some peace of mind to such people. But many people simply do not try hard enough, either because they are deficient in will or in intellect, or because they find some consolation in wallowing in resentment.

Even if one is prepared to grant that there is a special link between love and the acceptance of certain kinds of authority, particularly the authority of God and parental authority, and that an understanding of that link helps us to appreciate how acceptance of authority is compatible with freedom, one may well be at a loss to understand how these points are relevant to our relationships with the various political and religious authorities with which we have been concerned throughout our investigation. Is one obliged to love politicians? Is one even obliged to love the pillars of orthodoxy who dominate one's religious community? Is one obliged to "accept" in some sense the leadership of corrupt individuals and elites?

While it may be possible to love such authorities, even when they are thoroughly corrupt, I cannot see how it is obligatory or appropriate to love such figures. Nevertheless, we can see that freedom is to some extent a function of one's attitude towards such authorities. There are many possible degrees to which one can accept authority. A person who is committed to such radically anti-authoritarian notions that she is led to despise any form of authority is destined to be tormented by her constant awareness of her bondage. A more positive, less grudging, attitude towards actual authority, even if it requires a certain amount of self-deception, can bring one some of that spiritual freedom associated with peace of mind. The intense hatred of actual political and religious authorities can serve as an incentive to undermine their genuinely destructive influence, but being irrational by nature, it may involve blindness to the positive qualities of those authorities, and can lead to forms of resentment that are paralyzing or self-destructive. So, even if one is not obliged to love most actual authorities, one may be prudentially as well as morally well advised to be open to a more generous appraisal of their suitability for leadership. Such openness may well require less in the way of self-deception than one fears. One way of being free is not being constrained by the resentment that prevents one from recognizing the true worth of others. Related forms of bondage are the inabilities to trust our fellows, to accept graciously the guidance of those who know things that we do not, and to overcome envy, narcissism, and false pride.

But openness to a deeper understanding and appreciation of the positive qualities of actual authorities does not require a refusal to understand and appreciate the qualities of those who might be more suited to lead; neither does it require a refusal to understand and weigh the negative qualities of actual authorities. Men and women are not gods, and most authorities do not warrant from us the same degree of gratitude and concern that our parents do. The degree to which we accept and support existing and potential authorities, whether in the political, religious, or any other cultural sphere, must reflect in part a basically realistic appraisal of their qualities. While a little self-deception may be necessary for our own good, more than a little is irresponsibly indulgent. Our final appraisal of actual and potential authorities must take into account the demands of other authorities, perhaps higher ones, and the interests of our neighbours, our fellows in the community and in other communities. And it is natural to attach particular importance to our own interests and our own existential commitments, and those of people especially close to us.

To the extent, then, that we are capable of contributing to the resolution of conflicts between political and religious leaders, or conflicts between religious leaders and their critics within our religious community, we must be guided by careful, disciplined evaluations of the character of the competing authorities. Our evaluations should be as generous as possible without being irresponsibly unrealistic. Appreciation must always be based on understanding. We need to be able to see beyond false, packaged charisma to what may be the genuine article, or is at the very least the closest to it that we are likely to find at this point in history. In considering our own freedoms and those of others, we need to be mindful of the extent to which the acceptance of authority involves some degree of personal commitment.

So, these considerations may be added to the others, gathered at the various stages of our investigation, that we might bring to any institutionalized or informal procedures for resolving the various kinds of conflict that arise with respect to religious freedom. With these last considerations, our investigation comes to an end. As one completes the reading of a book on moral and religious subjects, one may be moved to reflect on what may seem to be an immense gap between ideals and realities, and between the thought provoked by a book and the action demanded by the exigencies of everyday life and the many forces over which one has little or no control. One's respect for men and women of action may even bring with it a concomitant suspicion about the value of philosophical reflection. Yet ideals are realities in their own way; and, as thought is what makes action possible, disciplined reflection is ultimately what makes significant action possible.

When we look at the so-called "real world," it may sometimes seem, as I suggested earlier, that authentic power is so securely in the hands of false charismatic authorities, and other operators and schemers, that there is little that idealistic people can accomplish in the way of improving the quality of communal life. If we dwell on that notion, we risk becoming cynical. Cynicism is a very destructive force: it robs us of the opportunity to attain any form of spiritual freedom, and it alienates us from our fellows. We must not ignore human evil; we have to be able to recognize it in all its forms so that we can fight it with whatever weapons are available to us. But we do not have to dwell on it, and sometimes we need to give our vexed spirit a rest by reminding ourselves of all the true nobility manifested in the world.

Consider, then, a transcendent Spirit, One perhaps "merciful and gracious, long-suffering, and abundant in goodness and truth." If you are unable to form such an image in your mind, think of all the wise, just, and vital people who have inhabited this world, including those we have recalled in this inquiry, such as Sebastian Castellio and Roger Williams of Providence. If you cannot relate to these figures from another age, then look around you for people like the young woman in Duffy Square, and when all else fails, think of the Divine mystery of the love of a mother who would be prepared to sacrifice her happiness or even her life in order to secure yours. If you are one of those rare, extremely unfortunate people who are not even in a position to do that, then think of yourself, and particularly about the fact that here you have taken some of the limited time allotted to you in this life to think about spiritual things instead of material ones, when you might just as well have been thinking about trivialities, such as commercially packaged pleasures and how to "succeed" at the expense of other human beings. My point is not that you should be congratulating yourself, or looking down at people who are of no substantial value because they value nothing substantial. Rather, I have reminded you of your own spiritual concerns so that there will be less chance of your being immobilized by the cynicism that tests the worthy as well as the worthless, and so that you will be less likely to undervalue the fact that, though you and I have little in the way of social power, we are obliged to do the best we can, using whatever special gifts are available to us, to uphold the cause of freedom and kindred ideals. This task is mainly to be accomplished through personal influence. In the words of John Henry Newman, "such considerations lead us to be satisfied with the humblest and most obscure lot; by showing us, not only that we may be the instruments of much good in it, but that (strictly speaking) we could scarcely in any situation be direct instruments of good to any besides those who personally know us, who ever must form a small circle; and as to the indirect good we may do in a more exalted station (which is by no means to be lightly esteemed), still we are not precluded from it in a lower place...."[36]

Notes

Chapter 1

1. John Courtney Murray, "Religious Freedom," in John Courtney Murray, ed., *Freedom and Man* (New York: P. J. Kenedy and Sons, 1965), p. 135.
2. Maurice Cranston, *Freedom: A New Analysis* (2nd ed.; London: Longmans, Green, 1954 [1953]), p. 14.
3. Jacques Ellul, *The Ethics of Freedom*, trans. and ed. Geoffrey W. Bromiley (Grand Rapids, Mich.: William B. Eerdmans, 1976), p. 438.
4. Cecil Northcott, *Religious Liberty* (London: SCM Press, 1948), p. 18.
5. M. Searle Bates, *Religious Liberty: An Inquiry* (New York: Da Capo Press, 1972), p. 295. This volume is a reprint of a work first published in 1945 under the auspices of the World Council of Churches.
6. *Ibid.*, p. 373.
7. John Kersey, *Dictionarium Anglo-Britannicum* (1708).
8. John Walker, *A Critical Pronouncing Dictionary and Expositor of the English Language* (1791).
9. Contrast the entries in *Klein's Comprehensive Etymological Dictionary of the English Language* (1971) and Eric Partridge, *Origins: A Short Etymological Dictionary of Modern English* (1961).
10. See, e.g., *The Oxford English Dictionary* (1933), *The American Heritage Dictionary* (1982), *Webster's Seventh New Collegiate Dictionary* (1965), *Chambers 20th Century Dictionary* (1982), and *The Concise Oxford Dictionary* (1982).
11. Peter Slater, *The Dynamics of Religion* (London: SCM Press, 1979), p. 6. The original is italicized.
12. Jean Holm, *The Study of Religions* (New York: Seabury Press, 1977), p. 18.
13. The concepts of world-view and commitment are discussed in detail in Jay Newman, *Fanatics and Hypocrites* (Buffalo: Prometheus Books, 1986), ch. 1 and 4.
14. Charles B. Ketcham and James F. Day, "Freedom as Experienced and as Thought" (postscript), in Charles B. Ketcham and James F. Day, ed., *Faith and Freedom: Essays in Contemporary Theology* (New York: Weybright and Talley, 1969), p. 249.
15. Walker, *Critical Pronouncing Dictionary*.

16. Cf. n. 10.
17. Cf., e.g., *Klein's Comprehensive Etymological Dictionary.*
18. Peter C. Hodgson, *New Birth of Freedom: A Theology of Bondage and Liberation* (Philadelphia: Fortress Press, 1976), pp. 8–9.
19. *Ibid.*, p. 10.
20. Herbert J. Muller, *Issues of Freedom: Paradoxes and Promises* (New York: Harper and Brothers, 1960), p. 3.
21. *Ibid.*, p. 5.
22. *Ibid.*, pp. 5–6.
23. *Ibid.*, p. 6.
24. *Ibid.*
25. Cranston, *Freedom*, p. 6.
26. *Ibid.*, p. 3.
27. Contrast Cranston, *Freedom*, p. 4, with Muller, *Issues*, pp. 5–6.
28. See, e.g., a parallel criticism of Cranston's analysis of liberalism in D. J. Manning, *Liberalism* (London: J. M. Dent and Sons, 1976), pp. 57–59.
29. Cranston, *Freedom*, p. 28.
30. *Ibid.*, p. 5.
31. *Ibid.*, p. 16.
32. *Ibid.*, ch. 5.
33. *Ibid.*, p. 21.
34. *Ibid.*, p. 5.
35. Joseph F. Rychlak, *Discovering Free Will and Personal Responsibility* (New York and Oxford: Oxford University Press, 1979), p. 10.
36. Daniel Callahan, "Freedom and the Layman," in Murray, ed., *Freedom and Man*, p. 155.
37. Christopher Dawson, *Religion and the Modern State* (London: Sheed and Ward, 1938), p. 128.
38. Austin Farrer, *The Freedom of the Will* (London: Adam and Charles Black, 1958), p. 107.
39. Yves Simon, *Freedom and Community*, ed. Charles P. O'Donnell (New York: Fordham University Press, 1968), p. 4.
40. *Ibid.*
41. *Ibid.*, p. 16. Cf. Jacques Maritain, *Freedom in the Modern World* (New York: Charles Scribner's Sons, 1936).
42. Simon, *Freedom*, p. 53.
43. Piet Fransen, "Grace and Freedom," in Murray, ed., *Freedom and Man*, p. 34.
44. Cf. Friedrich Nietzsche, *Beyond Good and Evil* (1886), sec. 6.
45. Baruch (Benedict) Spinoza, *Ethics* (1677), Part 1, definition 7, trans. William Hale White (1883), rev. Amelia Hutchinson Stirling (1894, 1899), and further ed. James Gutmann (New York: Hafner, 1949).
46. *Ibid.*, Part 2, proposition 35: demonstration.
47. Cf. Jay Newman, "The Compatibilist Interpretation of Spinoza," *The Personalist* 55 (Autumn, 1974), 360–68.
48. Spinoza, *Ethics*, Part 2, proposition 49: note.
49. Muller, *Issues*, p. 13. Cf. Newman, "Compatibilist Interpretation."

50. Bas van Iersel and Edward Schillebeeckx, "Editorial," *Concilium: Theology in the Age of Renewal* 3, no. 10 (March, 1974 [n.s.]), 7.
51. N. O. Lossky, *Freedom of Will*, trans. Natalie Duddington (London: Williams and Norgate, 1932), p. 10.
52. Jean-Yves Calvez, "Possibilities of Freedom in Tomorrow's Complex Society," in Murray, ed., *Freedom and Man*, pp. 176–77.
53. H. Richard Niebuhr, *The Responsible Self* (New York: Harper and Row, 1963), p. 101.
54. See, e.g., works by writers as different as Nietzsche, Berdyaev, Marcel, and Camus.
55. Muller, *Issues*, p. 9.
56. Reinhold Niebuhr, "The Commitment of the Self and the Freedom of the Mind," in Perry Miller, Robert L. Calhoun, Nathan M. Pusey, and Reinhold Niebuhr, *Religion and Freedom of Thought* (Freeport, N.Y.: Books for Libraries Press, 1971), p. 55. This volume is a reprint of a work first published in 1954 by Doubleday and based on a series of lectures at Union Theological Seminary.
57. Josef Neuner, "No Monopoly in Promoting Freedom," *Concilium* 3, no. 10 (March, 1974 [n.s.]), 37.
58. Hodgson, *New Birth of Freedom*, ch. 2.
59. Mortimer J. Adler, *The Idea of Freedom*, Vol. II: *A Dialectical Examination of the Controversies about Freedom* (Garden City, N.Y.: Doubleday, 1961), pp. 5–10.
60. *Ibid.*, p. 16.
61. Muller, *Issues*, pp. 3–4.
62. Lossky, *Freedom of Will*, p. 23.
63. *Ibid.*
64. *Ibid.*
65. Calvez, "Possibilities," p. 177.
66. Rychlak, *Discovering Free Will*, p. 7.
67. James A. Easterbrook, *The Determinants of Free Will: A Psychological Analysis of Responsible, Adjustive Behavior* (New York: Academic Press, 1978), p. 5.
68. Lossky, *Freedom of Will*, p. 9.
69. Diogenes Laertius, *Lives of Eminent Philosophers*, trans R. D. Hicks (2 vols.; London: William Heinemann; Cambridge, Mass.: Harvard University Press, 1950), II, 135.
70. Cf., e.g., Cranston, *Freedom*, p. 21.
71. Hans Hofmann, *Discovering Freedom* (Boston: Beacon Press, 1969), p. 1.
72. Kersey, *Dictionarium*; cf. n. 10.
73. Cf. n. 10.
74. *Webster's Seventh New Collegiate Dictionary*.
75. Massimo Salvadori, *The Liberal Heresy: Origins and Historical Development* (New York: St. Martin's Press, 1977), p. 23. The original is italicized.
76. Bates, *Religious Liberty*, p. 295.
77. Hofmann, *Discovering Freedom*, p. 1.

78. Calvez, "Possibilities," p. 176; John Gray, *Liberalism* (Milton Keynes, U.K.: Open University Press, 1986), p. 59.
79. Simon, *Freedom*, p. 53.
80. John Howard Schütz, *Paul and the Anatomy of Apostolic Authority* (Cambridge, U.K.: Cambridge University Press, 1975), pp. 14, 17.
81. Cf., e.g., Klein's *Comprehensive Etymological Dictionary*.
82. Kersey, *Dictionarium*.
83. Cf. n. 10.
84. Cf. Jay Newman, *Competition in Religious Life* (Waterloo, Ont.: Wilfrid Laurier University Press, for the Canadian Corporation for Studies in Religion, 1989).
85. Aristotle, *Nicomachean Ethics* 1109b–1110b.
86. *Ibid.*, 1110b.
87. Cf. Jay Newman, *The Journalist in Plato's Cave* (Madison, N.J.: Fairleigh Dickinson University Press; London: Associated University Presses, 1989).
88. Cf. William Hare, *In Defence of Open-mindedness* (Montreal: McGill-Queen's University Press, 1985).
89. Aristotle, *Nicomachean Ethics* 1103a.
90. Fransen, "Grace," p. 35.
91. Plato, *Theaetetus* 172c–176c.

Chapter 2

1. John Macquarrie, *Principles of Christian Theology* (New York: Charles Scribner's Sons, 1966), p. 308.
2. Hans Küng, *The Church* (Garden City, N.Y.: Doubleday, 1976 [1967]), p. 208.
3. Millar Burrows, *An Outline of Biblical Theology* (Philadelphia: Westminster Press, 1946), p. 231.
4. *Ibid.*
5. Northcott, *Religious Liberty*, p. 37.
6. Muller, *Issues*, p. 85.
7. Burrows, *Outline*, p. 227.
8. The translation of Hebrew Scripture and the New Testament employed throughout is that of the King James Version.
9. Genesis 2:16–17.
10. Genesis 3:22.
11. Genesis 6:9.
12. Cf., e.g., Exodus 32:7–10, Numbers 25:1–8.
13. Exodus 1:22–3:17.
14. Burrows, *Outline*, pp. 227–28.
15. *Ibid.*, p. 228.
16. Exodus 20:2.
17. Paul M. van Buren, *The Burden of Freedom: Americans and the God of Israel* (New York: Seabury, 1976), p. 39.

18. *Ibid.*, p. 62.
19. Leviticus 25:10.
20. van Buren, *Burden*, pp. 62–63.
21. *Ibid.*, p. 17.
22. Cf. Exodus 20:13–16.
23. Leviticus 11:4, 19:27.
24. Genesis 18:16–19:28.
25. Numbers 25:1–9.
26. Numbers 16:3.
27. Numbers 16:31–33.
28. Cf. Baruch (Benedict) Spinoza, *Tractatus Theologico-Politicus (Theologico-Political Treatise)* (1670), ch. 17–18.
29. Cf., e.g., 1 Kings 18:17–19, 21:17–29.
30. Exodus 28:1, Leviticus 8–9.
31. Numbers 18:6–32.
32. Numbers 22:1–24:25.
33. J. B. Bury, *A History of Freedom of Thought* (New York: Henry Holt; London: Thornton Butterworth, 1913), p. 53.
34. *Ibid.*, p. 54.
35. Cf. Jay Newman, *Foundations of Religious Tolerance* (Toronto: University of Toronto Press, 1982), pp. 112–18.
36. Northcott, *Religious Liberty*, p. 24. Cf. Muller, *Issues*, p. 91.
37. A. J. Carlyle, *The Christian Church and Liberty* (New York: Burt Franklin, 1968), p. 15. This volume is a reprint of a work first published in 1924.
38. *Ibid.*, p. 14.
39. Hodgson, *New Birth of Freedom*, p. 216.
40. Northcott, *Religious Liberty*, p. 37.
41. John 8:32.
42. Cf., e.g., Romans 8:2.
43. Burrows, *Outline*, p. 230.
44. Ephesians 2:8–10.
45. Mark 16:16.
46. Cf., e.g., Romans 12–13.
47. Matthew 28:19–20.
48. Cf. Newman, *Foundations*, ch. 5.
49. Carlyle, *Christian Church*, pp. 39, 44–45.
50. *Ibid.*, pp. 46–47, 49.
51. Leonard Griffith, *Illusions of Our Culture* (London: Hodder and Stoughton, 1969), p. 124. This quotation is italicized in the original.
52. F. J. Foakes-Jackson, "The Protestant View of Freedom," in Horace M. Kallen, ed., *Freedom in the Modern World* (Freeport, N.Y.: Books for Libraries Press, 1969), p. 80. This volume is a reprint of a work first published in 1928.
53. Bury, *History*, p. 55.
54. Bates, *Religious Liberty*, p. 376.
55. John Viscount Morley, *On Compromise* (London: Watts, 1933), p. 3.

218 *Notes to pages 50–61*

56. W.E.H. Lecky, *History of the Rise and Influence of the Spirit of Rationalism in Europe* (Revised ed.; 2 vols.; New York and London: D. Appleton, 1914), II, 21.
57. Northcott, *Religious Liberty*, p. 25.
58. See Bury, *History*, ch. 3, and Lecky, *History*, ch. 4, for two famous discussions of mediaeval persecution.
59. Neuner, "No Monopoly," p. 31.
60. *Ibid.*, p. 32.
61. Roland H. Bainton, *The Travail of Religious Liberty: Nine Biographical Studies* (Philadelphia: Westminster Press, 1951), p. 15. Cf. pp. 17–19.
62. Preston King, *Toleration* (London: George Allen and Unwin, 1976), p. 73. Cf. Bury, *History*, p. 78; Muller, *Issues*, pp. 14–15.
63. Northcott, *Religious Liberty*, p. 26.
64. John F. Hayward, *Existentialism and Religious Liberalism* (Boston: Beacon Press, 1962), p. 4.
65. *Ibid.*
66. Geoffrey E. W. Scobie, *Psychology of Religion* (London and Sydney: B. T. Batsford, 1975), p. 157.
67. See, e.g., Friedrich Nietzsche, *Beyond Good and Evil* (1886), esp. ch. 3, and *The Genealogy of Morals* (1887); Sigmund Freud, *The Future of an Illusion* (1927).
68. See, e.g., William James, *The Varieties of Religious Experience* (1902).
69. Immanuel Kant, "What is Enlightenment?" (1784).
70. Cf. A. Boyce Gibson, *The Religion of Dostoevsky* (London: SCM Press, 1973), pp. 182–93.
71. Muller, *Issues*, p. 88.
72. Nicholas Lash, "The Church and Christ's Freedom," *Concilium* 3, no. 10 (March, 1974 [n.s.]), 98–99.
73. Jean-Paul Sartre, "Existentialism" (or "Existentialism Is a Humanism"), trans. Bernard Frechtman, in *Existentialism and Human Emotions* (New York: Philosophical Library, 1957).
74. *Ibid.*, p. 45.
75. *Ibid.*, pp. 14–15.
76. *Ibid.*, p. 15.
77. Paul Roubiczek, *Existentialism — For and Against* (Cambridge, U.K.: Cambridge University Press, 1966), p. 27.
78. Cf. n. 67.
79. John Macquarrie, *Existentialism*, Theological Resources Series (Philadelphia: Westminster Press; London: Hutchinson, 1972), pp. 220–25.
80. See, e.g., B. F. Skinner, *Walden Two* (New York: Macmillan, 1961 [1948]), *Beyond Freedom and Dignity* (New York: Knopf, 1971).
81. Cf. Newman, *Foundations*, pp. 62–83.
82. Northcott, *Religious Liberty*, p. 49.
83. *Ibid.*
84. King, *Toleration*, p. 110.

85. Cf. Jay Newman, *Fanatics and Hypocrites* (Buffalo: Prometheus Books, 1986), esp. ch. 1–2.
86. Lecky, *History*, I, 354.
87. Cf. Newman, *Fanatics*, esp. ch. 1, 3.
88. Cf., e.g., Bury, *History*, p. 52; Lecky, *History*, II, 21.
89. Exodus 23:9.

Chapter 3

1. Fransen, "Grace and Freedom," p. 32.
2. Griffith, *Illusions*, p. 118.
3. *Ibid.*, p. 126.
4. *Ibid.*, p. 127.
5. Genesis 1:26–28.
6. Genesis 3:22.
7. Burrows, *Outline*, p. 232.
8. Genesis 18:23–33.
9. Genesis 32:11–14.
10. Cf., e.g., Numbers 6:22–27, Deuteronomy 27:11–28:68.
11. van Buren, *Burden*, p. 34.
12. Deuteronomy 26:18–19.
13. Cf. Burrows, *Outline*, p. 232.
14. Deuteronomy 11:26–28.
15. Cf., e.g., Leviticus 10:1–3.
16. Cf., e.g., Deuteronomy 17, Jeremiah 1:17–19, Hosea 4–7.
17. Genesis 20; Numbers 20:7–12.
18. Cf., e.g., Deuteronomy 4, 11, 17.
19. van Buren, *Burden*, p. 34.
20. Deuteronomy 6:5.
21. Exodus 34:6–7.
22. Leviticus 19:17–18.
23. Griffith, *Illusions*, p. 26.
24. Jonah 4:10–11.
25. van Buren, *Burden*, p. 80.
26. Romans 6:23. Cf. Küng, *The Church*, pp. 201–208.
27. Küng, *The Church*, pp. 201–202.
28. Macquarrie, *Principles*, p. 308.
29. *Ibid.*, p. 73.
30. *Ibid.*, p. 298.
31. Hodgson, *New Birth of Freedom*, pp. 128–40.
32. *Ibid.*, pp. 42–43.
33. *Ibid.*, p. 43.
34. *Ibid.*, p. 42.
35. Gustavo Gutiérrez, "Freedom and Salvation: A Political Problem," trans. Alvin Gutterriez, in Ronald H. Stone, ed., *Liberation and Change* (Atlanta: John Knox Press, 1977), pp. 3–4.

36. Carlyle, *Christian Church*, p. 25.
37. *Ibid.*
38. Cf. Robert O. Johann, "Authority and Responsibility," in Murray, ed., *Freedom and Man*, p. 148.
39. Matthew 16:18–19.
40. Matthew 28:19–20.
41. Mark 16:16.
42. Matthew 5:10–11.
43. Northcott, *Religious Liberty*, p. 38.
44. Ellul, *Ethics*, p. 443.
45. *Ibid.*, p. 444.
46. Muller, *Issues*, p. 87.
47. Foakes-Jackson, "Protestant View," p. 75.
48. Macquarrie, *Existentialism*, p. 215.
49. See, e.g., Søren Kierkegaard, *The Point of View for My Work as an Author: A Report to History* (1859).
50. Nicholas Berdyaev, *Truth and Revelation*, trans. R. M. French (London: Geoffrey Bles, 1953), pp. 112–13.
51. Immanuel Kant, *Critique of Practical Reason* (1788), trans. Lewis White Beck, Library of Liberal Arts (Indianapolis and New York: Bobbs-Merrill; Liberal Arts Press, 1956), p. 134.
52. *Ibid.*
53. William James, "The Moral Philosopher and the Moral Life," in *The Will to Believe and Other Essays in Popular Philosophy* (1897) (Cambridge, Mass.: Harvard University Press, 1979), p. 160.
54. William James, *Pragmatism* (1907) (Cambridge, Mass.: Harvard University Press, 1975), p. 40. The original is italicized.
55. "*Verjüdelt*" and "*verchristlicht*": Nietzsche, *Genealogy*, Essay 1, sec. 9.
56. Micah 6:8.
57. Psalms 138:6.
58. Proverbs 15:33.
59. Psalms 37:11.
60. Matthew 5:5.
61. Matthew 11:29.
62. Spinoza, *Ethics*, Part 4, proposition 53.
63. David Hume, *A Treatise of Human Nature* (1739–1740), Bk. 3, part 3, sec. 2.
64. Spinoza, *Ethics*, Part 3, proposition 55, and definition of the emotions no. 26.
65. Nietzsche, *Beyond Good and Evil*, sec. 46.
66. *Ibid.*, sec. 260.
67. *Ibid.*, sec. 287.
68. *Ibid.*, secs. 13, 25, 227.
69. François de la Rochefoucauld, *Maxims (Réflexions Morales)* (1678), no. 254.
70. Hume, *Treatise, loc. cit.*
71. Nietzsche, *Beyond Good and Evil*, secs. 199, 260.
72. *Ibid.*, sec. 267.

73. *Ibid.*, sec. 195.
74. Bernard of Clairvaux, *The Steps of Humility*, trans. George Bosworth Burch (Notre Dame, Indiana: University of Notre Dame Press, 1963), p. 125.
75. Spinoza, *Ethics*, Part 4, proposition 54: note.
76. Ludwig Feuerbach, *The Essence of Christianity* (1841), ch. 26.
77. Immanuel Kant, *The Metaphysic of Morals* (1797), Part 2, sec. 11.
78. Walter Farrell, *A Companion to the Summa*, Vol. III: *The Fullness of Life* (London and New York: Sheed and Ward, 1940), p. 464.
79. Thomas Aquinas, *Summa Theologiae*, II–II, q. 161, article 1. Cf. q. 129.
80. Exodus 20:2.
81. Farrell, *Companion*, p. 463.
82. Kant, *Metaphysic of Morals*, loc. cit.
83. Numbers 12:3.
84. Cf. Aristotle, *Nicomachean Ethics* 1105b–1107a.
85. Matthew 5:6–9.
86. Nietzsche, *Beyond Good and Evil*, sec. 202.
87. Cf. Newman, *Competition*.
88. Jean-Jacques Rousseau, *The Social Contract* (1762), Bk. 1, ch. 1.
89. R. G. Collingwood, *The New Leviathan* (Oxford: Clarendon Press, 1942), p. 176.
90. *Ibid.*
91. Cf. Plato, *Republic* 555b–558c.
92. John Acton, "Authority and Liberty," *The Rambler* 2 (1860), 146. This piece is reprinted in Lord Acton, *Essays on Church and State*, ed. Douglas Woodruff (New York: Thomas Y. Crowell, 1968), pp. 423–24.
93. Jay Newman, "Two Theories of Civilization," *Philosophy* 54 (1979), 483.
94. Muller, *Issues*, p. 95.

Chapter 4

1. H. G. Wood, *Religious Liberty To-day* (Cambridge, U.K.: Cambridge University Press, 1949), pp. 2–3.
2. *Ibid.*, p. 7.
3. Cf. Muller, *Issues*, p. 7.
4. Northcott, *Religious Liberty*, p. 18.
5. Franklin H. Littell, "Religious Liberty: The Present Challenge," in Charles Wei-hsun Fu and Gerhard E. Spregler, ed., *Movements and Issues in World Religions* (New York: Greenwood Press, 1984), p. 206.
6. Ursula Henriques, *Religious Toleration in England: 1787–1833* (Toronto: University of Toronto Press, 1961), p. 18.
7. Cf. Newman, *Foundations*, pp. 4–6.
8. Cranston, *Freedom*, p. 11.
9. Dawson, *Religion*, p. 108.
10. Littell, "Religious Liberty," p. 206.
11. Bates, *Religious Liberty*, pp. 124–28.
12. *Ibid.*, pp. 128–30.

13. *Ibid.*, p. 474.
14. *Ibid.*, p. 475.
15. Dawson, *Religion*, p. 124.
16. *Ibid.*, pp. 122–23.
17. Wood, *Religious Liberty*, p. 1.
18. Niebuhr, "Commitment," pp. 57–58.
19. Gray, *Liberalism*, p. 15.
20. Littell, "Religious Liberty," p. 199.
21. Bury, *History*, p. 76.
22. *Ibid.*, p. 77.
23. R. G. Collingwood, *The Idea of History*, ed. T. M. Knox (Oxford: Clarendon Press, 1946), p. 213.
24. Bury, *History*, pp. 92–93.
25. Gustav Mensching, *Tolerance and Truth in Religion*, trans., and augmented in collaboration with the author, by H.-J. Klimkeit (University, Ala.: University of Alabama Press, 1971), p. 20.
26. *Ibid.*, pp. 19–20.
27. *Ibid.*, p. 68.
28. *Ibid.*, p. 64.
29. *Ibid.*, p. 95.
30. Cf. Newman, *Foundations*, p. 114.
31. Genesis 9:1–6.
32. 1 Samuel 8:20.
33. 1 Samuel 8:10.
34. Bury, *History*, p. 22.
35. *Ibid.*, pp. 30–35.
36. *Ibid.*, p. 27.
37. *Ibid.*, pp. 40–42.
38. Cf., e.g., Mensching, *Tolerance*, pp. 47–48; Lecky, *History*, II, 21.
39. Cf., e.g., Bates, *Religious Liberty*, pp. 137–38.
40. Mensching, *Tolerance*, pp. 96–97.
41. Edward A. Synan, *The Popes and the Jews in the Middle Ages*, Quest Books (New York: Macmillan; London: Collier-Macmillan, 1965), pp. 1–3.
42. Cited in Synan, *Popes*, p. 226. Cf. pp. 92–93.
43. *Ibid.*, p. 217. Cf. pp. 43–47.
44. *Ibid.*, p. 231. Cf. pp. 79–81.
45. *Ibid.*
46. Manning, *Liberalism*, p. 34.
47. Bury, *History*, p. 76.
48. Lecky, *History*, I, 18.
49. Bury, *History*, p. 77.
50. Bainton, *Travail*, p. 29.
51. Joseph Lecler, *Toleration and the Reformation*, trans. T. L. Westow (2 vols.; London: Longmans; New York: Association Press, 1960), II, 485.
52. *Ibid.*, p. 486.
53. Bainton, *Travail*, p. 15.

54. Michael Novak, *Freedom with Justice: Catholic Social Thought and Liberal Institutions* (San Francisco: Harper and Row, 1984), p. 23.
55. Hayward, *Existentialism*, p. 4.
56. Bainton, *Travail*, p. 21.
57. Franklin Hamlin Littell, *The Anabaptist View of the Church* (2nd ed.; Boston: Starr King Press, 1958 [1952]), pp. 65–66. The original is partly italicized.
58. Cf., e.g., Northcott, *Religious Liberty*, pp. 28–29; Bury, *History*, p. 93.
59. Lecky, *History*, I, 371–74.
60. Sebastian Castellio, *Concerning Heretics* (1554), trans. and ed. Roland H. Bainton (New York: Octagon Books, 1965), p. 125. This volume is a reprint of a translation first published in 1935.
61. *Ibid.*, p. 126.
62. *Ibid.*, p. 133.
63. *Ibid.*, p. 134.
64. Bainton, *Travail*, p. 30.
65. Manning, *Liberalism*, p. 37.
66. *Ibid.*, p. 39.
67. Bury, *History*, p. 132.
68. Cf., e.g., Newman, *Foundations*, pp. 129–35.
69. Bury, *History*, p. 97.
70. Cf. Bates, *Religious Liberty*, p. 288.
71. Littell, "Religious Liberty," p. 199.
72. Bates, *Religious Liberty*, p. 544.
73. 397 U.S. 664 (1970): *Walz v. Tax Commission*, in Milton R. Konvitz, ed., *Bill of Rights Reader: Leading Constitutional Cases* (5th ed.; Ithaca, N.Y. and London: Cornell University Press, 1973 [1954]), pp. 180–81.
74. Lecky, *History*, II, 102.
75. Arthur E. Sutherland, *The Church Shall Be Free: A Glance at Eight Centuries of Church and State* (Charlottesville, Va.: University Press of Virginia, 1965), p. 40.
76. Plato, *Republic* 427a–c.
77. Bates, *Religious Liberty*, p. 374.
78. Cf. Manning, *Liberalism*, pp. 40–42.
79. John Locke, *A Letter Concerning Toleration (Epistola de Tolerantia)* (1689), trans. William Popple (1689), with modernization of spelling and punctuation by Patrick Romanell, Library of Liberal Arts (Indianapolis: Bobbs-Merrill, 1955 [1950]), p. 17.
80. *Ibid.*, p. 20.
81. J. W. Gough, "Introduction" to John Locke, *Epistola de Tolerantia: A Letter on Toleration*, ed. Raymond Klibansky, trans. J. W. Gough (Oxford: Clarendon Press, 1968), p. 35.
82. *Ibid.*
83. Locke, *Letter*, p. 39.
84. See, e.g., Patrick Romanell, "Introduction" to Locke, *Letter*, p. 9.
85. Spinoza, *Tractatus*, ch. 19.
86. *Ibid.*, ch. 12–14.

87. Locke, *Letter*, p. 35.
88. Morley, *On Compromise*, pp. 163–64.
89. 98 U.S. 145 (1878): *Reynolds v. United States*, in Konvitz, ed., *Bill of Rights Reader*, p. 30.
90. *Ibid.*, p. 29.
91. Cf. Newman, *Foundations*, p. 132.
92. Wood, *Religious Liberty*, p. 89.
93. *Ibid.*, p. 28.
94. Konvitz, ed., *Bill of Rights Reader*, pp. ix–x. Cf. pp. 26–110.
95. *Ibid.*, p. x. Cf. pp. 110–85.
96. Cf. Holm, *Study of Religions*, p. 18.
97. Cf. Wood, *Religious Liberty*, ch. 2.
98. See, e.g., Plato, *Euthyphro*.
99. Bates, *Religious Liberty*, p. 373.
100. Cf. Jay Newman, *The Mental Philosophy of John Henry Newman* (Waterloo, Ont.: Wilfrid Laurier University Press, 1986), pp. 70–77.
101. Cf. Newman, *Fanatics*, ch. 1, 4.
102. Spinoza, *Tractatus*, ch. 20.
103. Northcott, *Religious Liberty*, p. 40.
104. Morley, *On Compromise*, p. 160.
105. Bury, *History*, p. 235. Cf. p. 241.
106. John Stuart Mill, *On Liberty* (1859), in *Collected Works of John Stuart Mill*, Vol. XVIII: *Essays on Politics and Society* (Toronto: University of Toronto Press, 1977), p. 258. The original passage is divided into paragraphs.
107. *Ibid.*, p. 223.
108. Wood, *Religious Liberty*, p. 3.
109. Kant, *Critique of Practical Reason*, p. 30.
110. Donald Evans, *Struggle and Fulfilment* (London: Collins, 1979), p. 68.
111. Bates, *Religious Liberty*, p. 377.
112. Cf. Newman, *Fanatics*, ch. 1, 3.
113. Niebuhr, "Commitment," p. 63.
114. Roland N. Stromberg, *Religious Liberalism in Eighteenth-Century England* (London: Oxford University Press, 1954), p. 165.
115. Plato, *Republic* 420b, trans. Benjamin Jowett (1871).
116. See, e.g., Plato, *Republic* 592b.

Chapter 5

1. Hayward, *Existentialism*, p. 2.
2. *Ibid.*, p. 7.
3. See, e.g., J. Salwyn Schapiro, *Liberalism: Its Meaning and History* (Princeton, N.J.: D. Van Nostrand, 1958), p. 9; Manning, *Liberalism*, p. 9; Gray, *Liberalism*, p. ix.
4. Schapiro, *Liberalism*, p. 9.
5. Gray, *Liberalism*, p. 9.

6. Salvadori, *Liberal Heresy*, p. 14.
7. John Dewey, "Philosophies of Freedom," in Kallen, ed., *Freedom in the Modern World*, p. 243.
8. Gray, *Liberalism*, p. 9.
9. Manning, *Liberalism*, p. 58. Cf. Cranston, *Freedom*, Part 2.
10. Manning, *Liberalism*, p. 142.
11. Anthony Arblaster, *The Rise and Decline of Western Liberalism* (Oxford: Basil Blackwell, 1984), p. 55.
12. Gray, *Liberalism*, p. x.
13. *Ibid.*, p. 59.
14. Salvadori, *Liberal Heresy*, p. 27; cf. p. 23.
15. Dawson, *Religion*, p. 10.
16. Schapiro, *Liberalism*, p. 12.
17. Morley, *On Compromise*, p. 171.
18. Cf. Salvadori, *Liberal Heresy*, pp. 40–43.
19. Schapiro, *Liberalism*, p. 16.
20. *Ibid.*
21. *Ibid.*, p. 32.
22. *Ibid.*, p. 36.
23. Cf. Schapiro, *Liberalism*, Part I, ch. 2.
24. Salvadori, *Liberal Heresy*, p. 1.
25. Cf. Kersey, *Dictionarium*; Walker, *Critical Pronouncing Dictionary*.
26. Cf. ch. 1, n. 10.
27. Schapiro, *Liberalism*, p. 9.
28. Hayward, *Existentialism*, p. 7.
29. *Ibid.*, p. 24.
30. *Ibid.*, p. 12.
31. *Ibid.*, p. 7.
32. Foakes-Jackson, "Protestant View," pp. 76–77.
33. *Ibid.*, pp. 64–65.
34. Cf., e.g., *The American Heritage Dictionary*.
35. Novak, *Freedom with Justice*, p. 22.
36. Karl Rahner, *Free Speech in the Church* (New York: Sheed and Ward, 1959), p. 18.
37. Bernard M. G. Reardon, "Introduction" to Bernard M. G. Reardon, ed., *Liberal Protestantism* (Stanford, Calif.: Stanford University Press, 1968), p. 17.
38. Alan P. F. Sell, *Theology in Turmoil: The Roots, Course and Significance of the Conservative–Liberal Debate in Modern Theology* (Grand Rapids, Mich.: Baker Book House, 1986), p. 18.
39. Reardon, "Introduction," p. 64.
40. Adelaide Teague Case, *Liberal Christianity and Religious Education: A Study of Objectives in Religious Education* (New York: Macmillan, 1924), p. 11.
41. *Ibid.*, ch. 2 (title).
42. James Barr, *Fundamentalism* (Philadelphia: Westminster Press, 1977), pp. 164–65.

43. Case, *Liberal Christianity*, p. 14.
44. *Ibid.*, p. 16.
45. *Ibid.*
46. *Ibid.*, p. 19.
47. *Ibid.*, e.g., pp. 26–29, 47–48.
48. *Ibid.*, p. 29.
49. *Ibid.*, p. 71.
50. Sell, *Theology in Turmoil*, p. 90.
51. *Ibid.*, p. 11. Cf. Henry Aiken, *The Age of Ideology* (New York: Mentor, 1956), p. 15.
52. Donald E. Miller, *The Case for Liberal Christianity* (San Francisco: Harper and Row, 1981), p. 33.
53. *Ibid.*, p. 91.
54. *Ibid.*, p. 28.
55. *Ibid.*, pp. 15–17.
56. *Ibid.*, p. 37.
57. Cf. R. G. Collingwood, *Speculum Mentis* (Oxford: Clarendon Press, 1924).
58. F. M. Cornford, *From Religion to Philosophy*, Harper Torchbooks (New York: Harper and Brothers, 1957), p. v. This work was first published in 1912.
59. *Ibid.*, p. 126.
60. *Ibid.*, p. 127.
61. Translations of the fragments are from Philip Wheelwright, ed. and trans., *The Presocratics* (Indianapolis and New York: Odyssey Press division of Bobbs-Merrill, 1966). Numbers in the text refer to the standard numbering of Diels and Kranz.
62. Plato, *Laws* 716.
63. Bainton, *Travail*, p. 21.
64. Emil L. Fackenheim, *What is Judaism?: An Interpretation for the Present Age* (New York: Summit, 1987), pp. 75–76.
65. Heinz Moshe Graupe, *The Rise of Modern Judaism: An Intellectual History of German Jewry 1650–1942*, trans. John Robinson (Huntington, N.Y.: Robert E. Krieger, 1978), p. 113.
66. *Ibid.*, p. 114.
67. *Ibid.*, p. 77.
68. *Ibid.*, pp. 81–83.
69. Fackenheim, *What is Judaism?*, p. 74.
70. Morley, *On Compromise*, p. 85.
71. Barr, *Fundamentalism*, p. 344.
72. Simon, *Freedom*, p. 49.
73. Dawson, *Religion*, p. 135.
74. Novak, *Freedom with Justice*, p. 23.
75. Henriques, *Religious Toleration*, pp. 276–77.
76. Hayward, *Existentialism*, pp. 46–47.
77. *Ibid.*, p. 47.
78. Morley, *On Compromise*, p. 75.
79. Lecky, *History*, II, 357.

80. Miller, *Case for Liberal Christianity*, p. 152.
81. *Ibid.*, p. 34.
82. *Ibid.*, p. 14.
83. *Ibid.*, p. 98.
84. Barr, *Fundamentalism*, p. 164.
85. Macquarrie, *Principles*, p. 361.
86. Rychlak, *Discovering Free Will*, p. 255.
87. Cf. Newman, *Fanatics*.
88. Foakes-Jackson, "Protestant View," p. 78.
89. J. Gresham Machen, *Christianity and Liberalism* (Grand Rapids, Mich.: William B. Eerdmans, 1923), p. 2.
90. Hayward, *Existentialism*, p. 1.
91. *Ibid.*, p. 45.
92. Reardon, "Introduction," p. 63.
93. *Ibid.*, pp. 63–64.
94. Stromberg, *Religious Liberalism*, p. 27.
95. Reardon, "Introduction," p. 64. Cf. Dawson, *Religion*, p. 61.
96. Stromberg, *Religious Liberalism*, p. 173.
97. Machen, *Christianity*, p. 76.
98. *Ibid.*, p. 78.
99. Sell, *Theology in Turmoil*, p. 80.
100. Miller, *Case for Liberal Christianity*, p. 42.
101. Machen, *Christianity*, p. 144.
102. Dawson, *Religion*, p. 128.
103. *Ibid.*, p. 50.
104. *Ibid.*, p. 140.
105. James H. Mantinband, "Introduction to the *Clouds*," in James H. Mantinband, trans., *Four Plays of Aristophanes* (Washington: University Press of America, 1983), p. 2.
106. *Ibid.*
107. Aristophanes, *Clouds*, trans. James H. Mantinband, in Mantinband, trans., *Four Plays*, p. 74.
108. Plato, *Apology* 18c–d, 19b–c.
109. *Ibid.*, 31a–b, 37e–38a.
110. Plato, *Euthyphro* 3a–b.
111. Plato, *Apology* 41c–d.
112. *Ibid.*, 40b–41d.
113. *Ibid.*, 40e–41a.
114. *Ibid.*, 40c–d.
115. *Ibid.*, 41d.
116. Spinoza, *Ethics*, Part 5, proposition 42 (trans. White, with revisions by Stirling).

Chapter 6

1. Cf. Newman, *Competition*.
2. Newman, *Foundations*, pp. 143–45.
3. Cf. Newman, *Competition*, ch. 5.
4. Novak, *Freedom with Justice*, p. 23.
5. Lecky, *History*, II, 102.
6. Plato, *Republic* 459e–466d.
7. Collingwood, *New Leviathan*, p. 176.
8. *Ibid.*, pp. 160–61.
9. *Ibid.*, p. 161.
10. *Ibid.*, pp. 162–63.
11. Thomas Hobbes, *Leviathan* (1651), ch. 13–14.
12. Spinoza, *Tractatus*, ch. 16.
13. Hobbes, *Leviathan*, ch. 12.
14. G. E. Lessing, *Nathan the Wise* (1779), trans. William Jacks (Glasgow: James Maclehose and Sons, 1894), p. 131 (Act III, scene 7). The punctuation has been slightly revised.
15. Bury, *History*, p. 252.
16. Cf. Newman, *Fanatics*, ch. 4.
17. Schütz, *Paul*, p. 252.
18. *Ibid.*, p. 272.
19. Deuteronomy 34:10.
20. Cf. Plato, *Apology* 30d–31d, 33e, 37e–38a.
21. Cf. Plato, *Republic* 487e–489c, 557a–558c.
22. Cf., e.g., Friedrich Nietzsche, *The Genealogy of Morals* (1887).
23. Exodus 32:12.
24. Simon, *Freedom*, p. 53.
25. *Ibid.*
26. Nietzsche, *Beyond Good and Evil*, sec. 41.
27. Matthew 26:28.
28. John 5:42.
29. Matthew 22:37–38.
30. Deuteronomy 6:5–6.
31. Kant, *Critique of Practical Reason*, pp. 85–86.
32. Baruch (Benedict) Spinoza, Letter to W. van Blyenbergh, January 5, 1665, in *The Correspondence of Spinoza*, trans. and ed. A. Wolf (London: George Allen and Unwin, 1928), p. 151.
33. Baruch (Benedict) Spinoza, Letter to J. Ostens, February 1671, in *The Correspondence of Spinoza*, p. 255.
34. *Ibid.*, p. 257.
35. Job 2:9–10.
36. John Henry Newman, "Personal Influence, the Means of Propagating the Truth," in *University Sermons* (1871 [1843]) (London: SPCK, 1970), pp. 97–98.

Index

Aaron, 44, 197
Abbott, Lyman, 155
Abel, 38
Abelard, Peter, 148, 164
Abraham, 40, 47, 67, 68
Act of Toleration (1689), 97, 110
Acton, John, 89
Adler, Mortimer J., 15, 16
Age of Reason, 147, 164, 194
Aiken, Henry, 158, 165
Alexander III (pope), 106
Anabaptists, 108, 109
Anglicans and Anglicanism, 5, 192
Apology (Plato), 179, 180
apostasy, 27, 104, 168, 169
Arblaster, Anthony, 146
Aristophanes, 165, 179
Aristotle, 28, 29, 30, 31, 45, 79, 162, 178
Arminians, 112
asceticism, 53, 85, 171
atheists and atheism, 56, 57, 125, 177
Augustine (of Hippo), 50, 59, 62, 74, 137
authoritarianism, 2, 43, 50, 72, 96, 181, 182, 188, 196
authority:
    etymology of, 25
    in relation to religious freedom, 24–30, 186–211
autonomy, 14, 17, 18, 19, 22, 26, 33, 36, 37, 45, 47, 50, 59, 71, 75, 84, 147, 165, 172, 188, 205, 208

Bacon, Francis, 164
Bainton, Roland H., 51, 108, 109, 110, 164
Bakunin, Michael, 16
Balaam, 44
Baptists, 108, 153
Barr, James, 156, 169, 172

Barth, Karl, 74
Bates, M. Searle, 4, 16, 98, 99, 112, 116, 117, 127, 130, 137
Beatitudes, 73, 85
Belloc, H., 139, 178
Berdyaev, Nicholas, 75
Bergson, Henri, 164
Bernard (of Clairvaux), 80
Blondel, Maurice, 164
Blyenbergh, W. van, 206
Bodin, Jean, 108
Bonald, L. G. A. de, 139
Brahmanism, 102
Brothers Karamazov, The (Dostoevsky), 54
Bryce, James, 112
Buber, Martin, 74
Buddhists and Buddhism, 5, 31, 102
Bultmann, Rudolf, 74, 156
Burger, Warren, 113, 124
Buri, Fritz, 74
Burke, Edmund, 139
Burrows, Millar, 36, 37, 41, 67
Bury, J. B., 45, 50, 101, 102, 105, 107, 111, 132, 195

Cain, 38, 39, 66
Callahan, Daniel, 9
Calvez, Jean-Yves, 14, 17
Calvin, John, 49, 51, 74, 107, 108, 138, 139
capitalism, 149
Carlyle, A. J., 45, 49, 72, 73
Carlyle, Thomas, 147
Case, Adelaide Teague, 155, 156, 157, 158
Castellio, Sebastian, 107, 108, 109, 138, 139, 164, 211
categorical imperative, 135
Catholics and Catholicism: *see* Roman Catholics and Roman Catholicism
censorship, 123
charisma, 46, 197, 198, 200, 201, 210, 211
Charter of Rights and Freedoms (Canada), 100, 124
Chesterton, G. K., 178
Christ: *see* Jesus of Nazareth
Christians and Christianity, 5, 6, 28, 31, 35, 36, 37, 45, 46, 47, 48, 49, 57, 63, 70, 71, 72, 73, 87, 98, 105, 119, 137, 139, 143, 155–159, 163, 167, 171, 174, 175, 178, 179, 205
civilization, 1, 22, 33, 44, 57, 67, 69, 78, 81, 82, 84, 85, 87, 89, 91, 102, 107, 121, 145, 148, 150, 159, 172, 178, 187, 205, 206
Clouds (Aristophanes), 165, 179
Cohen, Hermann, 167, 169

Collingwood, R. G., 88, 102, 189
comparative religion, 4
compatibilism, 17
Comte, Auguste, 16, 77, 91
Concerning Heretics (Castellio), 109
conscience, 30, 72, 95, 98, 100, 105, 107, 108, 110, 114, 119, 123, 125, 127, 128, 129, 130, 135, 139, 165, 167, 170, 194
conscientious objectors, 123
Constantine (emperor), 105, 106
Constitution of the United States, 99, 111, 113, 120
contraception, 123
Corinthians, 206
Cornford, F. M., 160, 161
Cranston, Maurice, 3, 8, 9, 10, 13, 96, 130, 145
Critique of Practical Reason (Kant), 75
cults, 5, 58, 98

Darwinism, 164
Dawson, Christopher, 9, 97, 146, 170, 171, 172, 176, 178
Day, James F., 7
demythologization, 166
Descartes, René, 148, 164, 166
determinism, 11, 14, 16, 17, 30, 39, 54, 59, 60, 75, 76, 77
Deuteronomy, 42, 194
Dewey, John, 145, 155, 157
Diogenes Laertius, 17

Easterbrook, James A., 17
Ebeling, Gerhard, 74
ecumenical studies, 4
Eden, Garden of, 37, 38, 66
Eichmann, Adolf, 129, 139
election (theological doctrine), 40, 41, 47, 48, 49, 68, 74
Elijah, 44, 194
Ellul, Jacques, 3, 73
Empedocles, 161
Encyclopedists, French, 148, 164
Enlightenment, 54, 55, 102, 145, 147, 164, 168, 194
Ephesians, 47
equality, 146
Erasmus, Desiderius, 51, 107, 108, 148, 164
Ethics (Spinoza), 11, 12, 180, 206
Euthyphro (Plato), 162
Evans, Donald, 137
evolution, teaching of, 122
exclusivism, 45, 48, 104

existentialists and existentialism, 10, 23, 24, 47, 56, 74, 75, 77, 143, 164, 165, 166
Exodus, 40, 41, 42, 67, 197
Ezekiel, 167

Fackenheim, Emil, 167, 168
fanaticism, 62, 138, 172
Farrell, Walter, 82, 83
Farrer, Austin, 9
fatalism, 16, 47, 81, 84
Federalist Papers, 122
Feuerbach, Ludwig, 81
fictionalism, 164
Foakes-Jackson, F. J., 49, 74, 173
Fosdick, Harry Emerson, 155, 156
Franck, Sebastian, 108
Fransen, Piet, 10, 32, 65
Frederick II (emperor), 50
free will, 10, 14, 16, 17, 50, 75, 189
freedom:
    academic, 14
    definition of, 7–12
    economic, 14, 150
    existential, 14, 24, 40
    idea of religious, 1–34, 209–211
    psychological, 23
    spiritual, 3, 18, 23, 27, 31, 46, 48, 85, 86, 94, 122, 124, 163, 176–180, 182, 183, 187, 209, 211
"freedom of religion", 2, 3, 33, 100, 124, 138
Freud, Sigmund, 35, 52, 53, 58, 77, 202
fundamentalists and fundamentalism, 91, 154, 156, 164, 172

Galatians, 42
Genesis, 37, 38, 66, 104
Goethe, J. W. von, 147
golden rule, 135, 136, 137
Gospels, 46, 48
Gough, J. W., 118, 119
grace, 36, 42, 47, 51, 54, 71, 81, 128, 176, 177
Graupe, Heinz Moshe, 168
Gray, John, 102, 145, 146
Green, T. H., 147
Gregory I (pope), 106
Griffith, Leonard, 49, 65
Grotius, Hugo, 110
Guide for the Perplexed (Maimonides), 168
Gutiérrez, Gustavo, 72

Harnack, Adolf von, 156
Hayward, John F., 51, 107, 108, 143, 152, 153, 154, 170, 173
Hegelians, 164
Heidegger, Martin, 56
Henriques, Ursula, 97, 170
Heraclitus, 161
heresy, 27, 50, 188
Herrmann, Wilhelm, 156
heterodoxy, 27
higher criticism, 164
Hindus and Hinduism, 5, 103
History of Freedom of Thought, A (Bury), 195
Hobbes, Thomas, 110, 191, 194
Hodges, George, 155
Hodgson, Peter C., 7, 8, 15, 46, 71, 72
Hofmann, Hans, 18
Holm, Jean, 6, 124
Hooker, Richard, 110
Hosea, 206
Hubmeier, Balthasar, 51
Hume, David, 78, 80, 81, 128, 148, 164, 166, 203
Husserl, Edmund, 164
Hutcheson, Francis, 128, 165
hypocrisy, 62, 127, 137, 138, 173, 175, 180, 184

idolatry, 27, 41, 137, 191
Iersel, Bas van, 12
individualism, 45, 51, 58, 108, 130, 146, 147, 149, 150, 154, 158, 165, 172
inerrancy (of Scripture), 156
Innocent III (pope), 50, 106, 114, 139
Inquisition, 27
Isaac, 40
Isaiah, 41

Jacob, 40
James, William, 75, 76, 164
Jefferson, Thomas, 112, 123, 124
Jehovah's Witnesses, 95, 98
Jeremiah, 44, 206
Jesus of Nazareth, 36, 42, 46, 47, 48, 50, 54, 65, 70, 71, 73, 109, 110, 155, 156, 174, 175, 194, 205, 206
Jews and Judaism, 6, 37, 45, 47, 48, 57, 68, 80, 87, 98, 103, 104, 105, 106, 107, 121, 129, 143, 153, 159, 167, 168, 179, 192, 206
Job, 208, 209
John, 47, 206
Jonah, 69
justice, 22, 59, 62, 67, 76, 81, 84, 87, 89, 93, 140, 153, 180
Justin Martyr, 105

Kant, Immanuel, 54, 75, 76, 81, 84, 135, 136, 148, 154, 158, 164–168, 169, 199, 206
Kersey, John, 18, 25
Ketcham, Charles B., 7
Kierkegaard, Søren, 23, 74, 164
King, Preston, 51, 61
Konvitz, Milton, 122
Korah, 43, 44
Küng, Hans, 36

Lactantius, 105
La Rochefoucauld, F. de, 79, 80, 81
Lash, Nicholas, 55
Laws (Plato), 162, 179
Lecky, W. E. H., 62, 101, 107, 114, 138, 171, 172, 188
Lecler, Joseph, 108, 109
Lessing, G. E., 148, 164, 168, 192
Letter Concerning Toleration (Locke), 117, 120, 122
Leviathan (Hobbes), 191, 194
Levites, 44
l'Hospital, Michel de, 108
liberalism:
    idea of, 143–150
    idea of religious, 151–160
liberation theology, 32, 48, 72, 175
liberty:
    idea of, 18–19
    idea of religious, 18–19, 94–101
Littell, Franklin, 96, 98, 102, 109, 112
Locke, John, 110, 112, 117, 118, 119, 120, 122, 123, 124, 132, 138, 141, 145, 147, 148, 164, 185
Lossky, N. O., 13, 16, 17
Luther, Martin, 51, 75, 107, 108
Lutherans and Lutheranism, 5, 51

Machen, J. Gresham, 173, 174, 176
Macquarrie, John, 36, 71, 72, 74, 172
Madison, James, 112
Maimonides, 168, 169
Maistre, Joseph de, 139, 147
Manning, D. J., 107, 110, 145
Mantinband, James, 179
Manz, Felix, 51
Marcel, Gabriel, 74
Marcus Aurelius, 139
Maritain, Jacques, 10, 14

Marx, Karl, 16, 35, 58, 77
Marxists and Marxism, 13, 55, 74, 91, 126
materialism, 2, 17, 41, 171, 177, 179, 181
Mathews, Shailer, 155, 156
Matthew, 73
megalopsychia, 79
Mendelssohn, Moses, 168, 169
Mensching, Gustav, 103, 105
Metaphysics (Aristotle), 162
Methodists and Methodism, 21, 153
Mill, John Stuart, 96, 100, 128, 132, 133, 134, 135, 138, 141, 147, 164
Miller, Donald E., 158, 171, 175
Milton, John, 110, 132, 147
miracles, 43, 54, 157, 194, 195, 201, 203
monotheism, 5, 41, 45, 103
Montaigne, Michel de, 108
More, Thomas, 107
Morley, John, 120, 132, 147, 169, 171
Mormons, 120
Moses, 40, 41, 42, 43, 44, 67, 68, 82, 84, 115, 194, 197, 198, 201
Muller, Herbert J., 8, 10, 12, 15, 16, 36, 55, 74, 91
Müntzer, Thomas, 51
Muslims and Islam, 44, 95, 98, 126

Nathan the Wise (Lessing), 192
Neoplatonism, 168
Neuner, Josef, 15, 50, 51
Nevers, Count of, 106
Newman, John Henry, 12, 13, 170, 212
Nicomachean Ethics (Aristotle), 28, 31, 79
Niebuhr, H. Richard, 14
Niebuhr, Reinhold, 15, 101, 138
Nietzsche, Friedrich, 74, 76, 77, 78, 79, 80, 81, 84, 87, 164
Noachide Covenant, 104
Noah, 40, 104
nonconformity or nonconformism, 27, 102
Northcott, Cecil, 3, 36, 45, 50, 51, 61, 73, 96, 106, 107, 129
Novak, Michael, 108, 153, 170, 188
Numbers, 43, 84

On Liberty (Mill), 100, 132, 133
Ott, Heinrich, 74

Paine, Thomas, 148
Pascal, Blaise, 23, 74, 164, 209
Paul (apostle), 46, 47, 48, 49, 69, 74, 197, 206

Pelagianism, 50, 71
Pentateuch, 37, 41, 43, 47, 67
Pericles, 105
Peter (apostle), 73
Phinehas, 43
Pico della Mirandola, Giovanni, 164
Plato, 34, 79, 126, 140, 141, 162, 178, 179, 180, 189, 199
polygamy, 120, 121
positivism, 74, 164
Pragmatism (James), 76
pragmatists and pragmatism, 75, 76, 164, 166
predestination, 36, 47
privacy, 146, 150
proselytizers and proselytizing, 11, 20, 48, 73, 77, 104
Protagoras, 126, 162, 163, 166
Protestants and Protestantism, 5, 14, 20, 21, 36, 49, 51, 107, 108, 109, 153, 154, 156, 164, 167, 173
pseudo-religions, 5
psychoanalysis, 74
Puritans, 111

Quakers, 111, 120

Rahner, Karl, 74, 153, 154
rationalists and rationalism, 47, 74, 105, 107, 108, 147, 154, 164, 171, 172
Reardon, Bernard M. G., 154, 174
reconciliationism, 17
Reformation, 51, 102, 107, 108, 145, 147, 164
relativism, 45, 158, 162, 171
release time, 122
religion:
    definition of, 4–7
    etymology of, 5
    liberal, 160–180
religious studies, 4
Rembrandt, 12
Renaissance, 107, 147, 164
Republic (Plato), 179
responsibility, 11, 17, 28, 30, 37, 40, 56, 58, 59, 60, 72, 77, 85, 95, 130
Reynolds v. United States (1878), 120
Ritschl, Albrecht, 156, 175
Rock Edicts (of Ashoka), 102
Roman Catholics and Roman Catholicism, 10, 17, 20, 49, 51, 65, 89, 102, 107, 108, 114, 118, 153, 156, 168, 170, 192, 204

Roubiczek, Paul, 57
Rousseau, Jean-Jacques, 88, 128, 165
Rychlak, Joseph F., 9, 17, 172

Salvadori, Massimo, 18, 145, 146, 148
salvation, 23, 47, 61, 62, 63, 67, 70, 72, 85, 118, 120, 124, 180
Samuel, 104, 115
Sanhedrin (tractate), 168
Sartre, Jean-Paul, 24, 56, 57, 58, 74, 76, 77, 84
Saul, 115
Schapiro, J. Salwyn, 146, 147, 149
Schillebeeckx, Edward, 12
Schiller, F. C. S., 75, 164
Schleiermacher, Friedrich, 154, 156, 207
Schütz, John Howard, 25, 195
Schweitzer, Albert, 174
science of religion, 164
scientism, 146
Scientology, Church of, 94
Scobie, Geoffrey E. W., 52
self-determination, 7, 14, 15, 17, 19, 24, 82, 84
self-protection, 134
self-realization, 1, 15, 79, 81, 82, 83, 84, 148, 150, 165, 187, 195
Sell, Alan P. F., 154, 158, 175
Sermon on the Mount, 175
Servetus, Michael, 51, 107, 109, 138
Shaftesbury, A., 128
Shestov, Lev, 74
Simon, Yves, 10, 14, 22, 170, 202
sincerity, 78, 125, 127, 128, 129
Skinner, B. F., 59
Slater, Peter, 6
slavery, 8, 36, 40, 41, 42, 48, 49, 68, 176
Social Gospel movement, 48
Socinians, 108, 109
sociobiology, 74
sociology of religion, 4
Socrates, 34, 105, 126, 133, 148, 179, 180, 196, 199
Sodom and Gomorrah, 43
Sophists, 162, 179, 199
Spinoza, Baruch (Benedict), 11, 12, 16, 44, 77, 78, 79, 80, 81, 110, 119, 129, 132, 147, 164, 180, 189, 193, 194, 203, 206, 207
Stromberg, Roland N., 139, 174
subjectivity, 165, 195

Sunday observance laws, 123
Sutherland, Arthur E., 114
Synan, Edward A., 106

Taoists and Taoism, 5
Tenach, 167
Tertullian, 105
Thales, 161, 165
theocracy, 68, 90
Thomas Aquinas, 82, 164
Tillich, Paul, 74, 156, 158
tolerance, 22, 51, 63, 84, 86, 97, 103, 105, 108, 137, 143, 146, 149, 150, 152, 153, 154, 155, 164, 166, 171, 192
toleration, 50, 51, 62, 96, 97, 100, 102, 103, 105, 106, 108, 110, 111, 112, 117, 120, 137, 170
Torah, 36, 40, 44, 45, 69
Torquemada, T. de, 129, 139
Tractatus Theologico-Politicus (Spinoza), 79, 110

Unamuno, Miguel de, 74
Unitarians and Unitarianism, 109, 121
United Nations, 124
Universal Declaration of Human Rights (1948), 124
utilitarianism, 81, 132

Vaihinger, Hans, 164
van Buren, Paul, 41, 42, 68, 70
Varieties of Religious Experience, The (James), 76
vitalism, 164
Voltaire, 55, 62, 122, 138, 147, 164
voluntarism, 58

Waite, Judge, 120, 121
Walker, John, 7
Weber, Max, 25
Weiss, Johannes, 174
Williams, Roger, 111, 112, 211
Wood, H. G., 95, 100, 121, 125, 127, 134

Xenophanes, 161, 165

Zeno the Stoic, 17, 59
Zwingli, Huldrych, 108